TANTAMOUNT

THE PURSUIT OF THE FREEWAY PHANTOM SERIAL KILLER

BLAINE L. PARDOE and VICTORIA R. HESTER

WILD BLUE
PRESS

WildBluePress.com

TANTAMOUNT published by:
WILDBLUE PRESS
P.O. Box 102440
Denver, Colorado 80250

WILDBLUE PRESS is registered at the U.S. Patent and Trademark Offices.

ISBN 978-1-948239-49-3   Trade Paperback
ISBN 978-1-948239-48-6   eBook

Interior Formatting by Elijah Toten
www.totencreative.com

TANTAMOUNT

TABLE OF CONTENTS

INTRODUCTION

It is a simple yet deviously sinister document. Cut out of a notebook; it was just six lines, twenty-four words. For almost five decades, it has haunted the families of the victims and taunted the frustrated authorities. The note is the only confirmed voice of the killer of at least seven, potentially more, young women/girls in Washington DC in the early 1970s. Even more strange is that it was not written by the killer personally. The Freeway Phantom made one of his victims, Brenda Woodard, write it before he raped and killed her. He left it in her coat when he pulled her body from his car and left it alongside the highway…wanting authorities to find her and the message he left behind.

this is tantamount to my
insensititivity (sp) to people
especially women.
I will admit the others
when you catch me if you can! (sic)
<u>Free-way Phantom!</u>

The note tells us everything, and yet nothing about the Freeway Phantom serial killer who stalked Washington DC and Prince George's County, Maryland, for two years. It is a doorway into the mind of the murderer, while at the same time only cracks open the door just enough for us to see a bit of the horror that lies beyond. It is frightening because the killer admits his crimes and accepts the name that the local media had given him. It is also terrifying because he is taunting investigators, laughing at their failures to apprehend him, baiting them to do better. Up until the discovery of the note, investigators and the media only speculated that the victims were related. With this message all doubt was erased. A serial killer was stalking the Washington DC metropolitan area, though it would be years before that term was even invented.

Even more eerie, the killer is making it known that this is a game to him and that he is winning.

This note has misspellings and sloppy punctuation. The fact that it even has punctuation tells us something about the circumstances of its writing. There are corrections that the killer made to Brenda's handwriting. You can see where her murderer validated her work like a dominating schoolteacher. There is a correction made on the word "insensitivity" It was the first and last time the killer reached out to the authorities and to the cities caught in the frightening mayhem the killer ignited. As mysteriously as this serial killer began his reign of terror, he faded into the shadows.

Or did he?

To say that we, as a people, are fascinated with serial killers is an understatement. In the genre of true crime, the books on serial killers regularly outsell the others. Serial killers are the stuff that Hollywood movies and television series are based on. For many people, we can mentally cope with a single murder. Killing multiple, seemingly random people – that is something our sane minds cannot fully comprehend. As such, serial murders enthrall us. Serial killing cold cases are the most intriguing of all. Those stories draw you in out of the hope that you may be the person who can see something that the professional investigators missed. It was a matter of time before the Freeway Phantom cases became mainstream.

The investigators themselves often disagree amongst themselves as to which victims are tied to this murderer. Of course it wasn't helped that the media often attributed murders to the Freeway Phantom that were later disproved and their cases closed. Murders in DC were far too commonplace, and the knowledge of what serial killers were and how they operated only served to confuse the investigators even more. With multiple jurisdictions involved, the investigation seemed doomed from the start.

Washington DC's nightmare known as the Freeway Phantom started on April 25, 1971. Of the known victims, or at least those suspected linked to this killer, the last one occurred November 26, 1972. Twenty months, 579 days that this murderer was known to be stalking the children of strife-torn Washington DC. For many residents it was the end of DC's innocence. Children who were allowed to walk alone were told to go with someone and to avoid all strangers. Girls named Denise were even more frightened... since it appeared he may be targeting them. Everyone was a suspect.

The freeway in question refers to I-295 weaving through the District of Columbia for just over eight miles. It connects I-95 and the beltway that surrounds the capital,

I-495. Starting at the edge of the Potomac River, it passes Joint Base Bolling, the Anacostia Naval Station, and along the Anacostia River. Less than a mile of the freeway is in Maryland itself, where it ends, becoming the Baltimore-Washington Parkway, shooting up into the suburbs. Locals refer to the highway as the Anacostia Freeway. In 1971-1972 it was the primary dumping grounds for the Freeway Phantom. It was his road, his domain; its pavement was his jurisdiction. He acted with impunity and seemingly little fear of being seen or identified. Along this roadway he pulled his vehicle over, got out, pulled out his victims' bodies, and drove away. Countless people should have seen him but somehow didn't.

All we are left with are the questions. The most obvious of which is who did it? Was it a single killer or was it a pair of murderers? Did the killer really stop and if he did, why? How did he choose his victims? How did he snatch these girls off busy streets without being seen? Where did he take them? What did he do with them when he had secured them? Why did he dump the majority of his victims on I-295, one of the busiest freeways in the city? Why did he suddenly stop depositing his victims in the District of Columbia and start putting them in Maryland? What did he mean in the note when he said he would, "admit the others"? What "others" did he reference? Who were the suspects? Why was justice denied these families? There are other questions, dozens of them that demand consideration and answers.

One question rises to the top of all others: Was this a matter of race? If these had been young white girls gone missing, would it have garnered more attention than it did?

Muddying the waters were jailhouse confessions, lost evidence and records, and urban legends that persist to today. At the times of the killings, the nation's capital struggled with war protests, Watergate, and haphazard police work in an age before forensics. It seems incredible to us today that a serial killer stalked the streets of Washington DC and it scarcely merits mention. Only a few years out of the 1968 riots after the death of Martin Luther King Jr., Washington DC was not a capital at peace, but one in perpetual turmoil. Race issues, national politics, war and the space race dominated the headlines during the period of the murders. DC was the epicenter for chaos during the Freeway Phantom's reign of terror. He epitomized the violence that was straining under the myriad of tensions in the city.

Even to this day the Washington DC Metropolitan Police Department (MPD) steadfastly refuses to share information on the crimes, claiming, "We are actively working this case." It is a sad commentary on their police work, after nearly five decades that they are still hiding how badly this case was managed. Even the normally mute FBI was more than willing to share information on the cases. It makes one wonder what Washington's police department has to hide. As it turns out, plenty.

Lost in all of this are the victims themselves. With ages ranging from 10 to 18, their killer was somehow able to snatch them off the busy streets, often in broad daylight. Their stories seem as misfiled as the case files with the police. They are tied together by one thing, how they died.

- Carole Denise Spinks, 13 years old, disappeared on April 25, 1971, and found on April 30 off the Anacostia Freeway, I-295.

- Darlenia Denise Johnson, 16 years old, murdered July 8, 1971 – her body was found July 19 off I-295.

- Brenda Fay Crockett, 10 years old, murdered July 27, 1971. She called home from her captor's residence twice. Her remains are found on the grassy shoulder of the John Hanson Highway.

- Nenomoshia Yates, 12 years old, taken near a Safeway grocery store on October 1, 1917 – her remains are found on Pennsylvania Avenue.

- Brenda Denise Woodard, 18 years old, murdered on November 15, 1971 – her remains are left on the shoulder of I-295 on the entrance ramp to Route 202, along with the note she composed at the behest of her killer.

- Diane Dinnis Williams, 17 years old, taken and killed on September 5, 1972 – her body is found eight feet from the road.

- Teara Ann Bryant, 18 years old, abducted on November 26, 1972, while walking home from a nearby hospital in North Brentwood, Maryland, just outside of the District of Columbia. She is found two days later in the Anacostia River.

Some of the victims spent a few scant hours with their killer, while others may have been with him for days and were even fed by him. Almost all showed signs of sexual assault. There was, at one time, tangible physical evidence that linked five of the victims to each other, and their killer.

Were there other victims, ones who were not linked by the investigator to the Freeway Phantom? The murderer certainly alluded to it in his note. "I will admit the others when you catch me if you can!" Was this deliberate misdirection on his part, or were detectives in the dark as to which other murders he was responsible for?

To set your expectations up-front: If you are looking for us to definitively name the killer - this is *not* the book for you. Cold cases are rarely that easy for common citizens like ourselves to just crack, especially after nearly fifty years. If they were, true crime authors would be solving murders right and left. We are just authors, presenting facts and data.

We are here to take a jumble of information and make it digestible, perhaps even mildly entertaining. We will provide you names of suspects, where appropriate. One or more may be responsible for these crimes, or it can be another person who has slid under the radar of the investigators.

Where we can, we will give you, the reader, the key suspects and the cases for and against them. You are as much the detectives as we are. You have to decide for yourselves if the name of the Freeway Phantom is in these pages, or if it is someone else. Regardless, the killer has successfully eluded justice…for the time being. But you or someone you know may hold the key to cracking this case. Perhaps the killer talked to someone of his crimes, or perhaps you saw something on some dark night along I-295 that you are finally willing to share.

This story is a confusing journey of would-be confessors, gang rapes, and countless dead ends. The story is worth it though. The lives of at least seven girls are depending on us telling the story and you reading it. If nothing else, it ensures they are not utterly forgotten.

While these cases may never reach trial after nearly five decades, it is important that some answers are found. The real answer to these murders is out there with one of you, the reader. Someone out there knows something that could bring closure to the surviving family members and friends. Someone holds a secret that can finally give seven or more young girls solace.

The starting and ending point of it all is the note he left on young Brenda Woodard's dead body. Its contents were kept secret for decades out of fear that it might corrupt an already corrupted investigation. The note provides us with an incomplete picture of the murderer but a picture nevertheless.

PART I:

MURDERS IN THE NATION'S CAPITAL

CHAPTER 1: CAROL DENISE SPINKS

The body of a 14-year-old Southeast girl was found
yesterday 500 yards south of the Suitland Parkway,
near US Route 295, police said. Police said the victim,
identified as Carol Denise Spinks, 1058 Wahler Pl. EW
was discovered about 2:46 p.m. by an 11-year-old boy.
The girl was pronounced dead at 3:15 p.m.
in the DC morgue. Police said the cause
of death has not been determined.
—*The Washington Post*, May 2, 1971

Our nation's capital has always been an anomaly of cities
in the United States. Every other city in the nation resides
within a state. Washington DC has been carved out of
Virginia and Maryland, an urban island of sorts that was at
one time a worthless swampland. It sits astride the border of
northern and southern states, struggling with where it best
belongs.

In the 1970s, the biggest employer in the District was the
federal government. It was what drew a lot of families to the
city, in an era where government employment was seen as
an honored occupation. The District of Colombia residents
still do not have elected senators representing them, and
their vote has only been included in the Electoral College
since 1961. The founding fathers feared that making it a state
would be disruptive to government, and DC has wallowed

in that decision ever since. Even their current license plates defiantly reads, "Taxation Without Representation."

DC is managed by a mix of local officials with overbearing influence by the federal government. It is a complex city, not just because of its strange street layout (courtesy of the Freemasons) but even how peace is maintained. There are twelve different police forces currently in the city - ranging from the Park Police to the Washington National Cathedral Police to the Secret Service and the Washington DC Metropolitan Police Department (MPD). In 1971 the number was even higher, closer to twenty. To an outsider, it seems strange but to those who live in the city, these are indicative of the strange status that the city shares as the nation's capital.

By the late 1960s the city was becoming more divided among the lines of prosperity and race. Two-thirds of the city's population was black while at the same time 80 percent of the police force was white. The poorer neighborhoods in the southern parts of the city were populated almost entirely by black families. DC public schools had 92 percent black students; only one out of every three freshmen students in the DC public school system was expected to graduate high school. The divides in the city were deep and self-sustaining. In many respects it was a nuclear reactor, kept in a delicate balance to prevent it from going critical.

The control rods in that nuclear reactor were pulled on April 4, 1968, when Martin Luther King Jr. was assassinated. The black community, long frustrated by the inequalities in the city, turned to violence and vandalism to vent their anger. It started at U Street and 14th Street – the area known as the Black Broadway, spilling down the U Street Corridor. Fires were set and when first responders tried to intervene, they were attacked. Riots sprung up in Logan Circle, Chinatown, and spread to the Capitol Hill neighborhood. The rioting continued for four days, and eventually 13,000 troops from Fort Myer and Fort Meade moved into the city to restore a sense of calm...the most military in the city since the Civil War. The damage from the riots was staggering - at least $175 million in today's dollars. Close to a thousand businesses were damaged, including half of the city's 383 liquor stores. Almost 700 homes and apartments were burned. Police arrested 7,600 adults and juveniles on riot-related charges; thirteen people were killed in the skirmishes between police and rioters. In the end, the underlying problems that had led to the riots had not been resolved by 1971. The burned-out neighborhoods were like ugly scars on the city, charred reminders of the frustration felt by the majority of the population.

The day before the family of Carol Spinks lives changed forever, 500,000 protestors marched down Pennsylvania Avenue in the largest anti-war demonstration. April 24, 1971, was the start of a two weeklong demonstration opposing the Vietnam War that eventually shut down the US government. The protestors called themselves the "Mayday Tribe" with a mission to stop the government if the government wouldn't stop the War. Participants' goal was to nonviolently block traffic and bridges so that government officials wouldn't be able to get into office. The Nixon Administration had most of the protestors blocking traffic arrested before they even got into position using not only police force, but military force as well. It proved to be the largest of the anti-Vietnam war protests to ever hit the city.

The next day, on an unusually warm Sunday evening, Carol Denise Spinks ran into her mother just outside of the 7-Eleven about a half mile from their apartment building. Allenteen Spinks spotted her 13-year-old daughter before she entered the store. She reprimanded her for being out of the house and to return home immediately. It would be the last time Carol would be seen by her mother.

Carol was a typical seventh grader at Johnson Junior High School. She had seven siblings, including an identical twin sister named Carolyn. She was known as the shy and more insecure twin, as Carolyn was much more outgoing, but loved to show off her hula hooping skills. Her passion was jumping double-dutch jump rope, and she loved playing jacks with her siblings. She shared an apartment off Wahler Place with her siblings and her mother, Allenteen. Her older sister, 24-year-old Valerie, lived in the same apartment building and just across the hall from the rest of the family.

Wahler Place is located within the Congress Heights neighborhood of DC, nestled in the hills off the coast of the Anacostia River. After 1954 integration of schools, the number of white families living within Congress Heights rapidly declined. Congress Heights was previously closed to African American families due to segregation.

On April 25, 1971, Valerie asked Carol to go to the 7-Eleven store just seven blocks away to purchase five TV dinners, bread, and soda. Allenteen had strict rules for her children when she wasn't at home; they were not allowed to leave the apartment while she was visiting her aunt in Brentwood, Maryland. Carol decided to take the risk of getting in trouble and took a five-dollar bill to the store.

Carol walked the seven blocks down Wheeler Road, which happened to cross over into the Maryland state line. After running into her mother at the store, Carol was presumed to be heading home. Three hours ticked by without Carol returning to the apartment. The family began to worry and started to call neighbors and friends to ask if anyone had seen Carol. A phone call was made to the 7-Eleven, and the assistant manager said Carol had purchased the TV dinners and left the store at 7:40 p.m. Allenteen reported Carol missing to the Metropolitan Police Station's Seventh District.

In 1971, law enforcement treated missing children's cases differently than today. The police didn't take immediate action. There were no Amber Alerts, no contacting the news media to show pictures. Unless the child was missing for more than twenty-four hours, the police simply noted the call in a log. Chances are, sooner or later, the missing kid would simply return home.

A few witnesses had reported seeing Carol after leaving the store. A fourteen-year-old witness, on the way to the 7-Eleven with her own mother and sister, recalled passing Spinks on the sidewalk carrying a grocery bag. Another witness, Sicilia Diggs, reported seeing two black men jump from a blue car and snatch Carol off Wheeler Road. Diggs claimed that Carol was walking with her friend, Deborah Harrison, at the time and that the other girl had run away when Carol was abducted. Days later, after Carol's body had been found, Deborah Harrison was located and interviewed by police; she admitted to walking with Carol on the night she disappeared but denied watching her get abducted. Deborah also reported that she started receiving several threatening phone calls beginning the day after Carol disappeared indicating that she could be next.

Six agonizing days passed after Carol disappeared before a major break in her missing person's case. On Saturday, May 1, 1971, at 2:46 p.m. an 11-year-old boy wandered away from his friends while playing near the Suitland Parkway in Southeast D.C. Fifteen feet down a grassy embankment on the north bound lanes of Route 295, about 200 yards south of the Suitland Parkway near the Naval Research Lab lay the body of Carol Spinks. According to the FBI report, "The recovery site was along the northbound lanes of the highway was in the rear of the St. Elizabeth's Hospital complex. The boy and his friends stopped a traffic officer passing by on Interstate 295 to report the body."

Detective Romaine Jenkins was working in the homicide unit at DC Police Headquarters when a call came in that a body had been found on busy Interstate 295. Detectives John Moriarty and Roy Lamb were dispatched to the scene. Jenkins' supervisor assigned the 28-year-old detective along with two others to interview Spinks' neighbors and relatives. Just as Jenkins was about to head out, the district commander sent her to patrol the streets to help with Vietnam War protestors instead. The young dead girl was not the most pressing thing that the Washington MPD was coping with at the time.

The first officers on the scene were Captain Ellis and Lieutenant Like in Cruiser 219, joined a few minutes later by sergeants Ropel and Mussomele. Once they confirmed that they did, indeed, have a dead body alongside the highway, they called in Detective Sergeant Moriarty of the Homicide Squad along with Mr. Rayford of the Coroner's Office. Checks were made for missing children reports, and Carol Spinks was at the top of the Washington MPD's list.

Investigators at the scene where her body was found discovered that Carol was clothed in the same clothes in which she had disappeared six days earlier: a red sweater, blue gym shorts, and brown socks. Her size 8 and half blue tennis shoes were missing. Per the FBI report, "When found, the decedent was laying in a face down position, however the body was turned over by an on-looker prior to photographing by the police." As such, the crime scene had already been contaminated.

Her body was taken to the District of Colombia Coroner's Office for an autopsy. According to the medical examiner, she had signs of sexual molestation and abrasions to her hands and face. She had crescent-shaped marks on the left side of her neck, suggesting a ligature may have been used or perhaps these were fingernail impressions from her killer. Her nose was bloodied, and her lower lip was split open. She had been repeatedly sodomized.

The medical examiner estimated her death occurred two to three days prior to the discovery of her body, meaning she had been kept alive for three days before she was killed. The contents of her stomach included some type of citrus fruit, leading to the belief that she had been fed by her killer in the few days she had been kept alive. She had not been simply kidnapped and killed; she had been held prisoner. It should have been a clue, a hint, of the monster that the authorities were going to be up against.

Her official cause of death was asphyxia due to manual strangulation. Forensic examination showed Negroid hairs, unlike her own, on her shorts, sweater, underwear, and hair barrette. Synthetic green fibers were found on her shorts and inside her underwear. Blood was found under her fingernails, but the amount was too small for any conclusive blood-type testing or grouping. It told investigators that she had fought with her attacker. No semen was found anywhere on her body or clothing.

Police began an investigation into the abduction and murder of the petite girl. "Carol would never get into a car with strangers," stated Gloria Dent, a school counselor who worked with Carol.

To this day, Carol's twin sister remembers the day three detectives knocked on the door to inform the family of her death. Allenteen let out a bloodcurdling scream when she learned of her young daughter's fate. The Spinks family's agony was just the start, the beginning. No one knew that her death was the first link in a chain of victims that would terrorize and paralyze the nation's capital.

CHAPTER 2: DARLENIA DENISE JOHNSON

"She was found 11 days later - her face and body so badly decomposed that the medical examiner had to cut off her fingers to identify her. (Back then, there was no DNA testing, so authorities used fingerprints.) How she had died couldn't be determined. "Maybe," says [Detective Romaine] Jenkins, 'if they had located the body sooner, we could have had a cause of death.'"
—*The Washington Post*, May 2018

The next ten long weeks dragged by for the Spinks' family. Family members, friends, and Congress Heights neighbors answered every question from police, hoping to provide that small piece of information that would help solve Carol's case. The leads dwindled and tips were few and far between. If investigators thought that they were dealing with just a single young girl's brutal assault and death, that changed on Thursday, July 8, 1971, when another young girl disappeared into the darkness of Washington DC.

Darlenia Denise Johnson left her apartment on 3922 Wheeler Road SE in the Anacostia area between 10:30 and 10:45 a.m. for her job at the Oxon Hill Recreation Center, located in the Green School at Mississippi and Wheeler Road SE. She informed her family that she wouldn't be returning home that night; the Rec Center was holding an overnight trip for a group of children, and she had planned on helping out. Her coworkers never saw Darlenia arrive to work that day.

When her mother, Helen McNeal, hadn't heard from her daughter the next day, she filed a missing person's report with the Metro Police Department's Seventh District. As with Carol Spinks, there was no mobilization to look for Darlenia. There was no search for evidence or witnesses. All that the officer's confirmed was that she had not shown up for work. Her friends gave two variations of her plans – one that she was going on the overnight trip; the other was that she had planned to see her boyfriend instead.

Four days after she was last seen, on Monday July 12, a DC Department of Highways and Traffic employee had car trouble and pulled off on the side of I-295. When he got out of his vehicle, he noticed a body of a fully clothed, black female lying in the grassy area off the busy highway near the Suitland Parkway at 5:45 p.m. He immediately called police to report the body; it was the second phone call dispatchers had received that day regarding the same body. Officers had been sent to the scene earlier that day and reported back a "10-8", meaning they hadn't located anything and had moved onto other calls. "The officers didn't get out and look for the remains; they just drove by," stated homicide detective Romaine Jenkins.

As the days slowly passed, Darlenia's family knew there wouldn't be good news. "I prayed and I dreamed I saw her. I told my friends something had happened because the Lord has showed it to me," her mother told *The Washington Post.*

A full week after the phone calls came into the Washington MPD regarding the body on the side of the roadway, one of the callers drove by the area and saw that the body was still lying in the sweltering heat. The man became angry at the inaction by the department, so he informed his boss who drove by the area and called his friend, Charles Baden. Baden was a DC Police sergeant at the time who happened to be off duty that Monday. "He told me exactly where it was on the freeway opposite I-295, just north of Bolling Air Force Base," Baden recalls, "I asked him if he had called the police, and he said, 'Yeah, but nobody came.'" Baden rode to the site on his motorcycle and drove along the shoulder until he spotted the remains of Darlenia Johnson.

On July 19, a total of eleven days after Darlenia went missing, eerily, the location of this body was within fifteen feet of where Spink's body was found just ten weeks before, at the rear of St. Elizabeth's Hospital. The five foot, two inches, 110-pound young woman had lain exposed in the brutally hot July sun for days and was unrecognizable because of decomposition. By the time officers found her, identification was nearly impossible.

Her body almost appeared mummified, having been exposed for such a prolonged period. She was wearing blue shorts, a green sweater over a blue blouse, and a red/white/blue horizontal striped mini skirt. Oddly, her brown loafer shoes were missing. Detective Richardson arrived on scene with the mobile crime lab. The remains were taken to the medical examiner's office to be identified, but an autopsy would be inconclusive because of decomposition. The Medical Examiner had to cut off fingers for fingerprints to help identify the body. The official cause of death would be inconclusive as well as any evidence of rape or sexual molestation. Her mother was able to identify her 16-year-old's body by her clothing.

Very little evidence was able to be taken from her body. Negroid head hairs were found on her shorts, sweater, underwear, and barrettes in her hair. Blood was found under her fingernails and on her barrettes, but the amount was too small to be tested. No one knows what kind of trace evidence may have been lost simply because police officers had not found the body earlier. Even her date of death could not be determined.

About seventy-five residents of Congress Heights held a street corner press conference to draw attention to, "Poor police protection and failure to apprehend the murderers." Just three hours before the press conference was held, a 17-year-old girl was raped at knifepoint just two blocks away.

The protest was called together by Calvin Rolark, the editor of the weekly *Washington Informer* and president of the Washington-Highland Civic Association. Rolark led the meeting, accusing police and the news media of failing to give equal attention to crimes in Southeast DC. "If it was a blue-eyed, white girl from Silver Spring, her picture would have been all over page one. We are demanding from the police the same kind of services you get in Georgetown. Now it takes three or four and sometimes six hours before police respond. If they won't protect us, we'll have to protect ourselves by forming vigilantes," Rolark stated to the crowd. The group encouraged men to arm themselves with rocks and to run out any suspicious persons seen in the area. Darlenia's mother spoke at the event, "I think somebody picked her up, took her away and then killed her—I thought this was a nice neighborhood. We want protection out here. We're a bunch of forgotten people." The fear of the residents was palatable.

Lt Charles Light, of the Sixth District Police Department, stated that police patrols had not been increased in the Congress Heights area. He stated that the general crime rate in the area was "about average" and as far as he was aware, there was no known evidence linking Spink's and Johnson's deaths.

The police investigation seemed to focus on Alfred Holmes. While she had not gone to work as planned the morning she was last seen, it was believed that she had instead spent the day with Holmes at his home on the 300 block of F Street NE. According to FBI documents, if this was true, she would have been with her boyfriend from 2 p.m. on July 8 until 3 a.m. the next morning. Holmes was interviewed repeatedly by police and even given a sodium pentothal test after several witnesses claimed to have seen him with Darlenia on July 9. Holmes preached his innocence, claiming the last time he saw Darlenia was on July 4.

Bizarrely, Darlenia's mother reported to police that she had received several odd phone calls during the time her daughter was missing. Crank calls were not uncommon in an era before Caller ID. But who would crank call someone whose daughter was missing?

On July 21, about 125 Congress Heights residents held a street meeting in the 1000 block of Wahler Place regarding the deaths of both Darlenia and Carol. The meeting was called together by CHASE, an antipoverty agency in Congress Heights, that had helped organize search parties for Carol. "The police are committing crimes by not taking care of our children," said Congress Heights resident Glendora Thomas. Helen McNeil, Darlenia's mother, spoke at the event: "Somebody fooled her and killed her, or maybe she resisted what they wanted to do and killed her. I thought I lived in a nice neighborhood. I didn't think nothing could come about. I've been sitting up all night 'til before day in the morning. I'm so tired I feel like an old shoe." While the police had not yet started to connect the deaths of Darlenia and Carol, their families were drawn together by their common anguish. Carol's mother, Allenteen, came out of her home to address the crowd but broke down and had to walk away. "All parents should get together because we are sick and tired of the deaths of our children," Dorothy Wheeler said to the crowd.

CHAPTER 3: BRENDA CROCKETT

"Brenda Fay Crockett, considered by friends, neighbors and teachers to be a polite, friendly 10-year-old girl, spent Tuesday playing games, sewing and splashing in water from a fire hydrant. In the evening, after seeing a movie sponsored by a community program, Brenda was sent to the store for dog food and writing paper. She never returned home."
—*The Evening Star*, July 29, 1971

Ten-year-old Brenda Fay Crockett lived in Northwest DC and was enjoying a summer off from Harrison Elementary School in July of 1971. Brenda was a bright fifth-grade student and an active member of the school's safety patrol. She had lots of friends and loved attending church. Her mother reported she was well aware of the dangers of getting in vehicles with strangers. As such she seemed to be an unlikely potential victim to the killer operating in the District.

Nine days after Darlenia Johnson's body was found, Brenda disappeared into what would become a hellish night for her family. "My little girl went to the store and never came home," her mother, Reutha Crockett, told *The Washington Post*.

Those in the city at the time remember that July 27, 1971, was a hot and humid day in the District, with temperatures soaring to the low 90s. Kids played outside to simply stay cool in an era where many homes didn't have air conditioning. Just the day before, Apollo 15 launched, carrying with it, the lunar rover – man's first all-terrain vehicle for use on another planetary body. After the moon landing of Apollo 11 and the averted catastrophe of Apollo 13, people were beginning to treat trips to the moon as routine. While on the evening news, they were no longer as captivating as they had been only two years earlier.

During the day on that fateful Tuesday, Reutha Crockett was chatting at work with her coworkers regarding the recent murders in the area. "We were trying to imagine how we would feel if something similar would happen to us and we were faced with the same situation. That same afternoon, it did happen to me."

After work that evening, Reutha arrived home and her five children had gone outside to play. Brenda had spent the last evening of her life playing games outside, cutting a hot pants pattern to sew, and splashing in water from a fire hydrant. Reutha sat down to do her own homework from the evening school she was attending. She called Brenda inside and sent her to the Safeway at 14th and U streets NW around 8 p.m. Reutha needed typing paper and dog food for the family's three dogs: Ringo, Rex, and Romeo. When her mother sent her to the store, just five blocks away, she had assumed at least one of Brenda's siblings had gone with her. It was still daylight out, so her level of worry was low. After all, Brenda had been going to the store for years with family members. About thirty minutes had passed, and the twins came inside without Brenda. Reutha asked where Brenda was, and the children responded, "We don't know."

"Boy, I was upset. Because everything was running through my mind," Reutha recalled to the *Washington Star*. She began to search for Brenda around 9 p.m. Earlier that evening, Brenda had mentioned to her mother that she was waiting for it to get dark outside, so she could watch a movie with her friends in the neighborhood sponsored by a community group. "When I asked her to go to the store, she didn't refuse but said, 'Okay, Ma, I'll go.' I told her to hurry back." It wasn't like her to simply wander off.

Brenda was conscientious and attentive. She was a graduate of her school's, "Officer Friendly" program that instructed children to be aware of their surroundings and not talk to strangers. Her fourth-grade teacher, Allie Robinson, told *The Evening Star*, that although she was an average student, "she participated in extra-curricular activities to a remarkable degree. She was one of the most reliable school patrols we had."

While searching the neighborhood for Brenda, her mother stopped to ask a passing police officer if she could report a missing girl. The officer informed her that it wasn't "his beat" but would put her in touch with someone to help her. While she was out looking for Brenda in the neighborhood, she had no idea that Brenda was calling home.

The phone rang at the Crockett household around 9:40 p.m.; Brenda's younger sister, 9-year-old Bertha, answered the phone. Bertha immediately recognized Brenda's voice on the line. Brenda told her sister that a "white man" had picked her up near the Safeway and had taken her to Virginia. She also said she would return home by a taxicab. Bertha reported that her older sister was "crying a little bit" on the phone.

Just five minutes later, at 9:45 p.m., the phone rang again. This time, a family friend, Theodore Cadwell, answered the call. Cadwell heard Brenda whimpering on the other end as she told him she had been picked up by a white man, taken to his home in Virginia, and he was sending her home in a cab. Brenda asked if her mother had seen her. Cadwell asked Brenda to put the man she was with on the phone, but she said he was, "outside." Cadwell reported hearing movement in the background, footfalls on a floor, and the call abruptly disconnected after Brenda said, "Well, I'll see you." Her voice was oddly calm given what she had relayed. Brenda's mother arrived home, after searching for her daughter, and was informed of the mysterious phone calls. She called the police and filed a missing person's report with the Third District Metropolitan Police. Reutha Crockett stayed up all night, just waiting, hoping, praying.

"It was the most horrible night of my life," she would later tell the media.

The phone calls to the Crockett home were significant. While they could not be traced in the 1970s, the killer did reveal some important information. Brenda was in a house – such a call would not have been done on a payphone, and Mr. Cadwell heard footsteps in the background. The killer was concerned that Brenda's mother had seen him with his daughter, possibly able to identify his car. That meant while Brenda's mother was out looking for her, Brenda may have seen her mother, and it frightened her kidnapper.

Also, the call was disconnected. Not hung up. This indicates that the killer may have had a means to disconnect the phone, or simply unplugged it to end the call rather than hanging up.

The references to a "white man" and "Virginia" were clearly aimed at misleading the Crockett family, and subsequently the police. This was the first move in a game of chess between the investigators and the killer. Brenda's abductor had already planned on killing her and knew the authorities would be looking for him.

It would be another nine agonizing hours after the last phone call to her family, before Brenda's lifeless body was found. At around 5 a.m., a 24-year-old hitchhiker, Donald Ray Carter, of Alexandria, discovered a small body lying in the grassy shoulder of Route 50 (John Hanson Highway) and Kenilworth Ave in Prince George's County, Maryland. The body was just five feet from the curb of the road, lying face-up. Carter flagged down a passing motorist, hitched a ride into DC and was able to call police to report the body. A

Washington MPD patrol car was sent to the scene and Prince George's County Police arrived at around 6:30 a.m.

The final fate of Brenda Crockett fell to Dr. John Kehoe, deputy Medical Examiner for Prince George's County, who examined the body. He estimated that she had been deceased for at least five or six hours. The small four foot, eight inches, 75-pound girl was wearing a blue and white blouse, blue-flowered shorts, and some pink plastic curlers still in her hair. Her shoes were missing. A neighbor had reported seeing Brenda barefoot the evening she went missing, but her feet were noticeably clean when her body was recovered. Dr. Kehoe reported to *The Evening Star* that Brenda's body was found with a piece of cord, a scarf, both knotted, around her neck. Interestingly, a piece of cord was not found but just a scarf itself, tightly wrapped and knotted, such were the errors common in the newspaper at that time. Dr. Kehoe could not confirm cause of death until the autopsy was completed.

Prince George's County Homicide Detective Hilary Szukalowski was the first detective on the scene. He was a native of Hamtramck, Michigan, and had served in the US Navy before securing a job on the Prince George's County Police Department and becoming a detective in their ten-man Homicide Squad.

Szukalowski remembers the night well. "No one wanted to work the third shift. Our job, when a homicide came in, was to do the preliminaries. We would hand it off to the next shift to do the investigation. I was on two-week rotations at the time.

"I was close to getting off shift when the call came in. A hitchhiker found Brenda's body alongside the road. I got there and issued a Signal 81, Deceased Person Found.

"I remember everything vividly," he recalls. He placed clear plastic bags over her tiny hands to preserve any evidence before placing her body into a black, body bag for the drive to Prince George's Hospital's Morgue. Szukalowski said it had appeared that her body had been thrown from a vehicle. "I shot the breeze with the DC Detectives for a few minutes. At that time, we didn't use the name 'Freeway Phantom'; that came after she was found. They told me they had other girls that had turned up like her."

Szukalowski reflects back on finding Brenda's body, "People talk about soldiers having PTSD. With me it is the kids that I found that still haunt me."

Along with her shoes, several pink curlers were missing from her body. From a confidential police report on her death, "She had been vaginally raped, and there were ring-like contusions around her nipples, suggesting they had been bitten. There was a small contusion in the left temple region of her scalp." A few small Negroid hairs were found on the palm of her right hand but were too small for any sort of comparison. Synthetic, black textile fibers were recovered from her scarf. Green synthetic fibers were also recovered from her blouse, shorts, and underwear. Blood mixed with semen was found in the crotch area of her underwear but could not be conclusively grouped. While DNA evidence was something that was over a decade into the future, the Washington MPD had their first sample of it from Brenda's killer.

Prince George's County Police were able to quickly identify Brenda from the missing person's report just hours before. Reutha called her estranged husband, Lewis Crockett, to tell him the horrific news. Lewis had last seen his daughter six days prior to her death, when she had handed him a picture of her in her Easter dress and made him promise not to lose it. "She was a sweet kid," he said.

Brenda's school reported her as being an, "Obedient, lovely student" who participated in extra-curricular activities. "She was one of the most reliable school patrols we had," said one of her teachers. Three young boys each claimed to have been Brenda's boyfriend and were choosing not to play games after her death out of respect for her.

The tight-knit neighborhood came together to comfort the Crockett's. Women filed into the small, two-story, red-brick home to offer support to the family. A neighborhood who was typically full of frolicking children now only had a few playing ball on the block. "It's a shame you can't send your own child to the store and expect them to get home all right," said Barbara Dorsey, a neighbor of the Crockett's. Eva Artis, another neighbor in the close-knit neighborhood who often babysat for the Crockett children while Reutha worked, said, "We usually have a lot of games going on the street, but nobody's been acting right today. I think everyone is disturbed," she told *The Washington Evening Star*. Ms. Artis, who lived across the street from the family, told the same newspaper that Reutha, "Is a good mother; one that was concerned that her children grow up properly."

The crime made no sense. The fact that Brenda had been sexually assaulted was disturbing. This was not a girl who appeared older than she was. She was a child. The game the killer played with the family, having Brenda call the house more than once, feeding them misleading information, attempting to find out if he and Brenda had been seen by her mother... was cold and calculating.

With the brutal assault and death of Brenda Crockett, the Washington MPD found itself facing a cold grim fact. It was entirely possible that the same person was responsible for killing Brenda, Carol, and Darlenia. The phrase, "serial killer," didn't exist in 1971, but the concept of a repeat-murderer was not new.

CHAPTER 4:
NENOMOSHIA YATES

"Near YATES' body was a ladies loafer, believed
to have been shoved out of the car along with her
body. Recall that loafers were missing from the
JOHNSON body. It is not known if the loafer was
ever identified as belonging to victim JOHNSON."
—Confidential Police Report on the
Freeway Phantom Cases

Nenomoshia is a genus of moths, belonging to the subfamily
Olethreutinae of the family Tortricidae. belonging to the
subfamily Olethreutinae of the family Tortricidae. The name
is uncommon, but when used for a person's name it means
power, great humanity, a person who is a stimulator who
inspires those around them. Names often personify those
that have them, and such was the case of Nenomoshia Yates.

The hot summer months ticked by with little update from
police officials regarding the three young girls' murders.
A new school year started, and the temperatures started to
drop. The neighborhood children slowly started getting into
the school year routine, spending most evenings playing
outside after school. Life in Congress Heights seemed to be
going back to "normal"…until October 2, 1971.

Nenomoshia Yates, known as "Neno" by her friends
and family, was a quiet and serious 12-year-old sixth grade
student at Kelly Miller Junior High School. She lived in an
apartment with her father at 4952 Benning Road NE. Neno

spent most of her time riding bikes and roller skating with the girls in the neighborhood. "If they weren't on their bicycles, they were on their skates," said a neighbor. Neno loved school and "was one of the few children around here who said, 'thank you.'"

Neno lived in the Hanna Terrace Apartments, a three-story, yellow-brick apartment building in a lower-middle class, black neighborhood. Neno's father, a construction worker originally from rural Culpeper, Virginia, moved the family into the second-story apartment six months prior. "She loved to listen to records. She studied a lot. Sometimes I had to send her to bed," William Yates said of his daughter.

Change was in the air at the Yates home. Neno's stepmother was in the hospital after giving birth. Neno hadn't yet gotten to meet her days-old baby sister, LaShaun. The family was celebrating the arrival of the newest family member – what should have been the happiest of times.

On Friday, October 1, Nenomoshia was given a five-dollar bill to buy a bag of sugar, flour, and paper plates. Her destination was the Safeway at 5801 Benning Road, just a block's walk away from her apartment. Around 7 p.m., Neno started on the short trek to the Safeway.

She made it to the grocery store without an issue; witnesses in the store recalled seeing her inside. The clerk remembered ringing her out. Later, one witness reported to have possibly seen her get inside a blue Volkswagen with a yellow strip down the side with a Fauntroy political bumper sticker on it. The witness, who knew the Yates family, thought nothing of the sight at the time as he knew Neno's mother drove a similar vehicle.

Neno's father waited for her arrival back from the store. When she didn't return, he started to comb the neighborhood for her. William Yates knocked on neighbors' doors in the apartment building, searching for anyone who had seen Neno. Her mother was contacted, and she reported her daughter missing to the Fourteenth Precinct when she found out her Nenomoshia hadn't arrive back home.

At 8:45 p.m., Steven Patopi, a 15-year-old hitchhiker, spotted a body lying in the east-bound grassy area of Pennsylvania Ave SE. The area was just three tenths of a mile inside the Prince George's County line, with the body lying about 1,500 feet in the state of Maryland. Although it had been raining periodically throughout that October evening, the lifeless four foot, nine inches, 104-pound body was dry within the tall grass. The indication was that she had not been there long. Patopi had likely missed her killer depositing her remains by a matter of minutes.

She was lying face-up clothed in brown shorts, a sweatshirt, white tennis shoes, and socks. An extra shoe, a single brown loafer, was found near the body. Her body was still warm when she was found, with only forty minutes passing since the time she was last seen walking along the street. Prince George's County Police were able to quickly identify Neno Yates and called the crime lab from Metropolitan Police onto the scene. Detective Richardson started to follow what had now become standard procedure in the use of movie film of the area. Romaine Jenkins, now a nightshift supervisor in Homicide at the Washington MPD, dispatched Otis Fickling and Ronald Ervin to the scene.

The Baltimore Medical Examiner's Office completed Neno's autopsy. It was noted that she was violently raped, and her official cause of death was manual and ligature strangulation. Semen samples were able to be recovered from her body. Interestingly, the FBI lab report dated December 15, 1971, analyzed the same stained vaginal smears and reported that no semen was found. She had fingernail markings on her neck and face, an indication that she may have put up a fight against her attacker.

Negroid head hairs were collected from her underwear, sanitary napkin, sweatshirt, and jeans. Green synthetic fibers were also collected from her clothing. It was clear that someone else had redressed her. Her sanitary napkin was haphazardly placed…not by her, but by her killer.

A tire track was found near her body, which was noted to have been made by a smaller vehicle. Investigators suggested the vehicle could have been a Volkswagen, determined in part by a witness's account of seeing Neno get into a Volkswagen that evening. A photograph of the tire track was taken, but the imprint was not sufficient to make a cast.

A Safeway employee coming into work the next day found a grocery bag of sugar, flour, and paper plates. The bag was found on the sidewalk next to the woods in the 1900 block of Benning Road; the route she would've been taking home that evening, giving investigators a fairly solid positioning as to where she had been abducted. Detective Richardson believed Neno was forced into a vehicle with the thought that if she had gotten into a vehicle willingly, she would've brought the groceries with her.

Things changed in the District with the horrible murder of Nenomoshia Yates. The Washington MPD admitted that this case and those of Brenda Crockett, Darlenia Johnson, Carol Spinks, and (at the time) Angela Barnes were connected. They had been killed by the same person or persons. The press latched onto this, dubbing the killer, "The Freeway Phantom."

Three days after Neno's body was found, *The Washington Daily Press* ran a story on her murder. "We've got to get something on this before there's another victim," said a spokesperson for Prince George's County Homicide. District detectives released to the public that there was "a possibility" that the recent cases of the murdered girls were the work of a single person. The newspapers and television and radios stations referred to the cases as the work of the "Freeway Phantom."

Police scrambled to follow each small clue in Neno's case. The witness who had seen Neno get into a blue vehicle was a boy who lived in the same apartment building as the Yates family. He claimed the car had Maryland license tags. "If she got in that car, it was someone she knew. It had to be. She wouldn't even speak to me. That little girl would pass you and not even open her mouth. She would smile, but if you spoke to her, she would start running. Everywhere she went, she ran," said Alfred Aiken, the resident manager of the apartment building, to *The Washington Post*. It seemed that everyone who knew Neno knew she wouldn't speak to a stranger. So how did her killer get her into his vehicle?

Detectives roped off a section of the heavily wooded area across from the apartment building to search the area thoroughly looking for any other evidence. Neighborhood children reported several times that a man hiding in that wooded area had exposed himself to kids going to or from school. Karen Parmenter, a 16-year-old, who lived in the same apartment building as Neno, said the man scared the kids, which caused the children to walk the long way to school. Was this the killer, stalking his prey in advance?

CHAPTER 5: BRENDA DENISE WOODARD

"[The Freeway Phantom] Just dragged them out and left them. This girl had a winter coat, and it was just left on top of her. It didn't conceal her person, but that black coat really stood out when my headlights hit it. I knew that something was there that was out of the ordinary. I was probably going 35 to 45 miles per hour when I went by her on the curve. So I had to go back and get out of the car and shine my spotlight on her and take my flashlight and go and look. When I was about ten feet away, I could see that it was a girl under that coat. Her eyes were fixed, her pupils wouldn't dilate. Her arm was up, when they took the coat off you could see that it was propped up by her body rather than being held up. When I first looked, that alerted me, like "Whoa! Is she still alive? Is she holding her arm up?" Well, she wasn't holding her arm up."
—David Norman to the authors.

With a name now attached to the killer, the Freeway Phantom, the police tried to walk a dangerous tightrope between keeping the civilians and media informed and trying to track the killer. While the police were actively working each murder, the information they released to the local newspapers was anything but promising. "From all the information we have, we don't have a composite picture that points to any type of individual," said a district detective to *Washington Daily News*. Congress Heights residents continued to voice their frustrations with police, demanding more police patrols and protection. The families were frustrated by the silence they were getting from the Washington MPD.

The investigators were faced with problems they usually didn't with 'normal' homicides. Not only were they looking at each of the cases individually, but they knew they had a killer who was responsible for most if not all of them. That meant looking for connections between the victims, the crime scenes, and witnesses. Today, investigators have a wealth of knowledge and experience to tap on how to search for a serial killer. In 1971 there was no precursor for the Washington MPD to follow. They were making it up as they went along.

Six long weeks ticked by as investigators attempted to follow every lead in each of the cases. Tips came in from the public, but all proved to be dead ends. The cases were losing momentum, despite the increased publicity…until another girl went missing.

Brenda Denise Woodard had gone through a great deal in the past few years of her life. At 18 years old, she moved in with a neighbor, Brenda Schumpert, after ongoing conflicts with her family. She had moved into the apartment across the courtyard from her parent's apartment, at 2105 Maryland Avenue NE just three weeks before she went missing. The arguments were almost always over whether she was allowed to date, which her father wouldn't allow until after she graduated from high school. Brenda wasn't always obedient to the rules of the house and would go to parties and pursue boys, like many rebellious young women. Although she had physically moved out of her family's home, she visited her family daily and seemed to be getting along with her parents. On the day that Neno Yates had been found, she called her mother at work and cautioned her to take extra care of her sisters. She was well aware a killer was on the streets of DC.

Brenda had been held back two years in school due to low grades and high absences, so she was already much older than her classmates. Although she was the oldest of six children, she was in the same grade as one of her younger sisters. She got along with all her siblings and aspired to be an elementary school teacher, specifically first grade. She often babysat for friends in the apartment building and had worked as a playground assistant at the Youth Center on North Capital Street during the summer.

She had an almost obsessive crush on a boy named Walter Clark. Walter had a girlfriend and would occasionally sleep with Brenda, but he would always stay with his girlfriend instead of dating Brenda exclusively. Brenda had public episodes of crying outside of his home for hours at a time, becoming so hysterical that she was once hospitalized in the psychiatric ward at DC General Hospital. During that hospital stay, she was characterized by doctors as, "emotionally immature."

Earlier that year, in May, Brenda had gotten in trouble at school. She had attended Spingarn High School at the time and gotten into an argument with her boyfriend, eventually throwing an empty beer can at him. This incident, along with similar outbursts, caused Brenda to transfer schools. When she didn't return to Spingarn in the fall semester, many of her friends suspected she had been expelled. According to Edward Woodard, his daughter transferred schools after being heckled by other girls at school. Brenda had gotten a part-time job with the Recreation Department and had decided to complete her remaining classes at Cardozo High School's night program. She had planned her class schedule out to graduate by spring of 1973.

A few people who knew Brenda reported that she would frequently get in the cars of men she didn't know. Her parents said the exact opposite of Brenda, "She wouldn't get in a car with anyone unless they knew or unless they forced her to," according to her father. "I wouldn't say she was a saint or anything like that, but she was trying to improve herself. She wasn't into drugs or anything. I think that she was just a person, a person who didn't deserve to get murdered," said classmate, Anita Harrell.

On November 15, 1971, Brenda stopped by her family's home after babysitting at a friend's house to have dinner with her family. After dinner, she played a few records on her new record player she had bought the day before. She asked her father if her younger sister, Diane, could take her to school that evening. He told her no because Diane was an inexperienced driver. He offered to take her to school instead, and if she didn't have a ride home from school, he could pick her up as well. About 6:30 p.m. on that Monday evening, Brenda's father drove her to attend evening classes at Cardozo High School.

"I kissed her, and she smiled and got out — that was the last I saw of her," Brenda's father said. Her father, a porter at a Giant Foods store, noticed that Brenda was unusually happy when he had dropped her off that evening because she had an appointment for a job interview the next day.

After the classes let out for the evening, she left the school around 9:45 p.m. with Sherman Mitchell, a male classmate. The two stopped to eat at Ben's Chili Bowl, an iconic DC restaurant, in the 1300 block of U Street NW. After eating a small meal of two half-smokes, they boarded the DC Transit bus around 10:25 p.m. Carrying her four textbooks, she transferred to another bus at 8th and H streets NE, heading home for the night. Sherman remained on the first bus, heading to his own home. After arriving to his bus stop at 8th Street and Virginia Avenue SE, he walked to a 24-hour grocery store near his home. He got change for a dollar and called Brenda's home to make sure she got home safely for the night. It was after midnight, and her roommate answered the phone and told Sherman she hadn't seen Brenda yet.

Brenda would typically stop by her parent's home after class. When she didn't stop by on that Monday night, her parents assumed she had just gone straight back to her nearby apartment. At 11:30 p.m., her roommate called the Woodard's and said Brenda hadn't come home yet from night classes. Clearly something was wrong.

The next morning, Brenda's mother had left work early for a doctor's appointment at 6:45 a.m. She waited at the bus stop for about an hour before asking the guard what the long wait was for. The guard informed her that a body had been found off Route 202, on her way to work. She decided to start walking down the hill to get on another bus. On her way, she passed the body located on the other side of the street but couldn't see enough to tell what was going on. She continued to walk down the street and noticed a wig lying on the street. "It looks just like the wig my daughter has," she told a younger woman walking with her. After seeing the wig, it stayed on her mind even after her doctor's appointment.

"I still couldn't get that wig out of my mind. I arrived home around 11:45 a.m. When I opened the door, the phone was ringing. It was one of my coworkers telling me about a girl's body that was found near the hospital. I hung up on my friend because of the wig. I caught control of myself, and before I could call my friend back, the lady that Brenda was babysitting for called and asked if I had seen my daughter. I became very upset and called my husband at work to tell him that our daughter did not come home. When my husband entered our door, I burst into tears and said, 'Our daughter is dead!' and he asked me how I knew. I told him about the wig I saw near the body that was found, and I knew it belonged to Brenda. He told me not to get upset and that maybe it wasn't. He called the police, and they came out to our house."

At 1:45 p.m., the Woodard's filed a missing person's report for Brenda. While filing the report, they were shown a photograph of a young girl found in Maryland. They were able to identify Brenda based on the police photograph.

Around 4:50 a.m., a rookie Cheverly police officer found an unidentified body "appearing to be about 15 years old," fully clothed and facing up. Officer David Norman, badge number eight, spotted something dark in a rough grassy area of the service roadway between Baltimore-Washington Parkway and Route 202 Landover exit ramp, nearby to the access road to Prince George's County Hospital and only about a mile inside the Beltway.

David Norman had been with the Cheverly police department since 1970 after serving in the US Army as a paratrooper in Vietnam. "I was in the Army at Fort Meade, and I looked to get into law enforcement. So I went to Cheverly and got in. It was in the paper, you know, a job posting. I applied for it, and all of my credentials I had in the military kind of slid me right into that job, you know? Being a combat soldier, part of an elite military unit – that's why I was familiar with firearms and explosives and all that stuff."

As he recalled the crime scene to the authors: "Her body was found in Cheverly on the side of the road. The actual property itself is Prince George's County but is in the jurisdiction of Cheverly because we are on both sides of it. The particular side of the road where this body I found was out of the hospital territory, but it was in Prince George's County.

"So I was making a legal jurisdiction. As it was, finding a body is finding a body, but as it turned out I needed to have power over that particular spot, so the County police detectives could investigate it.

"Whatever time it was in the morning, I had just left the duty officer at the hospital, and I was driving down towards Maryland Route 202 – Landover Road. Well, to get there, I had to use the ramp leaving the hospital which also intersected with a ramp leading to the B and W Parkway. The body was on the right side, not on the parkway egress, but in the town of Cheverly. So I spotted the body, and I didn't know what it was. I just knew it was something black.

I went down to the intersection, made a U-turn, and came back up and pulled into the little section where the roads intersected going down to the Parkway or to 202.

"There's a place there for you to pull over on the side of the road and take pictures or whatever, on the right side, where I found the body. The other parts wouldn't be safe to pull over by. I wouldn't be there long either.

"When I pulled my cruiser into the space provided for coming off of the parkway or going back onto the parkway or going down to Route 202 – it's a little section of open roadway. I shined my spotlight onto the body. The killer had placed her coat over top of her. It was a shiny black coat. It covered her body except for her head and one arm. Her arm, her left arm, was sticking up. I thought at first she was holding her arm up. As it turns out it was propped up, the way she was laid down. I shined my light into her eyes, and, of course, there was no response at all – the pupils or anything. I decided to call in the homicide, so the county police were responding, which they are the investigative agency for the town of Cheverly.

"So the [Prince George's] county police showed up. Well, the first thing to show up was the United States Park Police. Now the Park Police have jurisdiction of the Baltimore Washington Parkway, including, to some extent, an exit ramp or any on-ramp. Municipalities have more power than the county or the federal government – it goes to jurisdiction. It's the town of Cheverly before it's Prince George's County, before it's the State of Maryland, before it's United States federal property.

"The Park Police had set up some sort of a van; it had all kinds of crime scene materials in it, and there were several cars pulled over. This particular detective, whose name was Dick Hart, from the Prince George's County Police Department, he approached me and saw all of the Park Police stuff being set up. He said, "Norman, can I talk to you for a minute?" I said, "Sure." He knew me by name, and

I knew who he was, he was famous as a detective. He puts his arm around my shoulder and says, "Norman, are we in the town of Cheverly?" I said, "Yes sir, we are." He asked, "How do you know?" I said, "There's Cheverly on the right and Cheverly on the left, and this is a state road other than leaving the parkway. And when you take the ingress cross this road and go into the parkway, then you're back on the federal parkway."

"He said, "Oh, but it IS the town of Cheverly then?"

"I didn't really know where he was going then. I said, "Yes sir, it is."

"He asked, "When you have a major crime, who investigates your major crimes?" I said, "The Prince George's County Police Department."

"He said, "Okay, I need to have a talk with this Park Police lieutenant over there." So the detective walked over to them, and he had me follow along. He approached the Park Police lieutenant and said, "I need to talk to you for a minute."

"The lieutenant said, "Yes."

"He said, "This is Officer Norman of the Cheverly Police Department, and he's the one that found the body. And for what it's worth, it's in his town. And he's giving the investigation to the Prince George's County Police."

"The Park lieutenant started arguing. Saying, "No, no, no, no. This is United States Park Property, and WE are the primary investigative unit.

"Detective Hart said, "I don't know how up you are on jurisdictional issues, but this is the town of Cheverly before anything. The town of Cheverly has the power to give this to whatever agency it wants."

"The Park Police lieutenant was fuming. He told his men, "Pack up the truck, we're getting out of here!" So he did. Hart said, "Good job Norman! Good job!"

"So I am there, and I had not touched this body. I didn't see any reason to touch it. I certainly didn't want to tamper with any evidence like her coat or whatever was under it. I could see that she was dead. Hart was talking to me, and his crime scene people were doing their jobs, taking photographs, whatever, and they used 35mm film canisters to mark the general area around the body. If you saw the photo of her with her coat still on, it has those little shiny things around the body. They are 35mm film canisters. They were trying to prevent anyone from tampering with that spot, inside those canisters. Also, if the body was moved, we needed to know exactly where it was – so that was somewhat marking where the body was.

"So when they removed the coat, her shirt was pulled up at her stomach, over the top of her belly button, and I believe you could see some blood there, and she had several non-life-threatening wounds to her stomach area, I believe. They didn't produce a lot of blood, in fact they couldn't – they were after the fact. The wound that actually killed her was a knife that went into her armpit, so the other wounds would have been after death – postmortem. That's probably why they didn't bleed much.

"The man had completely undressed her and put her clothes back on her. They weren't put on properly, that's how detectives knew that. Detective Hart told me, 'Norman, you helped me out, so I'm going to keep you in the loop,' and he did – though there wasn't much he could tell me. But he did give me a complete set of the photographs."

Investigators noted that her clothing wasn't put on properly, indicating that her killer possibly attempted to redress her. Her sweater was on inside out and her skirt wasn't properly zipped. Buttons were missing from her long coat. Four rings were still intact on her fingers and a green ribbon still in her hair. The afro wig she had been wearing when she was last seen was missing from the crime scene. The schoolbooks she had been carrying were also missing. A hole in her sweater corresponded with her abdominal wounds. The wound that took the young woman's life was an apparent knife wound that entered her armpit area. The textbooks stood out to the authorities. For some unexplained reason, her killer had kept them – perhaps as trophies, or by complete accident.

She was found lying on her back in a black turtleneck, a blue and white checkered mini skirt, black wet-look boots, and a burgundy, three-quarter length coat. Her sweater was turned inside out. Her body was faced perpendicular to the road with her hands clasped behind her head. No purse or identifying papers were found near her body. The still unidentified body was sent to Baltimore where the assistant Maryland Medical Examiner, Dr. Charles Springate, performed an autopsy.

Her cause of death was a stab wound to her right chest. She had also been strangled; her neck was bruised and broken according to the autopsy report. She had defensive wounds to her hands and had signs of rape that showed some degree of force. Green synthetic fibers were recovered from her socks and underwear. Negroid head hairs were located on her coat, boot, shirt, and bra. Two Caucasian head hairs were also recovered; although it's speculated that they came from the detectives on scene opposed to the perpetrator. It is unknown if the Caucasian hairs were ever compared against samples from officers on the scene.

The black afro wig missing from Brenda's body was located about thirty yards away. It was found lying in the left turn median of Landover Road. Detectives believed that the killer may have discovered the wig in his car after he had dumped Brenda's body and threw it out the window of his vehicle. From where it lay, it seemed that he had found it in his car after depositing her body, then had callously discarded the incriminating wig.

A report from police was published in *Washington Daily News* that a note was found pinned inside the coat pocket of the body. The note contained two handwritten lines on white notebook paper that, "…represented a real breakthrough for us, because it's our only communication with the suspect so far." While the exact contents of the note weren't published at the time, the newspaper reported that the note "contained a confession to several other similar crimes of young, black girls whose bodies have been found dumped near area highways."

Senator Charles Mathias of Maryland issued a statement during a press conference: "The murders of six Washington girls since May have shocked, alarmed, and saddened the entire Washington Metropolitan area. As a community we extend our deepest sympathy to the victims' families… sympathy, however, is not enough. Today I join with DC Police Chief Jerry Wilson and Chief Roland Sweizter of the Prince George's County Police Department in asking all area citizens to help police as they seek a solution to these slayings. In addition, I urge all parents of young girls and young women throughout the metropolitan area, to heed police warnings and take extra precautions until the person or persons responsible for these vicious and heinous crimes have been apprehended. Finally, I want to offer my praise to the men and women of both the Metropolitan and Prince George's County police departments for the excellent operation they have exhibited over the past months and which they continue to exhibit in the investigation of these crimes. Citizen cooperation can help bring about a solution."

No witnesses could be found who saw Brenda get into a vehicle that night. Detectives checked the whereabouts of known metropolitan area sex deviates at the time of her murder. Recent inmates of St. Elizabeth's Hospital in Anacostia were investigated. It was the murder of Brenda Woodard that caused the FBI to get involved with the Freeway Phantom because of the dispute over whether she had been found on federal land. The FBI made out of town checks on persons of interest who had left the area, widening the search across the United States. The Metropolitan

Police and the FBI released a photograph of a mannequin designed to look like Brenda Woodard dressed in her own clothing to the Washington DC newspapers. Police had hoped that publishing the mannequin's picture would help any witnesses come forward who may have seen Brenda the night she was killed.

The day after her body was discovered, Dr. Sheldon Freud reached out the media to warn girls named "Denise" that their lives were in danger. Dr. Freud was an internationally known psychologist who worked with the Prince George's County Police Department. "I would think that any girl with the name 'Denise' would be particularly careful. Random killing is not very common. Assuming that this is one man, we might suppose that he has some hostile association with the name Denise or even the letter D."

Six days after her body was found, Brenda Woodard's funeral was held. Reverend Jennings, the same reverend who married Brenda's parents and had christened Brenda, read her eulogy. Guests lined up to view Brenda, dressed in a new blue lace dress. At least ten of the girls who had signed the guestbook were named "Denise". One mourner sobbed loudly, "Oh Jesus. Oh Lord. I hope he doesn't see those names!"

The note found pinned to Brenda's body was the biggest clue investigators had. The FBI believed that Brenda herself had written the note; the theory was confirmed when the note was matched up with Brenda's handwriting. The note was written on lined notebook paper, clearly cut from the notebook it had come from. It was discovered that the note was written in Brenda's own handwriting with her typical punctuation, with no visible signs of nervousness in the handwriting.

Detective Romaine Jenkins believed that the note's contents were either dictated to Brenda by the killer or she copied it from a previous note the killer had written. Jenkins believed that someone in Woodard's tight-knit Northeast neighborhood may have seen or heard something. Jenkins herself had grown up in the same area, gone to Spingarn High School, and some of her cousins knew of Brenda.

Interestingly enough, Lt Joseph O'Brien, Chief of the Washington Homicide Squad, reported to the media on November 17 that despite other reports, the note found was "absolutely not signed: The Freeway Phantom." The specific note's contents continued to be withheld to the public.

The Washington Daily News reported on December 2 that the note had been dictated by the killer and written by Brenda. Although the entirety of the note wasn't published, the phrase "catch me if you can" was released along with the signature "the free-way phantom." Leaks were already occurring in the Washington MPD to add confusion to the public.

Another press conference was held on November 18, just two days after her body was found. Mayor Walter Washington along with Police Chief Jerry Wilson led the gathering at police headquarters. The *Washington Daily News* covered the press conference to ask for public assistance on the cases. Chief Wilson believed the killer must have tried to abduct a girl who got away or refused. "If such a girl exists, she should confer with her parents and then come forward with a description of the car and the man." Deputy Chief Pitts said, "There's got to be a clue out there, somewhere. Someone may be afraid to come forward with this information, possibly because he's afraid of his own safety. All names will be kept in confidence and the callers can remain anonymous." A general profile of the suspect was given: "Someone on the block who has a reputation of inviting children into his home, and he lives alone. Somebody knows a sex deviate or a child molester. Somebody knows something. These are generally the types of clues that will solve this case. We'll run out every anonymous lead we get," Deputy Chief Mahlon Pitts reported. The Denise name theory was also addressed, "I can't conceive that the killer is out looking for girls with the middle name Denise."

DC Police assigned six full time homicide detectives for the murders along with the 100 detectives assigned from Prince George's County, Cheverly Police, FBI, and the US Park Police. Six special phone lines were created. All calls, even cranks, will be checked," said Pitts. In the first seven hours the hotlines were open, officers received more than 500 calls from people with possible tips. The hotlines ran out of the fourth floor of police headquarters and ran around the clock. Callers were told they did not have to give their names during the call. *The Washington Daily News* set up a specific delivery box for information to be mailed in the case that a tipster might not want to speak directly to police.

Very little was offered about the status of the current investigations, but it was publicly announced that police weren't optimistic about finding the killer. The phrase "totally stalled" was used to describe the current investigations. Police did not believe there was any connection among the murdered girls.

The obsession with the Denise Theory continued to be topic in the media. *The Washington Post* consulted mathematicians regarding the theory that the killer was targeting girls with the middle name Denise. The paper reported that three of the four victim's parents were contacted to see why they chose the middle name 'Denise' for their daughter; all of them reporting they had no particular reason for the name. Although it is unlikely that the killer was targeting girls named Denise, the statistics are mind-boggling that it was mere happenstance. According to professors at Georgetown and George Washington universities, the chances that the common middle name is a coincidence in the murders is between 1:6 million and 1:60 billion. The Chief of the DC Division of Vital Statistics estimated that no more than 1 out of 100 girls would have the middle name Denise.

While theories on the victim's themselves floated, the public seemed to be fed up with the status of the cases. Christian Service Corps pled on the radio and television stations, asking the killer of any or all of the young girls to turn himself in: "This is an appeal to the person or persons responsible for the deaths of six young girls. Please call this number; this is a pay phone, and it is not tapped, and you will hear my voice only. Here's why I'm asking you to call. Right now, I'm more concerned about you. You probably feel the whole world is after you. You may be scared. You may be just plain tired. If you are, there is someone you can turn to without fear." One hour after the message was aired, a total of eight people dialed the number. Three of those callers didn't say a word, only heavy breathing was heard on the line. The other callers gave theories about the killer. One caller, who identified herself as being named "Denise," was hysterical when she called. The hope was that this personal appeal to the killer would cause him to confess.

A vigilante group, composed of 200 Vietnam War veterans in the District, formed a "Veteran's Protective League" with a goal to help protect citizens in freeway areas. The men broke into groups that patrolled the Baltimore-Washington Parkway, Capital Beltway, and George Washington Memorial Parkway areas 24-hours a day, with more men patrolling during dark hours. According to the group, the men carried two-way radios, infrared glasses, and floodlights. The group planned to set up roadblocks if any suspicious activity or vehicles were seen. "When we get out, since we're in uniform, it will look just like a military police barricade," said an informant. A district police official took to the *Washington Daily News* to respond to the group: "We need all the help we can get, there's no question about that, but let the police, who are paid to take the risks, take them."

By early December, more than 7,000 phone calls had been made to the six hotlines. Each call was taken seriously; at one point, police released that a tipster had mentioned seeing a flashy red Mustang with a dark-colored racing stripe near the grassy area Brenda's body had been found.

While the hotline calls had been ringing off the hook, by early April, only a few calls were being taken a week. "After months of intensive investigation, police say they have run out of solid leads in the slayings. Homicide detectives in the District and Prince George's County acknowledged for the first time that little credence was ever given to speculation that a single killer was responsible for all six deaths," *The Evening Star* reported. Sergeant Leo Spencer, of DC Homicide Squad, stated that some of his detectives believe they may be looking for as many as four killers; Prince George's County reported they consider the possibly of two to four suspects to be involved in the murders. With all the investigations occurring within different departments, it is easy to believe how each department had a different theory. Each tip was investigated thoroughly, but when each one didn't pan out to be credible or didn't offer an answer, investigators had no choice but to report to the public: "Nobody saw any of these girls abducted. It's unbelievable, but I guess that's the case," Spencer said.

Edward Woodard, Brenda's father, accused the media of publishing details of Brenda's life and neighbors for being too willing to supply information to the media. "People have a whole lot of criticism, but whatever you do as a parent, there's going to be criticism. People said I was hard on her, but it wasn't that…she was the oldest and she was my heart." Edward also made a public plea to Mayor Walter Washington to take an interest in the cases, "In the past, he hasn't had time to worry about us because we are poor people. The police have been very nice and polite, and I don't want to criticize them, but all isn't being done by the police and the Mayor."

CHAPTER 6: DIANE DINNIS WILLIAMS

"During her reinvestigation, [Detective Romaine] Jenkins learned that Johnson's mother got odd phone calls during the time her daughter was missing. Williams's parents also received a call, with the caller saying, 'I killed your daughter.' Police determined that Johnson likely was with her boyfriend before she vanished, but his mother refused to let police interview him. 'That's a little-known fact,' Jenkins says."
—*The Washington Post*, May 2018

Ten months passed after the death of Brenda Woodard. The ten-month pause was the longest cooling off period the Freeway Phantom had during his reign of murder. While much conjecture can be made as to why this was the case, it is clear the murder of Brenda Woodard did not go as he had planned. This is evidenced by his use of a knife to kill his young victim. She had fought, harder than the others. It had resulted in a loss of control; her struggle had forced him to resort to using a knife to kill his victim. Perhaps this and this alone was enough to shake him, to make him worry that he might get caught.

By early September 1972, the world was fixated on the Munich Olympics in Germany. On September 5, a group of eight Palestinian terrorists attacked the Olympic village, killing two Israeli Olympians. The terrorists wanted the release of 200 Palestinian prisoners in Israel. With the gunman holding the Israeli team members hostage, the West Germans attempted a failed rescue mission that cost the lives of all the hostages, five of the terrorists, and a policeman. The world was stunned by the sheer brutality half a world away.

On September 6, 1972, the Olympics resumed under the somber cloud of remorse. It was on that day that DC's Freeway Phantom began to listen to that nagging urge in the back recesses of his dark mind…that urge to kill again. As it had happened before, it began with the finding of a young woman's body on I-295.

Diane Williams had been planning to attend Ballou Senior High School where she would have started her eleventh-grade year. Just a few months before her death, in May, she along with her four sisters and brother, accepted Christ as her Savior and was baptized. As the oldest child, she would take charge and assume responsibility of the house and her siblings while her parents went to work. During the summers of 1971 and 1972, she was an employee at the Department of Recreation as a recreational aide at Savoy Elementary School in Southeast. She opened her own savings account and had enough money to purchase her own school clothes. She had dreams of becoming a model; with her soft, delicate features and trim build, modeling very well could have been in her future.

The Williams family lived in a two-story home in a tree-lined street in Congress Heights. The family had lived on Halley Terrace for the past three years. "She wasn't the type to get in a car with anyone she didn't know. She wasn't the type to go running around on the streets," said Margaret Williams, Diane's mother. "She was the quiet type. She hardly went out but had lots of friends at work. I knew where she was most of the time," Leon said of his daughter. Diane was a bright student and liked to draw. She was a member of the Youth Center at Bolling Air Force Base and a social group at Assumption Church. She was known to trust people in general and wasn't afraid of anything or anyone. She would walk anytime of the night and not be afraid.

The only thing that stood out in Diane's life was she had recently been sad and depressed, causing her to seek help from a doctor. She had reportedly undergone an abortion in the recent months before her death. She did not enjoy living in the DC area, after moving around the United States multiple times throughout her life. A newspaper claimed Diane was seen at local bars and nightclubs. Margaret Williams did not believe her daughter would go into a bar or nightclub, although Diane did not always tell her mother where she was going.

Diane's life was destined to cross paths with another man, the Freeway Phantom in September of 1972. It was not an encounter she was destined to survive.

Her fate began when the body of a young black female was found lying face down just off Interstate 295, between the District line and the Capital Beltway. The body was found just eight feet off the shoulder but not easily seen from the roadway due to a slight grade. A tractor trailer driver had stopped to check on his equipment and noticed the body in the grassy area and notified Armed Forces Police at 8:04 a.m. The Armed Forces Police lacked jurisdiction in the area and notified Maryland State Police Headquarters in Forestville.

Lieutenant Richard Stallings, of Maryland State Police, responded to the call. Once Lt. Stallings reached the scene, the truck driver led him to the body. "I thought she must have lain there overnight due to her clothes being wet," he said. Stallings notified Prince George's County Police who immediately reached out to the specific "Phantom Division" working under Deputy Police Chief Mahlon Pitts. The mobile crime lab was sent to the scene, and the crime scene was quickly roped off. A systemic search of the entire area within a quarter-mile radius was completed. Hundreds of feet of 8mm motion picture film was used. Both film and investigation findings were compiled into a report and taken back to the Phantom Division to be studied by the various law enforcement agencies involved.

The black female was described as in her mid-teens to early twenties, lying with her hands at her sides. She was wearing a yellow top and blue jeans. "DIANE" was written on one of her white sneakers and $1.26 was in the pocket of her jeans. Although her shoes were found with her body, the shoelaces were missing. The unidentified body was sent to the morgue in Baltimore for autopsy by Prince George's County Police. Dr. Peter Lipkovic, assistant medical examiner for Maryland, performed the autopsy. The cause of death was reported as "manual strangulation." She had a minor bruise to her rib cage and abrasions on her left elbow. Fingernail markings were found on her neck. It was estimated that she had been dead for nine to twenty hours prior to the body being discovered. Diane Williams had been reported missing the day before, on September 5, by her father. Detective Robert Granham, of the Maryland State Police, contacted Diane's parents and invited them to Baltimore. Diane Williams, who was actually 17 years old, was positively identified by her parents later that afternoon at the city morgue.

Semen was present on her body, but it was reported by her boyfriend that they had sex the night before. It is unclear if the semen recovered was positively matched to her boyfriend or from her attacker at the time. Brown Caucasian and Negroid head hairs were collected from her body. As with Brenda Woodard's case, the Caucasian hairs were believed to have originated from the detectives on the scene. Green synthetic fibers were found on the inside of her bra.

Although her parents had identified her body, they had not gotten home in time to inform her siblings. The television stations had picked up the information from the Baltimore Police Department; once the media understood the body had been identified by her parents, they felt no further obligation to suppress the information. Diane's five siblings waited at home for their parents to return with news of their oldest sister. Suddenly the name "Diane Williams" flashed on the television screen. According to a neighbor, the normally quiet and mannerly Williams children were screaming at the news.

The painful task of reconstructing the last known events of the life of Diane Williams began. The day before Diane's body was found, the Williams family had gone to the Recreation Department where Diane worked to pick up her paycheck. Diane stopped at the bank to deposit her paycheck, then the entire family shopped at Sears, Roebuck and Company for some school clothes. Diane volunteered to paint the stair walls, and the family took part in choosing a paint color. "All that day, Diane seemed very happy," her mother said. When they arrived home from shopping, Diane took a nap while her mother started painting the walls. Diane made the family dinner that night, fried chicken, sweet potatoes, rice, and gravy. During dinner, Diane's boyfriend, James, called to say he had bought some new records and wanted to invite her over to his house. "I was not in favor of her going but because Diane wanted to, Diane wanted so very much to go, I told her to check with her father. Leon and I both agreed that Diane could go if she promised to be back by 10:30 p.m.," said her mother. Before she left, she borrowed some change for the bus fare. "I remember telling her, 'if you are not here by 10:30, don't bother to come back.' That was the last time I talked to her or saw her alive."

The curfew time of 10:30 p.m. came and went and Diane was not home. Right before Leon Williams left for his nightshift job as a prison guard at Virginia's Lorton Reformatory that night, he reassured his wife that Diane would be home soon. Her mother continued to worry when she had not come home by 11 p.m., so she called Diane's boyfriend. "When he stated he had escorted Diane to the bus stop and waited until she boarded the bus over an hour ago, the nightmare that later turned into reality began. An hour later, James telephoned me and learned that Diane had still not arrived home. To avoid a false alarm, I didn't telephone Leon at work. I sat alone and wondered what happened to Diane. The anger that I had felt because she had not kept her promise to me turned into anxiety and anger," recalled her mother.

On his way home from work the next morning, Leon drove along the route where six other young girl's bodies had been found. He noticed a truck pull over and a few men standing nearby. At the time, he didn't notice anything significant of the sight. Later that day, he would realize he passed by the discovery of his daughter's body. When he arrived home that morning, he learned that Diane had not returned or phoned home. He immediately called the Metropolitan Police Department to report his daughter missing.

James Pryor had watched Diane board a Capital Transit bus at Martin Luther King Avenue near Howard Street NE. The bus driver, a 28-year-old man, was interviewed by police for five and half hours.

The testimony of the bus driver, Warren A. Williams III, the last person to see Diane other than her killer, was less than helpful. He was adamant that she had gotten off his bus at 19th and Benning Road. But for investigators like Detective Romaine Jenkins, that didn't make sense. "The bus driver said she got off at 19th and Benning Road. No, she didn't. If she got off the bus and she was going home, she got off at 21st. That was leaving her closer to her house. She wouldn't have gotten off at 19th Street…he made a mistake. If she got off at 19th Street, she wasn't going home. That would have caused her to walk too far to get home. Twenty-First Street – go straight up 21st Street until she hit Maryland Avenue."

Williams was adamant in where he let her off. He told *The Washington Post*, "The only reason I remember the young lady was because she was so good looking and because she was dressed so neatly. She could have been a model." He claimed that she was accompanied by two youth who, "looked like hoodlums. They were pretty shabbily dressed." The two men the bus driver had described were tracked down by police and questioned. Neither one of them could add anything to help in the investigation.

What investigators did note was that the streets were poorly lit near Halley Terrace, and if Diane had gotten off at her regular bus stop, she would have had to cross a dark parking lot to get home.

"It was unusual for a girl to get on the bus by herself at that hour of the night," the bus driver Williams said. She got off the bus at Martin Luther Avenue and South Capitol Street. From there, she would have walked across a dark parking lot and poorly lit street.

The tight-knit community reacted with anger towards the police departments and at the mayor. Much of the community raised a racial issue, believing that if the young women had been white, their murders would have been solved. The Williams family received phone calls around the clock, including the same person calling at 2 a.m. on four separate occasions, saying "I killed your daughter" in a sinister voice. Other crank calls came in, asking for Diane by name.

During the investigation, police found that two of Diane's younger sisters and a couple of neighborhood girls had told their parents about a man that had exposed himself to them just three weeks before Diane's death. At the time, the teenagers found it funny and didn't think anything of it. After Diane's death, they decided it may be significant and informed detectives. Detectives requested that the girls come to headquarters to assist a police artist with establishing a description of the man. When the officers arrived at the home of the neighborhood girls to take them to police headquarters, the girls' father refused to allow his daughters to participate. The girls' mother ended up bringing the girls to headquarters later that day. With all the girls' help, the police artist drew a face of a foreigner of Hispanic or Indian in nature. Police never did locate the man nor was it known if he was responsible for her subsequent murder.

Diane's body was taken to Mason's Funeral Parlor prior to her funeral. The mortician noted a piece of evidence she thought was worthy of investigation by police. She insisted pathology tests be made the night before the evidence was to be destroyed by the embalming fluids. Semen and Negroid hair were found in Diane's mouth. The previously performed autopsy conducted in Maryland had not discovered this critical information.

The Evening Star offered a $5,000 cash reward the day after Diane's body was found for any information leading to an arrest in any of the slayings. A special phone line, "Tips Anonymous." became open six days a week from 7 a.m. to midnight. If a tipster didn't feel comfortable calling, mailed information was also accepted. Local radio station WUST offered a $1,000 reward, and Warehouse Employees Union offered a $3,000 reward.

Leon Williams religiously had made payments on a $4,000 educational policy for Diane. The policy was presented as collateral to pay for her funeral expenses. Diane's funeral took place on Tuesday, September 12, 1972. To accommodate the large number of visitors, her viewing took place on Sunday and Monday evenings. A total of seven books were filled with names of visitors. Among the visitors was the Woodard family, showing respect and support of another potential Freeway Phantom victim. Plain clothes detectives were present during the funeral to watch for any suspicious activity and used movie cameras to film the funeral. An "x" was placed next to any visitor's name who acted any different than suspected. A spectator who had accidently knocked over a basket of flowers was later questioned by police.

James Pryor, Diane's 16-year-old boyfriend, was known as a shy, sensitive young man with a bush haircut. James and Diane liked to spend time together just sitting and listening to music. Although Diane had been to James' home a few times, he would typically come to her home to visit her. When Diane's family told James that arrangements had been made for him to ride in the family car during her funeral procession, tears rolled down his face.

Jennifer Woodard, the 16-year-old sister of Brenda Woodard, read a letter during Diane's service. "I know that all the sympathy cards and notes of condolence in the world cannot erase away any portion of the pain that you must feel at this moment. Some people can only guess about how it must feel to lose someone very close in such a violent way. But, I do not guess. I know. I was the first one of my sister and brothers to find out about my sister Brenda's death. It was a moment of numbness. My whole world seemed to have shattered before me. The only thing I could say was 'why couldn't have it been me?' A big part of living includes accepting the bad with the good, but why in god's name does such a large part of it have to be bad? One day, and I hope very soon, this insane maniac will be found. But until then, I hope and pray that another innocent girl will never fall in the hands of such evil and purposeless death."

Diane's flower-covered, pale blue coffin was lowered into the ground at Arlington National Cemetery. Since her father was a twenty-year veteran of the Army Quartermaster Corps, she was laid to rest at the historic cemetery.

The investigation ratcheted-up immediately. Captain Robert Boyd led the Washington Metropolitan Police and assigned thirty officers to the case. Detectives went door-to-door in Diane's neighborhood; talking to neighbors, friends, and anyone who knew Diane. Each morning, the Phantom Division held a briefing on developments in the investigation from the previous day.

"She was my second mother. I went to her for love and answers. I hated when she had to work because she was gone away from me," said her sister Patricia. Patricia Williams joined the Metropolitan Police Department in October 1982 with a goal to help solve the Freeway Phantom murder cases.

The public made their own assumptions that Diane's case was most likely related to the other young girls' murder cases. Even Lt. Richard Stallings of the Maryland State Police was quoted saying Diane's murder fit "the same pattern as the murders last year." Washington MPD Detectives made sure to report that there was no definite link with the other murders but "because of the similarities, you have to follow it up."

The similarities between the girls was indeed hard to ignore. Four girls shared the name Denise, one named Diane. Six girls were in school, with one attending night classes. Three of the girls played or worked at the same parks. All the girls were last witnessed walking along major streets. All the girls were young, healthy, and athletic. All the girls lived in the Congress Heights and Anacostia areas in Northeast DC and came from middle-class families.

Frustrating the detectives was that during the investigation, police were unable to find a single trace of Diane from the time she left the bus until her body was found in Maryland. Even at the hour of night she was walking that last leg home, there were people on the streets – but no one seemed to see her or her assailant. The Washington MPD added an additional thirty men to assist Maryland State Police and the FBI during the investigation. The rewards for information continued to climb to more than $9,000. More than 1,000 persons were interviewed by police. Thousands of phone calls came into the six specific telephone lines with all tips being checked out. In mid-October, *The Washington Post* reported that Metropolitan police "blame the public for the inability to find the killer or killers of seven Washington girls found strangled over the past seventeen months along expressways." Police continued to believe that someone had to have seen each victim getting into the killer's vehicle. Detective Louis B. Richardson of homicide division gave a general update on the cases. "I'm positive somebody knows something in each and every case. We're pleading with the public to come through." Two detectives were assigned to each case, treating each as an individual murder. "Maybe the detectives can communicate more clearly with the victim's families. These cases could be isolated," he said, "As long as they are out there, you don't know who the next victim is going to be."

At first glance, the Denise theory wouldn't be able to be applied to Diane Williams' case. Her middle name was Dinnis, a variant of Denise, which continued to fuel many rumors that the killer was obsessive with names that start with the letter "D" or the name Denise. Newspapers carried every theory, no matter how ridiculous, to try to apply a level of clarity around the twisted mind of the killer.

A generalized idea of the type of suspect police were looking for was released to the public. They believed the killer was middle-class, only due to strangulation killings being typically associated with middle- and upper-class killers. This man looks for a certain type of young girl: black, well-dressed, thin, and walking somewhere alone. It was also believed that the killer was someone in the Anacostia community who knew the area well. Maybe he lived in the area or worked in the area. Lt. Richardson continued to plea to the public, "This man has confided in a close relative or a friend. We're seeking this person to come forward to save an eighth victim's life. This man is a bonafide freak. He is mentally unbalanced."

Maryland State Police publicly delegated the investigations of Prince George's County homicide and rape cases to Prince George's County Police Department in early November. Although the Maryland State Police claimed that they didn't have the manpower to investigate the cases, it was rumored to be due to "professional jealousy" between the two police agencies over the Freeway Phantom cases. A source went to the media and reported that state police refused to let county police on crime scenes "until they had completed processing the scene." Prince George's County Police reported these incidents, which forced a meeting between the two police chiefs. The investigative change caused more than thirty-five state troopers to request job transfers.

Newspaper accounts reported that DNA testing was completed in 2006 by Prince George's County Police Department to determine the identity of the semen sample recovered from Diane's body. According to unconfirmed reports, this DNA sample was linked to James Pryor, Diane's boyfriend. Allegedly he admitted to having sexual intercourse with Diane the night of her disappearance once confronted with the evidence. These allegations have not been validated by the current officers assigned to the case, however. Nor is it clear if the DNA recovered from her mouth was the same as the DNA recovered from her vaginal area.

And now comes the quandary. Most lists of the victims of the Freeway Phantoms stop here. Even the current poster from the Washington MPD shows Diane Williams as the last of the Phantom's victims. But that may not be true. There is possibly another and the distinct possibility that the Freeway Phantom struck again in the 1980s. Before going there, one must first look into the tragic murder of Teara Ann Bryant…

CHAPTER 7: TEARA ANN BRYANT

In loving memory of my sister who passed away
one year ago today, November 26,1972
As flowers rest upon your grave
May the Lord be with you through the day
It seems like yesterday, when you passed away
We think about you every day.
Your loving Brother, Terrance Bryant
—*Washington Evening Star*, November 26, 1973

Teara Ann Bryant is a name that is not often associated with the Freeway Phantom cases, at least not publicly. Even the different police agencies cannot fully agree whether she is part of the spree of murders claimed by the Freeway Phantom. Different officers from the Washington MPD do not concur, and the Prince George's County Police have long claimed that she is not part of the spree of crimes. The FBI, however, does include Bryant in their analysis of the Freeway Phantom cases as do some of the most respected authorities who have investigated these crimes. It is well-worth considering her as a Phantom victim.

On Sunday, November 16, 1972, 18-year-old Teara Ann Bryant was taken to Leland Memorial Hospital by her mother for a "minor medical problem." Her mother dropped her off and told her to call her for a ride when she was ready to be picked up. "I left her at the hospital at 3 p.m. I told her to call me to get a ride home, and I gave her a dollar for bus fare in case she missed me. But I never saw her again," sobbed her mother, Sadie Bryant.

At 5:30 p.m., Teara called home and spoke with her brother and informed him that she did not need to be picked up from the hospital and that she would be taking a bus home instead. She was witnessed to have stopped at Dunkin Donuts after leaving the hospital. Between 6 and 6:30 p.m. a neighbor who knew Teara, reported seeing her carrying a bag and walking south along Route 1 near Suburban Trust Bank heading towards her home. "I don't know why she wouldn't have taken the bus. I gave her money for it, and it would have taken her right to the door," said Mrs. Bryant to *The Washington Post*. When she didn't arrive home, Teara's mother called her boyfriend and other friends to see if she was with one of them. Sadie Bryant reported her daughter missing at 3:55 a.m. Monday morning.

An entire day passed until Teara's lifeless body was found floating in the shallow Anacostia River in Bladensburg about twenty feet from the bridge over the river. Raymond Alston, a 19-year-old, Cottage City Vocational School senior, spotted her body as he was crossing the Bladensburg Road Bridge in Anacostia Park on his way to school that morning. "I thought it was a doll, a big toy, until I got closer and knew it was real." He ran to the school and told his teacher about the discovery. The principal of the school went with Alston back to the river to verify the body before calling police.

The location of her body was about two miles from the hospital. She had noted bruising on her neck; her cause of death was strangulation. One of her loafer shoes was discovered upstream in Anacostia River Park, only about 200 yards from Teara's home in North Brentwood. It is believed that her body floated downstream to the location it was found, based on authorities locating one of her shoes washed up on the embankment. Teara was clothed in her red, white, and blue horizontally striped dress, red nylon, three-quarter length jacket, one brown loafer, and white knee-length bobby socks. A gold band was still on her left hand, which seemed to rule out robbery as a possible motive.

Police believed Teara met her assailant as she walked south on Rhode Island Avenue between 5:30 and 6:30 p.m. She was last seen, alone at the time, on the 5000 block in Hyattsville, which also is the location of the Hyattsville County Police Station. When her missing brown loafer was found, it reinforced the police theory that she had been attacked as she walked home. The tide levels in the basin supposed the theory that her body had been dumped into the river at the bridge and then drifted downstream to the location her body was later found.

Teara was an unmarried devoted mother of an 18-month-old son, Anthony L. Jeter. She had been senior at Northwestern High School in Brentwood, just restarting school after dropping out for a few months to take care of her young son. "She wanted to finish school so that she could get a decent job. She tried to get a job without finishing, but she couldn't, so we talked it over this fall, and she decided to go back to school, even though it was hard for her with the little boy and all. She was so devoted to her son. He was almost her whole life," said Teara's mother.

She had spent her whole life growing up in Brentwood, and her friends recalled her as outgoing and friendly. "She was a very talkative and friendly girl. She had her problems—going to school and taking care of the child at the same time and trying to get a job—but she was a strong person, and she was doing all right," a friend recalled of Teara.

Adding to the hell that the family was going through, The Metropolitan Life Insurance Company, initially voided Sadie Bryant's $1,000 life insurance policy claim for Teara's death. The insurance agent, Ralph Vawters, informed Mrs. Bryant that because Teara's physical description wasn't on the original contract, it would be voided. It took considerable effort to finally get the insurance company to pay the grieving family.

Prince George's County Police and Metropolitan Police detectives quickly discounted reports that Teara's death was in any way linked to the Freeway Phantom cases. "Her death doesn't have any of the elements," said John Hoxie spokesperson for the Prince George's County Police. Authorities announced that since Teara's killer had tried to hide her body instead of dumping her roadside, that it differed too much to be considered connected to the other cases. "You don't have the transporting and dumping aspect. This looks like the killer didn't want the body found. It was more conventional."

It is understandable to believe that Teara Ann Bryant may not have been part of the Freeway Phantom killings. There was no tell-tale green synthetic fiber evidence, which would later link five of the six known victims, though her immersion in water may have washed it away. Her killer is not believed to have taken her somewhere to have killed her, which was part of the Freeway Phantom's modus operandi. It is believed she was killed either where her body was placed in the river, or between there and where she was last seen. Lastly, Teara Bryant was not stalked in the District of Columbia, but was intercepted, assaulted, and killed entirely in Maryland. The biggest assumption that Teara was not considered a Freeway Phantom victim at the time was the fact that she was found in a body of water and away from a major roadway.

At the time, Teara was strangled, and there is evidence, specifically her teddy being opened, that there had been some sort of sexual assault. Also, the Freeway Phantom, as will be explored later, bathed his victims. Teara was thrown in the river – either to conceal her body or to remove trace evidence. Was it possible that she was indeed the last victim of the Freeway Phantom?

Her case, like the others, remains open and frigid cold to this day.

PART II

THE HUNT FOR THE FREEWAY PHANTOM

CHAPTER 8: EARLY IN THE HUNT

"I've got some information for you."
"Well, what is it?"
"When you find the Phantom, you'll be surprised
because the Phantom wears a policeman's uniform."
Click
—From the Phantom hot line, *The Washington
Daily News*, November 19, 1972

To say that the Washington MPD was unprepared for having a serial killing case in their jurisdiction would be a gross understatement. Initially they did not connect the crimes and confused the list of victims, unsure of just who was truly linked the cases. The waters were muddied by the death of Angela Barnes. Shot in the head execution-style in the middle of the Phantom's killing spree, she appeared on most of the early lists despite having a different mode of death than the other victims. She also lacked the tell-tale green fibers that connected most of the Freeway Phantom's dead.

Making matters worse, when Angela's killers were found, they were in law enforcement. To a community that had strained relations with the police, going far past the recent 1969 riots; it only served to fuel the fires of a theory that someone in law enforcement may be involved. The Freeway Phantom continued to kill once Angela's killers had been arrested, leading authorities down another dead end.

The Mayor's office got involved with the case, making inquiries for the public. Maryland Senator Charles Mathias took to the media to warn young girls to, "take extra precautions," until the killer could be apprehended. Even the White House contacted the police to inquire about the case and offer federal resources. Community groups held meetings and organized early forms of neighborhood watches. Young black girls volunteered to serve as bait, under the watchful eyes of undercover officers, to attempt to lure out the killer. In many ways the tragedy of the Freeway Phantom brought together the city residents in a way like nothing before. One resident summed it up bluntly, "All parents should get together because we are sick and tired of the deaths of our children."

Multiple jurisdictions being involved in the investigation did not help. The killer's operating in both Prince George's County and the District, with the involvement of the Park Police and the FBI, both enabled and complicated some of the efforts of the investigators on the street. Was this the intent of the killer, or fortunate circumstance?

Some of how authorities spoke to the media did not reassure the public. Chief Jerry Wilson of the Washington MPD told *The Washington Daily News* that the department had sifted through a lot of evidence, but he was not optimistic that they could find the killer. Lieutenant Joseph O'Brien, head of the Homicide Squad said he, "...couldn't concede that the killer sought out victims with the name 'Denise.'" This made some families much more concerned than others, fearing their daughter with that name might be targeted.

The Washington MPD felt the public pressure and tried to respond. Thirty homicide detectives worked the cases, augmented with an additional twenty-one detectives pulled from other duties. Overtime was authorized, but this was not a case that was going to be solved by throwing manpower alone at it. At the urging of Deputy Chief Maholn Pitts, hotlines were established after the death of Brenda Woodard and were immediately swamped with phone calls. "We feel that because the girls are over in this area," he said pointing to the Southeast quadrant of Washington DC on a map, "that someone in the community, there are individuals or an individual, who has a clue to help us in these cases." Pitts was convinced that the killer had tried to approach other young girls and had likely failed. Perhaps if some of them came forward, it might help investigators. His hinting at this in media press conferences seemed to only stir more anxiety in the community rather than calm the situation.

The Washington Star and *The Washington Daily News* all established post office boxes where tips could be mailed in and phone numbers that could be called into. *The Washington Daily News'* Phantom Finder received more than 500 calls in the first seven hours of operating. By the end of two days, they had received more than 2,000 tips, most of which were pure speculation and guessing on the part of tipsters.

Many of the calls were useless. Typical of this: "My father is the Freeway Phantom," one little girl called in. When asked for his name, she hung up. Others told the tip lines that the killer drove a Corvair, a Mustang, a Bonneville, a Ford pickup truck, a green station wagon, a convertible… every make and model that could be conceived of. The tips included family members turning each other in, ex-wives fingering their former husbands as the killer, and women who had been flirted with or approached by men in automobiles.

When the tip line leads proved fruitless, they tried other techniques. The police poised a black unmarked car at the church of Diane Williams' funeral to film everyone attending, thinking that perhaps the killer was one of the mourners.

The reward for the killer started at $10,000 and was raised to $15,000. Radio station WUST offered an additional $1,000; the Warehouse Employees Union Local No. 730 offered $3,000; the Mecca Temple Number 10 of the Ancient Egyptian Arabic Order of Nobles and the Mystic

Shrine offered $1,000, and *The Washington Star* offered $5,000. While the amounts do not seem like much by today's standards, in 1972 dollars it was equivalent to nearly $145,000. Despite the money being offered, the tips slowed to a trickle.

Other groups did what they could to maintain interest in the cases. The Christian Service Corps went on several radio station urging the killer to turn himself in. "We want to help you, if you'll turn yourself in." To their credit, several DC councilmen got involved at a neighborhood level, both attempting to calm the public and generate tips. On one radio program, Dr. Sheldon Freud, a Prince George's County clinical psychologist tried to analyze the killer on the air. "The killer cannot control his impulses and may or may not want to, but that an atmosphere of panic and appellations such as 'Freeway Phantom' are likely to feed is psychosis. This is not a horror movie. We are dealing with a human being who probably cannot control himself. He should be told that, if he'll give himself up, he'll get treatment." These pleas did not bring the Freeway Phantom to surrender.

Detective Richard Thorton of the Washington MPD told reporters in a press conference, "It's like looking for a needle in a haystack. We don't have any more than we had the first day, except that we've eliminated some people as suspects. I can't say we're not getting somewhere, though, because every time you eliminate someone you get somewhere."

Investigators went to the local mental hospital, St. Elizabeth's, and began to comb the wards for any violent patients who were unaccounted for during the time of the crimes. Further, during this pre-HIPAA era, doctors were interviewed and turned over patient records in the search. While some proved tantalizing, most ended up being more blind alleys for the detectives.

The Washington MPD believed that this was a matter of finding the killer's pattern. If they could dissect how he operated, they could somehow apprehend him. This led them to following some tips that made little or no sense. One was that five of the victims (Carol Spinks, Darlenia Johnson, Angela Barnes, Brenda Woodward, and Diane Williams) had all frequented a nightclub, The Shelter Room, in the 1300 block of Savannah Street SE. Given the ages of the girls involved, this seemed borderline absurd, but officers clutched onto any possible thread that might connect the girls, not realizing that their only real relationship might be that their murderer selected them.

The families of the victims understood one thing, keeping the cases in the press was the best way to ensure they would not be forgotten. They spoke at various community functions like the Congress Heights Citizens Association. The parents and family members formed the Freeway Phantom Organization, Inc. aimed at continuing the pressure on authorities and informing the community as to the risks the killer posed. They went on television and the radio to warn the Washington DC community to be mindful of their children, that the predator was in their midst. The organization brought in law enforcement officers to talk about defending oneself against a rapist assault. Their efforts led to an increase in the reward for the killer.

Two true crime magazines covered the case – *Crime Detective* and *Official Detective*. The reporting of the stories in the magazines was usually along the lines of contemporary true crime articles, often authored by reputable reporters or even investigators tied to the cases. The covers of these magazines in the 1970s were almost always salacious, with semi-nude women, often shown in bondage or with a knife at their throats. Most places selling them put them next to *Playboy* and *Penthouse* on the magazine racks. The family members were incensed that their young girls were being published in "pornography" magazines, so they took matters into their own hands.

One of the officers of the organization, and an aunt of one of the victims, Diane Williams, Mrs. Wilma Harper, wrote a self-published book, *The Mystery of the Freeway Phantom*. The proceeds went into the organization. Much of the book is gleaned from newspaper accounts and deals with crime prevention; it did serve as another avenue to keep the story going.

As with all cold cases, the issue becomes one of tips and resources. As the leads slow to the authorities, the resources to follow up on them are not needed and diverted to other cases. It is a sad story that plays out with such crimes repeatedly. The massive manpower thrown at the Freeway Phantom cases dwindled down to a handful of officers.

That changed on February 11, 1973, with the arrest of several men as part of a string of rapes that had plagued the District. Suddenly, the Freeway Phantom case went from frigid to raging inferno in terms of priority.

CHAPTER 9: THE GREEN VEGA GANG – PREDATORS IN THE NIGHT

"Until the missing links in the case
emerge, the case is stymied."
—*The Washington Afro American*, June 19, 1976

The story of the Green Vega Gang and its involvement in the Freeway Phantom cases is one involving unsavory if not horrible people, investigators striving to give the families a sense of closure, and the blatant manipulation of the legal system. It is a story that meanders through seedy sections of our nation's capital and through the back alleys of people's imaginations. Fanned into a flame at one point by the press, it was a fire that burned quick and provided little comfort to the city. Much like the final season of *Game of Thrones*, despite the incredible build up and long-awaited anticipation, it fails to fully deliver.

Like any major metropolitan area in the 1970s, Washington DC had an unmanageable number of open rape cases. Even obtaining statistics from that period is nearly impossible. What was known was that there were well over a thousand unsolved rapes in the District by the early 1972. Combined with a sharp rise in drug use, it was nearly overwhelming for the Metropolitan Police Department.

Rapes were easy to prosecute if the victim knew her attacker – but many of the cases that stacked up in the Sex

Squad's files were rapes of opportunity. Their assailants were total strangers, sometimes pulling their victims in right off the streets in broad daylight. In an era where there were no surveillance cameras and no cell phones for tracking, victims could be abducted, raped, and dropped off somewhere else in the city with little idea of where they were or who had attacked them.

It was clear there were serial rapists at work as well, though that particular phrase would not come about for another decade. Such was the Green Vega Gang rapes. The name of these particular rapists was tied to the emerald Chevrolet Vega car used in the crimes. These rapes stood out, not just because of the vehicle used in their crimes, but based on the descriptions of witnesses, it was upwards of five different men involved with the rapes.

The driver of the vehicle was always described as the same man, a "Negro male, medium complected, stocky and bearded. His height was estimated between five foot, nine inches and five foot, eight inches." His age was guessed to be between 25 and 30 years. Some described him as a good looking, well kept, and his initial approach with his victims was not threatening – but almost charming.

There were others who rode with the driver. The most often described man was a Negro male, in his twenties with short bush haircut. One victim said he had two broken front teeth, was about five foot, nine inches, clean shaven, and about 23 years old. Another said the passenger in the Vega had a chipped tooth, a scar, pimples, and was dark complected, clean shaven, tall, and wore a dashiki and glasses. Yet another said he was dark skinned, in his mid-twenties with a scar on his face.

Their modus operandi was indelibly linked to the car they used. The driver would appear as less threatening as possible and was driving alone. The well-dressed man would pull up in a green Chevrolet Vega alongside the sidewalk in DC and offer a ride to a young woman hitchhiking, waiting at a bus stop, waiting for a taxi, or somebody simply walking alone in the dark. Their victims ranged in age between 15 and 26 years, with the vast number of them on the older end of that spectrum. The driver would ask them if they needed a ride. Most agreed willingly, not realizing the risk. They were lulled into it by the lack of a visible threat.

Those few women who sensed something was not right, would be shown a pistol and ordered into the passenger seat of the car. If there was a chance that the victim would be spotted, the driver would point the gun at her and have her lay her head in his lap as he drove.

A few blocks away the first of his accomplices would be standing, waiting for their driver/partner, usually pretending to hitchhike. They would flag their compatriot down and would say they needed a ride. It all seemed innocent enough. The new male hitchhiker would get in the small car with the girl in the back, effectively trapping her. Then a few blocks away, the pair would sometimes pick up at least one other man.

The victim didn't realize something was wrong until she wasn't taken to her destination. Her kidnappers would drive to an abandoned building or apartment. The victim would be taken to a filthy room, or a place where her cries could not be heard... even an empty laundry room would suffice for the gang. The girl would be threatened with a knife and or gun. The men would rape her and threaten her not to talk. She would either be let free or be driven to another location in the city and unceremoniously dumped. The Green Vega Gang would set out again, trolling the dimly lit streets, looking for more prey.

The police began to piece together countless such assaults, all involving a green Chevy Vega, sometimes described as blue...all described as having Maryland license plates. Sometimes the rapists struck more than once a night. They stalked the streets of DC with impunity, operating in the primarily black neighborhoods where they would not stand out.

Most rapists do not operate with accomplices, which stood out and meant that these men were even more dangerous if encountered together. The numbers of potential rape cases that might be linked to this pattern were not small; there were dozens, if not hundreds. The first such instances of this gang appearing were as early as 1969. The majority occurred in 1971-72, right in the middle of the Freeway Phantom murder spree. In fact, some of the abductions took place only blocks from where Phantom victims had been kidnapped.

Today the police would have issued photographs of the car, composite sketches of the suspects, and enlisted the aid of the community to help identify these men or at least warn the females of the city about the risk. For some reason, the Metropolitan Police Department did not do that. It is possible that they didn't want to tip off the rapists and force them to change cars or alter their MO. Perhaps it was something as simple as they didn't want to admit that this was a major problem and that they had no lead or progress on the cases. So many unsolved rapes attributed to the same gang would not reflect well on the department.

That isn't to say that the police were oblivious to the danger. They did have composite sketches made up, and officers were briefed to be on the lookout for a green Vega. It paid off on February 11, 1973, when officers spotted a green Vega and a driver who fit the description of the rapist. Officers started talking to the driver, John Nathanicl Davis – peppering him with questions.

Another large man, Morris J. Warren, saw the officers at the car and came down the hill where the car was parked. Davis spotted him and said, "Hold on, I'll only be a minute… if you wait a few minutes I will drop you off at home." The burly man turned and started to walk away while Davis tried to explain why he had been pulled over in DC, while living in Landover, Maryland.

Raymond Banoun, the US Attorney who would eventually go on to prosecute the men would later reveal the comedy of errors unfolding. "Warren, like an idiot, came back. And he said, "What are they doing to you dude?" or something like that." Police noticed that the larger man also fit one of the descriptions of the rapists. When asked for identification, Warren only had a social security card, and it wasn't his; it was for a Morris Saunders. Quickly it appeared his story was not holding up, especially since Davis had already told officers his true name. Saunders was the name of his common law wife's family.

Officers jotted down his name, and Warren told Davis that he would take the bus home. The entire interaction struck the officers as awkward and wrong.

Davis was arrested and his car impounded. He was driven to the Fifth District substation. Two of the rape victims were brought in and positively identified him from his booking photograph as the driver of the car and the leader of the rapists who had assaulted them. John Davis did not ask for a lawyer. He used his one phone call to call his wife to tell her that he was being charged with rape but would be home, he expected, in twenty minutes. Nine days later, two of his victims, Marilyn Reed and Linda Jenkins both identified Davis as one of their attackers.

It would take longer for Morris Warren to be arrested... April 21, 1973. His apprehension triggered the arrests of the other members of the gang.

For the first time in years, police had finally started to crack the Green Vega Gang's nefarious and hideous activities. Little did they realize that this string of rapes would forever be intertwined with both the Freeway Phantom cases and a never-ending controversy as a result.

Calling them a "gang" was more of a metaphor for the media than reality. Gang implies a level of organization and structure, a common bond. The only real bond these men shared were the terrible crimes they committed together and their pasts.

The Green Vega rapists all met at Kelly Miller Junior High and then Springarn High School. Not all of them completed high school, but their unofficial leader, John Davis was a math major at Federal City College, taking night classes. Where the others were rough around the edges in terms of personality, Davis was almost suave in his demeanor prior to his arrest. That changed once he found himself in jail however, and he let his true nature be revealed. To the casual observer he dressed sensibly and was well groomed.

In many respects Davis didn't fit the profile that one might think of as leading a gang of rapists. He had married Sandra Latson and was the father of two children. Her family considered him a "stand-up" man who was family focused, especially on his children.

He was a man who had two personas, one with his family, and one when he was away from home. While his relatives basked in Davis's image as a "family man," there was a darker side to his personality. Prior to his arrest he was having a sexual affair with his daughter's babysitter, a teenage girl of 16. Even sicker, he initiated the same illicit physical relationship with the babysitter's younger sister of 13 years.

Davis had a prior arrest record but nothing that might tie him to sex crimes. He had been arrested for car theft and spent time in Lorton Prison in nearby Virginia. Still, this crime didn't hint at his violence.

John Davis had two jobs. One was at the Department of Health, Education & Welfare, the other was a community service organization, Project Start, where he was an intern supervisor. When the police dug into his background and talked to coworkers, they learned of his anger issues. A colleague at Project Start said that if Davis became frustrated in achieving a goal, he would become enraged and even violent. Davis's dark side manifested itself at times at work. His coworkers said that he seemed to get pleasure out of causing other people harm and misery. In almost every instance of the Green Vega Gang's activities, it was John Davis who usually wielded the gun on their victims – using it to force them into submission.

Morris J. Warren was better known by his nickname of Fatsy or Leon. He did not complete high school. He worked as the chief cook at Marjorie Webster Junior College. His personality at times could be off-putting and crude.

As he told the press in one jailhouse interview years after his arrest, his father was a gardener who did time in Lorton Prison for narcotics use. His father passed away when Warren was ten from kidney issues. He and his five brothers and sisters lived with their mother, cramped into tiny apartments where they often slept three or more in a bedroom. His mother was on welfare, unable to fully provide for her orphaned children.

Warren got into trouble several times during his youth, once for shoplifting and another time for running away from home. He dropped out of college in his junior year, not because of academics but because of real-world issues... namely his girlfriend. "She had two babies by me. When the third one came, I had to drop out and start working," he told *The Washington Post.*

Morris Warren tried to make a living, securing several odd jobs including being a porter, a dishwasher, and later a cook. Despite his efforts, he fell afoul of the law. At the age of 18 he was convicted of carnal knowledge and robbery and sentenced to a short term at Virginia's Lorton Prison. With little else to do with his time, he took training in prison as a medical technician. After two years of jail, Warren was paroled. Once more he tried to turn his life around, and at the age of 22, he was placed in a city-sponsored program that provided trade skills in bricklaying, carpentry, and plumbing.

After several jobs as a short order cook, he secured a full-time position at Marjorie Webster Junior College, where he made between $130 and $150 a week plus bonuses. "It was enough to get by, but it wasn't a good salary. By then he had moved in with Brenda Saunders, his common law wife.

Where John Davis tended to be close-lipped with authorities, Morris Warren talked, and his talking linked both him and Davis to the other members of the gang. One was Paul Fletcher. While he fit the description of one of the gang members, his personality did not seem to be aligned with what one might think of as a rapist. Police interviews with his family and friends indicated that he was a follower, a timid man who was easily manipulated by others.

Fletcher worked as a janitor in the Montgomery County Public Schools. He was far from being a good employee, frequently failing to show up to work and being written up multiple times for disciplinary action by his manager.

His brothers and sisters were stunned when Fletcher was arrested in connection with the Green Vega rapes. Some were outwardly angry with him, saying they would, "Kick his ass then call the cops," once they learned of his involvement. Even in his interviews with authorities, Fletcher came across more as man who was not the leader, but, "along for the ride," as indicated in one police report.

In stark contrast to Paul Fletcher was another member of the gang, Paul Brooks. Where Fletcher was timid, Brooks' default setting to deal with any situation was through violence.

His childhood was difficult. Brooks came from a poor family, and often he would visit a local woman's house in the neighborhood to beg for food. Brooks claimed that she was a known lesbian and that he had been molested by her on multiple occasions. He could not tell his mother about the abuse and over time developed feelings that no one in his family actually loved him.

Violence was his mainstay, his go-to-drug of choice. He bragged to friends about beating women and claimed that the only way he could get respect from the opposite sex was to "inspire fear." When his young wife told him she was leaving him, he stabbed her in the leg with a knife that was ten-to-twelve inches long.

Brooks lacked formal education and could not spell well. He tried to create the illusion of intelligence by using big words, but often in the wrong context. He worked off and on in the laundry room at DC General Hospital.

Brooks suffered from frequent headaches so horrific they made him cry and pull out his own hair. After his arrest he begged to see a psychiatrist while in custody, in hopes of curing them. He was the only one of the Green Vega rapists who underwent psychiatric analysis while in custody. The evaluation results were less than flattering. Analysis said he was functioning at a borderline level of intelligence. He blamed his mental slowness on everyone: his family, friends, etc.

Almost everyone who knew Paul Brooks was not surprised he was involved with the rapes, except his mother. She believed her son had been manipulated into the acts and would not have undertaken the crimes he was eventually accused of on his own accord. Like her son, she blamed everyone else for his crimes.

The final member of the Green Vega ensemble was Melvin Gray. Gray worked as a mail carrier, assigned to the Post Office at 16th and Irvin streets NW. According to his wife, Francine, he was a good father. She described her husband to authorities as "meek," where others that police interviewed described him as quiet and shy. He was talkative with coworkers about his family. Francine said that he was seemingly afraid of typical vices like alcohol or drugs – and that he was a good father.

Gray did have a temper. His wife said that he had "only" hit her once, when she was pregnant and visiting another man's apartment, leaving her with a black eye. Other than that single incident he did not come across as a stereotypical serial rapist.

How does a "normal" person go from school friendship to being in a gang of rapists? How does that subject even get raised in conversation? In looking at this motley crew, it is clear Davis was the ringleader. Paul Brooks was clearly prone to violence; it was his primary mode of operating. Morris Warren was dangerous, but unlikely to commit such crimes alone. Paul Fletcher and Melvin Gray were both described as family men. How did this group become the Green Vega Gang?

In the end, it doesn't matter. Individually, the majority of them wouldn't have probably committed rape under normal conditions. Together though, they became an organized criminal activity preying on the young women of the District. Together, they were responsible for the largest number of rapes in Washington DC history.

Initially it was John Davis and Morris Warren who would be charged by the US Attorney's Office. Standing up against them was Raymond Banoun. He was not a physically imposing figure, but a pit bull of thought and energy in the courtroom. His mind was quick, and he organized his thoughts almost bullet-point style, as if he had filed information in his mind. Banoun graduated the City College of New York in 1965, and George Washington University Law School, with honors, in 1968. He had started with the US Attorney's office in 1970, primarily working misdemeanor cases through 1971. By 1972 he was working felony cases. The Green Vega cases landed on his desk. They were not his first felony cases, but some of his more infamous.

Two well-respected Metropolitan Police Department detectives were involved with the Green Vega Gang cases as well. One was Virgil Hopkins of the Sex Squad. As Banoun recalls, "Virgil was a veteran Sex Squad detective who was the nicest gentleman you can imagine. He was just a wonderful guy who pleased the victims and worked with the victims, and he was just a delightful guy to work with." Given the nature of the crimes he investigated, he was perfect for the job.

The other investigator on the cases was Detective Sergeant Louis Richardson. Richardson was highly respected in the Washington MPD. He primarily worked homicide and had an arrest rate of 90 percent, impressive given the tools and techniques available in the 1970s for police officers. He was a cop's cop. Richardson had served in the Army and had weathered a trumped-up court martial in his short stint in the service. When he was 21-years-old, he had been living in Lexington, Virginia, working as a hotel porter when he decided to become a police officer. He moved to DC and worked for the Government Printing Office for a while as he went through the lengthy hiring process. The police offered him a job on one condition, that he have his tonsils removed. While he had never had problems with them, he was determined to join the force. Richardson hitchhiked to a veteran's hospital in Martinsburg, West Virginia, to get them taken out.

He trained under Captain Joseph O'Brien, another deeply respected officer in the force. In later years he would recall what it was like working in the police department as a black officer. "New white boys would ride in the scout cars, and I would walk. All of this was very frustrating and disgusting." Things had gotten better by the 1970s. "You've got a few of the old white officers of yesterday hanging on. A lot of them in supervisory or policy making roles. But all in all, 95 percent of the white officers are beautiful, but you've still got that five percent.

Ray Banoun describes Richardson in more simple terms, "He was very flamboyant. White hat, always dressed to kill."

Louis Richardson did not become involved with the initial investigation of the Green Vega Gang but was pulled in once there was a suspicion that they may be responsible for the Freeway Phantom crimes.

Eventually these three men, Banoun, Hopkins, and Richardson would be the bastions of law enforcement, standing like sentries between the horrific violence of the Green Vega Gang and the citizens of DC.

The decision had been made to try John Davis and Morris Warren together on the first of batch of rape and kidnapping charges. The stage was set; the actors all had their roles. The audience, the citizens of the District of Columbia, were ready to hear what had transpired with these rapes. At the start of the trial, in the autumn of 1973, no one realized that the Green Vega Gang may (stress may) have had anything to do with the Freeway Phantom cases.

CHAPTER 10: THE GREEN VEGA GANG – THE TANGLED WEB

"Rape is not primarily a sexual matter. Gang rape is no more than a sexual matter than individual rape. The prime dynamic of rape is the violent degradation and humiliation of women. Many rapes are not truly consummated. The rapist may find himself impotent or unable to achieve orgasm. "Rapists fear women, fear being controlled by women, are frequently married but henpecked by their wives or girlfriends and suffer from poor self-concept and lack of firm sexual identity. In that sense, he is no different from a woman who beats a child."
—Dr. Davis Langham, Chief of the city's Forensic Psychiatry Office, *The Washington Post*, July 13, 1975

Both Davis and Warren were out on bail as the police continued their investigations into their cohorts and connections to other rapes. While under suspicion for the rapes, Paul Brooks robbed a 7-Eleven in Palmer Park, Maryland, and was eventually arrested for that crime. Matters were complicated even more on September 9, 1973, when Morris Warren and Paul Fletcher robbed two 7-Eleven stores. In one, Fletcher had fired at the window, wounding one patron with a bullet resting just under his scalp. In the second robbery in nearby Cheverly, Maryland, Warren shot the store security guard, George Henry Stevens, standing at a refrigerator case, killing him. In his wild spray of bullets Warren hit Raymond Evinger with two bullets, puncturing his body with six holes...but he survived. James Ivison, the store manager, had been hit in the elbow with one bullet. The pistol used in the robberies was found in Morris Warren's apartment during the execution of a search warrant. On top of the rape charges in the District, Warren and Fletcher were charged in Prince George's County, Maryland, for murder (in the case of Warren) and armed robbery. It seemed that the Green Vega men could not help but get into trouble. Perhaps they had begun to realize that justice was slowly closing in on them.

The first trial of Morris Warren and John Davis garnered remarkably little press coverage. The tales of the victims were lost in the shadows of President Nixon's reelection. Washington DC newspapers were often boxed-in with their coverage of politics, seeing it both as a local and national story. Newspapers in the District struggled between being a local paper for the city and covering DC as the capital of the United States. The rapes of a few residents, however tantalizing, did not seem to initially garner much coverage initially.

The first trial involved seven victims, whose stories were almost the same. Two had been waiting for taxicabs, the others for a bus or walking the street, when accosted by Davis in his green Vega. All took place after sunset. A knife and revolver were used to intimidate and maintain control of the victims. The witnesses all described the driver as John Davis. Warren was a hulking accomplice, picked up after Davis got his victims into the car. Two victims who testified, Marilyn Reed and Sharon Williams, were kidnapped on the same night, about five hours apart. Both were raped in apartment buildings, one in a laundry room, another in an abandoned basement apartment. One of the Vega rape victims was taken from DC to Prince George's County near the Baltimore Washington Parkway and raped there. Davis's green Vega roamed the district and surrounding counties freely, stalking innocent victims of opportunity.

Their defense strategies were to sully and discredit the victims. In one instance, according to Warren, they had *not* lured one victim into their clutches. In the case of Marilyn Reed, according to Warren, she had asked them for a ride home. He alleged that during that trip, he asked her to have sex with him and she agreed. Warren claimed they stopped in an alley and had engaged in intercourse with both himself and John Davis. Even on the surface, as a defense, it was implausible – blaming Ms. Reed for her rape.

In the case of Sharon Williams, Warren put forth that Davis, Paul Fletcher, and Paul Brooks picked her up at 13th and U Street NW. Warren claimed he had known her previously and knew she was on dope and a junkie. They rode around the Cardoza neighborhood, and Miss Williams asked for some smoke. He gave her some, but she wanted some cocaine, so they went to find a friend who could provide it.

They went to an apartment building in Kenilworth Terrance. The friend was not at home, but he claimed Williams was high on beer and weed. He admitted asking her for sex, and she agreed, perfectly consensual in Warren's version of events. They went inside an empty building and engaged in intercourse. The other two men engaged in sex with Ms. Williams, but she was so high they could not get any sense into her – so they left her there.

US Attorney Banoun had his work cut out. He knew that the testimony of the victims wasn't enough, he also had to show them in the best possible light. "So there were seven victims, and it was very interesting. They ranged from really poor to students who were trying to better themselves. One of them seemed like a real hard core, tough girl, who just broke down. She was the one that broke down the easiest.

In fact, it was very interesting. She didn't have appropriate clothes. I remember before trial, one of the detectives and I had to take her to the department store near the courthouse and get her a bra, because she didn't have a bra. I didn't want her to appear before the jury like that. And so we got her that and I bought her a blouse or something to wear. She was the one that had the greatest impact. She was the toughest street girl; yet, she totally broke down.

"It was really tough getting two-or-three of them to testify. They didn't want to testify; they didn't want anything to do with it. They were embarrassed; they were terrified. So there was a lot of preparation work."

Davis was well represented. According to Banoun, "Davis had a very good lawyer who died only recently...Dovey Roundtree. Dovey was not only a very fine lawyer, but she was also a pastor – an ordained minister, who preached in a church. That's why it was so bad to go up against her in a courtroom because she often spoke as if she were a pastor. And a lot of the black jurors knew her. She was terrific. She preached essentially."

Banoun remembered Morris Warren's presence during the trial. "During the trial, Warren was just himself. He looked like a beast, literally. I don't mean that derogatorily. The way he was built—he was huge. You know, he used to say to us, 'I can do a hundred years in jail without a problem. I could be upside down on a tree and do my time.' Whereas Davis was very much involved in the case, he clearly had disagreements with his lawyer; he was arguing with her a lot."

Banoun recalls, "The judge clearly was on our side. You could tell because during the midst of one of the defense witness's testimony, I believe, there was this big fat fly, flying around the courtroom, flying around the bench. It mesmerized the jury. He (the judge) took a pad, and while the witness was testifying, clearly paying no attention, following the fly around. All the jurors are doing is following the fly around. He finally takes his pad and *smashes* it, kills the fly, and says, 'I got the damned thing!' That was the one thing that was clear as could be, that he did not like this case at all."

There were dramatics played out for both sides in the trial. As Banoun remembers, "By then some of the witnesses, the victims, had already broken down on the stand. One broke down so badly that the judge, he had boxes of tissues, and he would go to them and say, "Would you like a box of tissues?" When one broke down the judge took a break and excused the jury. And as the jury was filing out, Dovey said out loud, 'She's putting it on.' I turned around and said, 'Like hell she is! How dare you?' It was right as the jury was filing out of the courtroom. And the jury was glaring at her.

"But in any event, they got convicted. I don't know whether it was after the conviction or after the sentencing… but after one of those, the Marshal came out, and the judge called us to the bench. He told us they had just gotten a piece of paper out of Davis's mouth, the note said, 'I'm going to kill that bitch lawyer,' or something to that effect."

Davis continued to generate a stir in the courtroom. "… he [Davis] was having an affair with the babysitter of his daughter. The babysitter was a teenager. And the babysitter told us…he sent her letters. In the letters he told her he was going to 'pour hot tar down the throat of Judge Newmans' and that he was going to kill everyone involved in the case against him."

The connection to the Freeway Phantom began in that courtroom, with an almost off-the-cuff remark by Davis's attorney. As Banoun remembers it, "So in any event, during the pretrial suppression hearing, Dovey Roundtree said, 'It is obvious here that the police were not looking for a green Vega when they stopped them (Davis and Warren). They were looking for the Freeway Phantom.'" While this may not be an exact quote, Banoun was in the middle of a heated trial, it did attract attention of others in the courtroom.

"In any event, when she said that, Virgil (Hopkins) was in the courtroom and so was Louis Richardson. And related to me later or during the break, 'We've got to look at those.' That sort of triggered something.

"I was pretty skeptical – at first. Only because I had really read a lot about the Freeway Phantom cases, and there were so many attempts to solve them, all failing." But Richardson and Hopkins had latched onto Roundtree's comment. On the surface it seemed plausible. The Green Vega Gang operated in the same neighborhoods as the Freeway Phantom. While the rapists focused on older victims, most of the Freeway Phantom victims had been sexually assaulted. In that autumn courtroom in DC, the detectives felt they had just been handed their first substantial lead in months.

Dovey Roundtree had, with two sentences, kicked off a massive investigation that would embroil the US Attorney's office and multiple police agencies for close to two years.

On October 5, 1973, Morris J. Warren and John N. Davis were convicted in dizzying number of counts in connection with the rapes, kidnappings, and armed robberies. The investigation was ongoing, and more charges were destined to come as more rapes could be linked to the gang. The other members of the gang would stand trial separately while Morris Warren was sent to Lorton Prison in Virginia.

As Detective Richardson probed into the gang's potential connections with the Freeway Phantom, the families were struggling with the three-year anniversary of the start of the killing spree. *The Washington Post* interviewed some of the family members on February 17, 1974, and their angst, sorrow, and frustration were exposed for the public. Allenteen Spinks, the mother of Carol Spinks, the first victim, spoke out in deep shaken voice. "I don't forget it. I think about it every day. It's mine they've taken from me and I feel the hurt."

Edward Woodard, the father of Brenda Woodard, felt that race came into play. "I feel they should have caught someone by now. Why do you think that when white people are killed, they always seem to catch somebody?"

Calvin Rolark, publisher of the *Washington Informer*, added to the frustrations felt by the family members. "For years blacks have been at the mercy of white-run police departments who have held them at low priority as long as blacks were killing blacks, and I haven't seen much change in this...You find a pattern of young blacks being missing and murdered, and we're never able to bring the individuals to justice...But if white folks are murdered they don't stop investigating until they find who did it."

The reality was buried in the stark statistics that could not change perceptions in the black community. In 1972 in DC there were 255 homicides. Of these, 233 (91percent) were black victims and twenty-two white. Twenty-four of those cases remained unclosed from that year, twenty-two cases, or 9.4 percent involve black victims and two cases, or 9.1percent involved white victims. As such the closure rates are almost statistically identical between black and whites. These were statistics that did not convey the feelings that the community and the victim's families often felt and perception often trumps reality. With 71 percent of the city being black, the feeling was understandable.

With sixty officers working homicides, the police's reaction was they were doing their job, it was the newspapers and television that was not doing theirs. Captain Robert Boyd, the chief of the homicide squad, laid the blame with the media. "The media folk say, 'Anything happened?' and we say, 'Yeah, man, closed a case today. We worked like hell on it. Tough case.' Then we tell them the victim was someone in the Southeast, and they're not interested. They don't write it up."

Two days later in *The Washington Post*, Captain Boyd offered a profile of the Freeway Phantom. "My hunch is that he's a Negro male, above 30 – between 35 and 45. My ideal suspect is a good-sized male. I don't know why I know it, but I do. I don't see him as a small-sized person." He postulated in the interview that the killer had to gain trust of the victims. He could have worn the uniform of a fireman, or a security guard, or just drove a taxi. With all the military bases around Anacostia, he said that a military man, "would be a damn good suspect."

Allenteen Spinks did not play into the Washington MPD's speculation. "He's got to be sick, insanely sick."

The articles coming out in February had to have factored into the pressures on Detective Richardson to make progress on the Freeway Phantom cases. Their probe into the ongoing Green Vega cases had revealed some tantalizing hints that the two sets of cases might be connected. One of the Green Vega victims, a Ms. Spriggs, in her 1972 report of her rape to the Washington MPD, stated that the man she identified as John Davis had driven her to a wooded location and told her "This is where I kill little girls." That location was adjacent to the where Brenda Woodard's body had been found. Was it an idle threat aimed to intimidate her, or was it a confession?

The best way to proceed was to get one of the Green Vega Gang to cooperate. John Davis was too strong of a personality and too smart to be a target. As the leader of the gang, he would likely be a key prosecution target. The other members of the gang were in the middle of their own legal quagmires with rape and kidnapping charges. They needed someone in the gang who would talk; someone that could propel their investigation forward. That left them with Morris Warren.

As Banoun remembers it, "We basically looked into Davis and Warren. Somehow we connected two, potentially three other people to them. Paul Randall Brooks…and Paul Julius Fletcher. Fletcher was known as 'flathead.' That's very important because that was how some witnesses identified him. The back of his head was totally flat.

"We basically decided that Warren was clearly the weaker link. Davis was *never* going to cooperate. Davis was too smart. Because he was so smart, he was also the most dangerous because he was the planner. The others had no ability to really plan or organize anything. He clearly controlled the others. He was smarter than the others – at least that's what appeared."

In the spring of 1974, only a few weeks after the article ran in the *Washington Post* on the anniversary of the crimes, the MPD, led by Louis Richardson, visited Lorton Prison and met with Warren. They offered him an exchange for his cooperation with the authorities. They would grant him certain privileges if he could help them with outstanding rapes in the District as well as information on the Freeway Phantom cases.

Warren agreed. In Banoun's words, "He had a girlfriend. Very large. Bigger than he was, height wise and width wise. She loved the guy. And so, there were conditions. He wanted to get to see her…that was the most important thing. At first he really didn't really care if he got convicted of more rapes or not.

"We had already entered into an agreement with him that had to be approved by my supervisor's office, that basically it was more than use immunity. As I recall, we agreed that if he cooperated fully, and told us the truth, he would not be charged with any other rape cases, but would be open to be charged with murder if he did not tell the truth about all of them." Warren's other convictions still stood at the time, and he was facing charges related to the 7-Eleven robberies.

A task force had already been formed, and it had to be done without the knowledge of the media, otherwise it might tip off the other members of the Green Vega Gang. Ray Banoun is one of the few men still alive or willing to talk about their time on that task force. "I can *assure you*, in reality, I handled many similar, in terms of being very complex, fraud cases, but I *never* had an investigative group like this one or agencies committing the kinds of resources we had on this case. You're talking two FBI, two homicide, one Sex Squad, one-maybe-two, two PG County, and two Park Police officers. And they were full time on it. That didn't include all the backups they had.

"It is really amazing the amount of manpower we had on this case. I am not aware of any other investigation where we got that kind of support. I handled a lot of public cases but never had those resources.

"It's fascinating because obviously we didn't have technology then, no DNA. The amazing thing was that there could be 200 to 250 open sex cases, rapes cases, and kidnap cases, unsolved. It boggles my mind. And we really spent the time going through these, and comparing them to each other, comparing them to what we knew, the patterns we knew, comparing them to the homicides. Clearly the intent was not to solve rape cases. It was clearly to solve the homicide cases. Otherwise we wouldn't have gotten the FBI and these other agencies, the District, and Maryland, involved.

"I remember that during the winter month, we were driving around. We had a caravan, literally. For some reason, I remember I always ended up in the back seat with Morris Warren; in a police cruiser – in the back seat you can't open the back door from the inside. So I was stuck with him in the back seat of a detective car. We had no marked cars. An FBI car, a homicide squad car, a sex squad car, a park police car, and a PG County police car. Warren would take us around and he would say, 'There was this instance where we picked up a girl here, we took her here, we raped her here, so-and-so was with us.' We never showed him any of the files. This was his recollection. He would then add, 'We dumped her here.'

"Anyway, we would go around, in a convoy. Another thing that was frustrating was that there were elements in the descriptions that Warren was giving us that matched multiple unsolved rapes. He claimed that they could have possibly raped somewhere between 500 and a 1,000 women."

"Many of the facts in the unsolved cases fit the pattern of the Green Vega related cases. Except there was anywhere from two to four guys involved. With differing descriptions, we were led to believe that the number of perpetrators varied, that there were as many as six different guys. The detectives reviewed those open rape cases, studied them, and compare them to the homicides. Where were the girls walking, when they were picked up? Where were they left? And lo and behold, what we found was, in some of the rape cases, some of the girls were dumped in the same areas. One of whom was dropped off, believing she was dead. She was beaten to a pulp and strangled but survived. There were elements like that.

"There were places where they were raped in abandoned buildings. But there was information that resembled homicides, and the rapes that occurred elsewhere....We met with the medical examiner, a number of times to try and see if evidence in those open cases and the homicides matched. Some things matched; some did not. These were very old cases. There was a lot of homework going into it. Along the way, there was enough there to convince us to pursue... there was enough to pursue the investigation. We could tie the two matters in some instances. Secondly, the theory was that even if we can't tie the two, we out to at the least find all of the people, potentially involved and convict them of the rapes.

"I think what ultimately happened is that Warren loved the attention. He was the big star of this caravan. Until he realized it wasn't going to get him off completely, and he'd probably end up getting killed in jail, so he stopped cooperating, and we cut him off, stopped bringing him up from jail. He had been in our offices, day-after-day; the police would go pick him up from the DC jail...so he was out of the jail. So when he realized how cooperation was not going to help him, he started denying his involvement.

"I remember, we gave him on a couple of occasions, we had to provide him with lunch. We would stop at 7-Eleven, after the regular lunch time, when the store was pretty much empty. He was handcuffed, and the manager asked, 'What the hell is going on?' The police would go up and show their badges, they would stay in the corner, and he would get a sandwich to eat."

Morris Warren loved to talk and to other inmates as well and seemed to relish being an informant. Warren talked to James Arnold, another inmate at Lorton, telling him that he had, "Assisted John Davis in removing out of the latter's car the body of a young female who had been killed."

Throughout late May 1974 Warren sang a song that investigators loved to listen to. Brought before a grand jury, Morris Warren was drilled with questions. He denied any personal involvement with the Freeway Phantom cases, but he implicated his former friends, John Davis, Paul Fletcher, and Paul Brooks in not only some of the Freeway cases, but also in somewhere between 500 and a 1,000 rapes over a four-to-five-year period.

Years later, after the legal machinations had finished, Ray Banoun told the *Washington Post*, "Warren triggered our belief...that he knew about the homicides because he gave details of the rape of a girl behind the Pepsi Cola plant near Kenworth Avenue and Prince George's County Hospital.' Details given by Warren, Banoun testified in court, matched details of the rape and murder of Brenda Woodard, a Freeway Phantom homicide victim." Brenda had been found on a ramp that could be taken from the Pepsi plant as well as the hospital.

The task force had managed to operate under the radar of the media for weeks. That came to an end in early June of 1974. Prince George's County State's Attorney, Arthur A. Marshall Jr., went public with the investigation. He told the

Washington DC papers that, "A new break has come in the three-year-old intensive police investigation of the so-called "The Freeway Phantom" cases that could lead to solving of at least three of the brutal slayings.

"There have been major inroads and major developments in several of the homicides – at least three." District homicide detectives today were surprised by Marshall's confirmation.

"I would anticipate that if the information is corroborated within thirty to ninety days, we could present the (Prince George's County) grand jury with some information." While Marshall declined to say which cases may be impacted, he had effectively outted the investigation to the public. In one instance, he went so far as to say that there were upwards of six individuals who may be charged...a hint about the Green Vega involvement, which the media immediately latched onto.

Ray Banoun remembers the incident as a pivotal point in the investigation. "We were *livid*. How he could leak that information. We hadn't questioned Brooks or Fletcher at that point."

Damage control from the task force agencies tried to contain Marshall's statements. Captain Robert Boyd of the District Homicide Squad said that Marshall's comments were "Unfortunate." John Hoxie, a spokesman for the Prince George's County police said, "Anybody's irresponsible at this time to comment on it, and that includes the state's attorney." "We hope it won't, but it theoretically could, adversely affect an investigation. It's always dangerous to talk about informants."

Marshall, a Democrat, was up for reelection that year, and the investigators saw his leak for what it was, a way to reap in votes in the fall. For his part, Arthur Marshall attempted to backtrack his comments with the media. "Maybe I should have just given no comment, but I don't feel that any statement I've made has jeopardized the investigation. He felt that because he hadn't given the names of informants or suspects that he could not be accused of tainting a possible jury pool."

In many respects, Marshall's attempts to cultivate votes began the downfall of the Green Vega connections to the Freeway Phantoms. It cast doubt with the one person they needed to stay focused, and that was Morris Warren. By mid-June of 1974 Warren must have suspected that the deal he negotiated might somehow come back to bite him. He demanded that the US Attorney's office provide him a written statement of their agreement. Banoun was quick to respond in hopes of keeping Warren talking. But in exchange for his information; among them, Warren wanted release from jail, total immunity from prosecution, and part of the $10,000 reward. What Warren wanted and what he had agreed to with investigators did not fully jibe. The government could not agree to those demands. Prosecutors insisted that Warren would also be required to plead guilty to lesser charges related to any of the crimes that went to prosecution. Warren was given a signed agreement on June 4, 1974. Banoun recalled years later, "We agreed that we would not use anything against him that he would tell us regarding the homicides of…little girls." Warren had them delete the word 'little.'" Apparently he did not want to be known as a pedophile in prison.

John Davis proved himself smarter than most of the Washington DC media. When word of Marshall's announcement reached him in jail, he pieced together his former friend's betrayal and wrote him in prison, angry that Warren was trying to pin the Freeway Phantom cases on him. He demanded to know from Warren what he had told the police. The letter must have shaken Warren. In a letter to Davis he said that he hadn't told the authorities anything and would never try and "take Davis down" for the Freeway Phantom cases. The letters had the desired effect with Warren, he had been intimidated by Davis writing him and the prospects of being labeled as a jailhouse snitch.

Other members of the Green Vega Gang also began to see the handwriting on the wall. Why should Warren be the only person to cut a deal? Melvin Gray came forward to investigators expressing a willingness to cooperate. When he met with investigators, he was shown pictures of Green Vega and Freeway Phantom victims. When he saw the picture of Carol Spinks and Nenomoshia Yates, he offered confessions in both of their cases.

He claimed to have been involved directly with the death of Yates. In the confession of the murder of Carol Spinks, he and one Cassandra Horton, a close friend of his, wove a tale that crippled his credibility.

Gray and Horton described Spinks as appearing about 18 years old. They claimed that Morris Warren had contacted Carol by phone and told her to meet him at the 7-Eleven. At the store, she was forced into the car by Warren and Fletcher. They drove her to Gray's apartment where she stayed with her abductors for a week.

Gray's confession was clearly an attempt to try to broker a deal before Warren's testimony landed him in more hot water. The flaws in what he and Horton presented to authorities were numerous and glaring. Carol Spinks was five feet tall and barely weighed one-hundred pounds. She had not developed enough physically to ever be confused with being an 18-year-old...she looked every bit her 13 years of age. Horton said she had been wearing curlers in her hair when she had been kidnapped. Clearly Gray and Horton had confused details from newspaper articles about Brenda Crockett, who had been wearing curlers. They claimed that she had been carrying a grocery bag from the 7-Eleven that contained potato chips and a bottle of soda. The clerk at the 7-Eleven remembered that Carol had purchased the TV dinners that she had come in for.

In terms of the Yates confession, the authorities went to his place of work and determined he had been on the job at the time she had been abducted.

In other words, Melvin Gray's confessions were utterly bogus. He had tried to toss Morris Warren under the proverbial bus in terms of blaming him for a crime he didn't commit, apparently trying to beat him to the punch. His confession was deemed unreliable and unusable, leaving investigators with only Morris Warren to hang their hopes on…and those hopes were dwindling quickly.

In July the media began to report about members of a rape gang appearing before a grand jury in the District looking into the Freeway Phantom cases. One prominent article in the *Washington Post* on July 19, 1974, said that two members of a gang involved in string of sex offenses have appeared before a grand jury. Search warrants had been issued to obtain hair and fiber samples from others. The entire affair was about to be made public. With the proverbial shit about to hit the fan and his escapades now fully public for anyone, especially John Davis, to know about, Warren decided to renege on the agreement. He had members of his family hold a press conference. On August 29, 1974, the storm broke as Warren opted to no longer cooperate with the investigators.

As Ray Banoun recalls, "What happened at some point is that we realized that getting the chances of making the homicides became slimmer and slimmer, because even if we were convinced they were the perpetrators, we would never have the evidence to actually prosecute them. So we concluded that we had evidence to get them sentenced to sufficient time on the additional rape cases." In other words, Morris Warren's usefulness was dwindling, as were his chances to leverage his agreement with the US Attorney's Office.

Warren's sister, Cynthia, told the Washington news outlets that her brother knew nothing about the Freeway Phantom killings and had given false information to the investigators in return for their promises to not prosecute him. This false information included at statement that Davis, a Federal City College student, knew and dated Brenda Denise Woodard, one of the Freeway Phantom victims.

Cynthia Warren went on to say that she had received two telephone threats on the life of her family in recent weeks, no doubt from the leaks about the grand jury to the press. "We've all become more scared for our lives," said Morris's mother, Lorraine Warren. "It's come to the point now where they (the government) don't care who goes down the drain as long as they get somebody."

Cynthia further claimed that her brother was orchestrating a grand hoax with the authorities. "We have been made recently aware of these allegations and as part of the overall investigation of the Freeway Phantom cases, we have presented these claims to the grand jury for its evaluation of their validity." In one interview she gave with investigators, Cynthia Warren said that her brother, "Sought media attention and seemed to gloat about having 'put one over' on the district attorney."

Morris, she would go on to claim, had watched detectives for visual clues while they drove around the District and surrounding regions. Sometimes they would inadvertently coach him into saying what they wanted. In other words, Fatsy Warren had played the agencies that had been working with him.

Warren's flip-flopping had left the investigation exposed and vulnerable to public scrutiny. As details of the grand jury reached the public, Ray Banoun tried to execute damage control on the situation. He told *The Washington Post* that, with a promise of limited immunity, Morris J. Warren had appeared before a grand Jury in connection with the Green Vega and Freeway Phantom cases.

Banoun's arrangement with Warren was made public as he read the agreement, "Anything you [Warren] have told me in a signed statement of promises dated June 4 about the rapes and murders of girls will not be used against you in a court of law in the District of Columbia, provided that (what) you are giving us is complete, accurate and truthful… You will have to enter a plea of guilty to some offense in this case." In return the government "…will bring the extent of your cooperation to the attention of DC Superior Court Judge Theodore R. Newman who imposed a sentence of 15 years to life on Warren in four other rape cases." The statement was signed by Warren, Prosecutor Robert Zsalman, Detective Sergeant Louis Richardson, Detective Norman Brooks, and Detective Virgil Hopkins.

Sources close to the investigation leaked the modus operandi of the gang…hinting that their method of picking up rape victims could very well have been the same as the victims in the Freeway Phantom cases. One source kept the focus on the rapes, rather than the Phantom inquiries. "We have fifty 'hard' rape cases in the district alone, with an estimate of up to two-hundred cases the suspects may be involved in."

In the years to follow, people would say that the Green Vega investigations accomplished little. In reality, while they did not apparently crack the Freeway Phantom cases, they did solve a large number of rapes and managed to take a number of dangerous individuals off the streets for years. In November, the grand jury returned five indictments charging Paul Fletcher, Paul Brooks, and Morris Warren in the rapes of thirteen women between July 30, 1970, and December 2, 1972.

This was reported in the *Washington Star* as, "The first major step" in the prosecution of the Freeway Phantom cases.

Behind the scenes there was less optimism. One Washington MPD confidential report stated: "By August, Warren felt the AUSA (Assistant United States Attorney) office was reneging on their half of his deal, and began claiming that he had perpetrated an elaborate hoax on the office and that all his information was false. The AUSA office was forced to question the validity of WARREN's statements."

Oddly enough the hurt feelings were mutual, Warren publicly expressed that Ray Banoun had sold him out. He told a reporter for the *Washington Post*, "If the grand jury indicts me, it will only be on the word of the prosecutor." He went onto say that he, Davis, Brooks, and Fletcher had grown up in the same neighborhood east of the Anacostia. "We partied together. I know what they would do. They won't kill or hurt no little girls or woman…I wouldn't hurt no little girls. I've got three kids of my own."

The Washington Afro-American newspaper reported Warren's deal more bluntly. "Warren got partial immunity, special jail house privileges and even sexual liberties." The last part did not play well with many citizens, especially in light of Warren's refutation of the agreement.

Morris Warren's involvement with the Freeway Phantom investigation and the publicity that his grand jury testimony had generated was enough to force Prince George's County to move the murder case of George Stevens, the security guard from the 7-Eleven in Landover to Calvert County alone with one of the Green Vega related rape cases. Warren was dealing with fresh prosecutors in Prince George's County who were aware of his immunity shenanigans and unwilling to cooperate.

On December 10, 1974, John Davis returned to DC to appear in a lineup before six rape-kidnap victims. It quickly turned into a debacle. Ray Banoun recalls the entire strange series of events. "What happened was we could not get Davis to go to a lineup. We had to go before Chief Judge George Hart to get an order directing him to appear. We subpoenaed him for a lineup; he refused. He moved to squash the subpoena. Judge Hart ordered him to appear. But Davis refuses to walk across the street from the courthouse to police headquarters. He also objected to wearing the number four that the police gave him, claiming it was a code for the witnesses to identify him.

"So basically, we had to go back to Judge Hart, because he said he would not cooperate and refused to stand up at the lineup. Judge Park threatened him with jail for contempt of court and authorized the police to use whatever force was necessary to bring him to the lineup. I have *never* seen anything like it. He had to be dragged, from the detention at the Superior Court. The Superior Court detection block in those days wasn't where it is today. He had to be dragged, from the cell block across the street to Police Headquarters on Indiana Avenue, literally carried by five or six people, dragged! He was dragged up the stairs and into the lineup. The judge instructed us to, "Let him select the number he wants." So he selected the number nine.

"It was a scene. It was amazing. I've never seen anyone be physically dragged to a lineup. Davis claimed the officers broke his leg. The nurse had to testify in front of Judge Hart that he only had bruises, that nothing was broken. The police officer testified that he was so heavy, so limp, and it made their task very difficult.

"But once in the lineup, he would not turn to face the victims. He stayed with his back to the victims. So the officers had to seat everybody…he would not raise his head. So each person had to hold the head of the person next to him, pulling them up. All of the others were police officers, in the picture of the lineup, everybody is sitting down, holding everybody else's head."

Five of the six victims broke down crying hysterically after identifying Davis in the lineup room. One of them suffered an epileptic seizure and required medical attention. Another rushed back into the room which witnesses watch the lineup screaming, "I'm going to kill him!" It was one of the most bizarre, out of control lineups in the annals of Washington MPD history.

As a result of the lineup, new charges were leveled at John Davis, who was returned to Lorton Prison. When the identifications were in the media, reporters pressed Banoun for more details. He did his best to put a positive spin on Davis's performance. "The investigation is continuing, and more indictments are expected in the Green Vega and Freeway Phantom cases."

The charges coming out of the task force continued to pile up. In October 1974, Morris Warren and Melvin Gray were subpoenaed to appear in a lineup in front of more rape victims. By the first of November, indictments were issued to cover upwards of twenty of the hundreds of unsolved rapes that authorities thought could be attributed with evidence and witnesses to the Green Vega Gang.

Indictments issued to cover fifteen-to-twenty of the approximately 300 rapes believed to have been by the Green Vega Gang. In December, Marilyn Reed appeared in court along with Sharon Williams, facing off against their attacker, Paul Fletcher. He was convicted of the charges. Just before Christmas, the grand jury indicted John Davis and Melvyn Gray on additional charges of rape and kidnapping. For the first time, Gray's confession was hinted at, though the details have never been made public until this book's publication. Gray's attorney at the time was William Borders, who told the *Washington Post*, "I have some problem with the alleged confession which deals with the defendant being before a grand jury." John Davis's charges were from victims aged between 14 and 21 years of age.

By 1975, the legal machine was churning through the ruin caused by the Green Vega Gang. On March 25, 1975, Paul Brooks appeared before Judge Ugast to plead guilty to six armed kidnapping charges. He had been facing eighty-two counts of rape, kidnapping, and sodomy and had accepted a plea bargain. As part of that, he was willing to provide a sworn confession read in court, in which Brooks described how he and two other men picked up a 15-year-old girl at gunpoint in Northeast, Washington and raped her in an abandoned apartment. In part, Brooks said to another man in the car in which she and two other girls were being abducted, "Let's take them where we took Denise out on the freeway." Those words caught the attention of almost everyone. Was this a reference to Darlenia Denise Johnson, Brenda Denise Woodard, or Carol Denise Spinks? If it was, a solid link could be established to the Freeway Phantom cases.

The plea bargain almost fell apart as the reading of his confession had started. His defense attorneys, Durward Taylor and M. J. Cuff, protested the bargain that Banoun was offering them. Banoun responded curtly, "Well, let's go to trial then." Visibly angered, Cuff retorted, "I didn't agree to this!" A recess was asked for and the attorneys met in a conference room. When they returned to the courtroom a few minutes later, Banoun said he agreed to show the judge the additional seventy-six charges that were being dropped, only when Brooks was going to be sentenced on May 27. Per Banoun in an interview with *The Washington Post*, those additional charges were dropped because the convicted man agreed to cooperate with the government on "...other related cases." "The agreement basically consisted in Mr. Brooks entering plea to four counts of armed rape and two counts of kidnapping in the indictment that we had before the court. Also it consisted in his agreeing to appear before the grand jury and testifying about his involvement in criminal activities as well as the involvement of other people associated with him in various criminal activities. To that extent, as I stated in court today, he has appeared before the grand jury on Friday of last week. He will continue to appear if necessary. That was basically his agreement."

Chris Lorenzo of Washington DC's Channel 5, WTTG, pressed Banoun on the larger issue on everyone's minds, "Did these indictments come from the federal grand jury that is investigating the so-called Freeway Phantom murders?"

Banoun responded; "They came from a special grand jury which has been investigating a number of matters, including the Freeway Phantom cases and other related criminal activities. But it is not a grand jury that has been solely considering that matter."

Morris Warren was convicted on April 12, 1975, of the murder of George Stevens, the 7-Eleven security guard. The trial had taken place under the watchful eyes of Prince George's County Judge Perry Bowen. As a result of the botched robbery and murder, Warren was sentenced to a fourth life term plus forty-five years in prison. Out of bitterness, his family once more held a press conference that was covered by the *Washington Afro-American*. His common-law wife, Brenda Saunders, said that Warren had been providing investigators with false information on the Freeway Phantom cases. She went on to say that he had continued to feed police officials with false information because they allowed him to have sexual relations with her, as long as he kept providing information. While not true news, it seemed to cement two things. It gave people reasons to doubt the investigation, and it cemented that Morris Warren was highly unreliable as a possible witness.

Paul Fletcher went before court in May 1975 on numerous charges relating to two victims dating back to December 1971. One was kidnapped at gunpoint in the 5100 block of Wisconsin Avenue NW and thrown into the Vega where Fletcher was one of the three passengers. They drove the substitute schoolteacher to an abandoned house in the 3700 block of Hayes Street where she was raped.

Later than night a woman waiting for a cab on Georgia Avenue and Sheridan Street NW was offered a ride by Davis in the nefarious green Vega. The driver drove a short distance then picked up two men claiming their car had broken down. One of those men with Fletcher. She was taken to the basement laundry room in the 5100 block of Eastern Avenue NE and raped and beaten. One of the victims could not testify against him, but her sworn statements were used. She had died of causes not related to the crimes or her assailants. On May 10, 1975, Fletcher was convicted of rape, sodomy, kidnapping, and assault with a dangerous weapon. For Banoun it was yet another victory over the Green Vega Gang. While this conviction was being celebrated, the charges against Morris Warren were going to come to court in July and November of 1975…and the public was about to get a glimpse into the depths of depravity that the Green Vega Gang had inflicted on the city and their victims.

CHAPTER 11: THE GREEN VEGA GANG - FINAL JUSTICE

"It's ancient history to everyone but the victim's families and the police. The so-called Freeway Phantom is blamed for murdering seven young girls in 1971 and 1972. DC Police believe the Phantom was actually a gang of at least five men who are also suspects in literally hundreds of rapes. Two of those five suspects are now believed to be cooperating with the prosecutors; giving testimony to link the convicted rapists to the Freeway Phantom murders."
—WMAL News, July 9, 1975

Morris Warren's big day in court came on July 8, 1975. Judge Fred Ugast considered Warren's motion to dismiss all charges and had to deal with the question as to whether Warren had lived up to his end of the agreement with prosecutors. To arrive at that decision, Ugast would flip the tables on Ray Banoun. Rather than being a prosecutor, Banoun would be a witness in the court, discussing in detail what had been promised to Warren as well as what he had delivered on.

"I testified at length – hours – about why we concluded that he (Warren) had not been truthful to us, and therefore we indicted him for rape. And the judge disagreed. I remember at one point, I forgot something very important, and I knew Judge Ugast very well. Usually you can't rehabilitate a witness on direct examination. I mean that can only be done on cross. When I had *clearly* forgotten something – I remember the AUSA who was questioning me tried rehabilitating me, with my notes. The defense attorney was a very good lawyer and objected that he could not, 'You can't rehabilitate a witness on direct!' And I remember Judge Ugast saying, "This is Mr. Banoun, I know him, that's okay."

In later years, to the authors, Ray Banoun summed up his recollection. "By then, Warren was serving two life sentences for rapes, plus the murder case that he was about to go to trial on in Prince George's County." "Judge Ugast issued an opinion on or about July 8, 1975, in which he dismissed the new rape indictment against Morris Warren because of the agreement we had with him. He ruled that Warren had given enough truthful information about the rapes, that he [Warren] had therefore fulfilled his obligation on the rapes, but he had not fulfilled his obligation on the [Freeway Phantom] murders – that he had not given us enough truthful information – and, therefore, he could be prosecuted for the murders."

Judge Ugast agreed with Warren and his defense team, he had lived up to, at least in part, his plea agreement. Ugast said the indictment must be dismissed because of "the possibility that some use of information he gave while under immunity." Per Ugast, Warren had admitted that they were involved in anywhere from 500 to 1,000 rapes over a three-year period. The investigators, however, found the Green Vega Gang's involvement was likely much smaller. The District had 1,080 open rapes between 1969 and 1973. This was narrowed to 150 that fit the modus operandi of the gang. Warren laid the blame at the feet of his former friends, John Davis, Paul Brooks, and Paul Fletcher. The judge further concluded that only when Warren had stopped cooperating with investigators, Banoun filed the additional charges against Warren.

How had all of this started? The evidence that the judge released, stated that Morris Warren made comments to his probation officer and another inmate that led them to believe that he and John Davis may have been connected to the Freeway Phantom murders. While he had been contacted by the Washington MPD investigators, his own words had started this entire affair.

In his ruling, Ugast dropped two bombshells of his own that had been introduced under seal in evidence. In the course of the grand jury investigation, Ugast revealed that Warren had taken investigators to the locations where three of the Freeway Phantom's bodies had been left. Furthermore, Ugast revealed for the first time that Teara Ann Bryant was considered one of the Freeway Phantom victims, per the investigators own conclusions.

Teara Ann Bryant had been strangled and dumped in the Anacostia River on November 26, 1972. Not all the members of the task force agreed that Bryant was one of the Freeway Phantom victims. "As far as our detectives were concerned there was never any hard evidence tying the Bryant case to the others," said John Hoxie, Prince George's County Police spokesman, regarding the startling revelation. "It was a theory that was explored, but in our opinion they didn't feel it held up. The case is still open."

Morris Warren proclaimed his innocence in the matters. As he told *The Washington Post* on July 9: "To be truthful with you, I am really disgusted. I haven't did anything and I'm going through hell. I'm trying to hold myself together because I know I haven't done anything I'm charged with. I'm locked up for crimes I never committed." Warren tried to paint himself as the victim in the search for the Freeway Phantom.

Judge Ugast summed up his findings on the matter bluntly. "While Mr. Warren denied any involvement with the Freeway Phantom cases, he told Detective (Louis) Richardson that Paul Fletcher, John Davis, and Paul Brooks were involved in somewhere between 500 and 1,000 rapes over the last four years, and they were the ones that should be in jail." It was far from the absolution that Warren wanted.

Judge Ugast's release of the opinion provided the media with details for the first time of the links between the Green Vega Gang and the Freeway Phantom murders. As recounted in *The Washington Post*:

"On May 16th Mr. Warren began to direct the government agents to the locations he had described to them regarding the two Freeway deaths. On May 16th he took them to the areas where Brenda Woodard, a homicide victim, had allegedly been kidnapped, raped and murdered."

"On May 17th he showed them the alleged locations dealing with Darlene Johnson, although while showing them where her body was abandoned, he took them to the place where Brenda Crockett's body was found. Both Ms. Johnson and Ms. Crockett were victims of the so-called Freeway Phantom homicides.

"On May 17th while indicating where Ms. Johnson had been taken, Mr. Warren took the officers to the alleys behind Ely Place, SE, and 31st Streets SE. While in the alley between E Street and Ely Place between 31st and 32nd streets, Mr. Warren saw a barking dog and mentioned that he remembered that he and his cohorts were looking for a place to rape the girl when a man with barking dogs came out of the house or an alley."

Judge Ugast continued, "One of the rape victims also told investigators that she had been taken to the 3100 block of Ely Place SE and the driver of the car became frightened when an old man with three dogs came along."

The Washington Post reported that detectives

were convinced that Warren had confused at least two of the incidents. "…this factor merely bolstered his own opinion that Mr. Warren was a likely suspect in the rape case."

Paul Fletcher went back to court in Prince George's County on July 18, 1975, for the murder of George Stevens. Circuit Court Judge Powers sentenced Fletcher to thirty years in prison for the murder and fifteen years for the assault with intent to commit murder. Fletcher had been offered immunity to testify against Morris Warren in the trial but had decided at the last minute to not do so. Where Warren might sell out Fletcher, Fletcher would not do that to his former partner in crime.

A few short days after the stunning revelations of Judge Ugast and Paul Fletcher's sentencing, Paul Brooks' trial for three rapes came up. The portrait that the victims painted of the Green Vega Gang was that of violent sociopaths, a rape-machine of sorts, trolling the dull orange sodium lit streets of the nation's capital, striking almost at random. It was, sadly enough, a fairly accurate representation.

Brooks saw the handwriting on the wall and confessed, but in doing so only exposed himself for the vicious person he was. He described the events on Halloween, 1972, when the gang was looking for victims. They spotted two young women walking near Moten Elementary school in the twilight hours. They drove them to a condemned apartment on Congress Street where the women were raped.

According to Brooks' confession in court: "Me, Morris Warren, and John Davis were out riding in John Davis' Chevrolet Vega. We were riding around in an area which I am not familiar with, but anyway, we saw two girls standing by a school. John got out of the car and started talking to the girls, and he talked them into getting into the car. After they got in the car we drove around and stopped at an apartment building in Southeast, (on Congress Street). We took them into a vacant apartment building and took them up some steps into a vacant apartment in the building. Then we made them lay on the floor, and I had sex with one of them, and John had sex with one, while Morris just stood around the apartment. After I had sex, I left the apartment. A few minutes later Morris and John came out of the building and we left. The girls were still in the apartment when we left."

Brooks glossed over the grisly details, no doubt to make himself look better. Banoun was prepared for this, having the victims present to tell their side of the nights they had been kidnapped and assaulted by the gang. One of the victims, a 16-year-old at the time was questioned by Ray Banoun to tell more. "The 'slim one and the short guy' is Davis. The "heavy-set guy" was Brooks. Brooks had been armed with a knife and gun.

"He" (Brooks) kept rushing me, telling me to take my clothes off, and he came closer towards me like he was getting ready to hit me. So I said, 'Okay, okay,' I started taking off my clothes real fast.

"Then he laid me on the floor with a bunch of glass and dirt and everything."

Bonoun pressed the point as carefully as he could given the nature of the crimes. "Did he get upset at you at any point?"

"He said – kept saying I better do it good…and then he kept saying I'm going to kill you. I'm going to kill you. He just kept saying it over and over again and I was getting, you know, scared

"I kept saying, 'Please don't kill me. Please don't kill me.'"

"At that point, did anyone come into the room or had anyone come into the room?"

"Yes. The heavyset guy that had (the other woman) brought her in the same apartment building with me."

"Did you say anything to the other women when she came in?"

"No"

"Do you remember what you were doing?"

"I was just laying on the floor."

"Were you crying or anything at the time?"

"No, because if I did, he kept trying to hit me in the face."

"Now, what happened after he finished having intercourse with you?"

"He got up…he zipped his zipper up and he pointed down at me and said, 'I'm going to kill you. I'm going to kill you.' Then the heavyset guy, he said, 'Man I can't do anything with this one right here.' He took the other woman into the room – it looked like a bedroom to me. He took her in there and made her take off her clothes."

"The heavyset guy told me to take off my clothes again, because after the other one finished with me, I put my clothes on."

"Did the heavyset one have intercourse with you?"

"Yes."

Banoun continued the questioning, "What happened after he was completed with you? Were you taken into the other room where the other woman was?"

"Yes. Well, the heavyset guy made me watch (the other woman) and the slim guy on the floor."

"Did the slim guy do anything to you?"

"After he got finished (with the other woman) and I, he started kicking and beating all on us."

"What do you mean by that? How did he kick you?"

"Like he knew karate, throwing karate kicks."

"…he kicked me in my stomach and my head hit the wall. He kept hitting all on her. He kicked her in the stomach and the face.

"After he got off (the other woman) he threatened her with a piece of glass, he pushed me in the glass and said he was going to kill me. So, I was trying to tell the heavyset guy – I was begging, really, I said 'Please tell him don't kill me,' and he pulled a knife out of his pocket and said, 'Man, come on. Don't do that.' You know, he was just trying to reason with him."

"Who was?"

"The heavyset guy. So, the slim guy had pulled me out of the closet, and they were talking, and they both left, and they told us to take off our clothes – that's when he started really beating us, and he said if we moved he was going to be sitting in the hallway with a gun. He said if we moved, he was going to come back in there and kill us."

Her story of brutality by Brooks was merely that of one of the five women that testified as to the nature and depravity of his actions. They painted a grim portrait of a group of men, devoid of compassion, who brutally assaulted women almost at random.

With his confession and guilty plea ratified, all that remained was the sentencing. For that, Banoun and investigators had a bombshell from their arsenal against Paul Brooks. During his own cooperation with the authorities, he had agreed to undergo sedation with sodium amytal, in layman's terms, "truth serum." While under the influence of the drug, for almost six hours, Brooks talked about not only the rapes he was involved with, but allegedly he made statements that indicated that he and the Green Vega Gang were responsible for the Freeway Phantom killings.

Decades later, Ray Banoun remembers the sessions where the truth serum was administered and his lack of confidence that it obtained meaningful results, "He's [Brooks] basically in one room with them, you see them through a one-way mirror, and it was fascinating.

"During one session, as Dr. Yochelson, the expert, was questioning Brooks about one of the murders. Brooks was lying down, supposedly relaxed from the drugs, and yet as Dr. Yochelson was holding Brooks' arm, Brooks was pulling it back, fighting Dr. Yochelson, who remarked, 'You're fighting me!'

"That's why I'm telling you my faith in truth serum is weak." So weak in fact, that the testimony that Brooks gave while under sodium amytal was not submitted to the grand jury for their consideration. But for Brooks' sentencing, it was fair game.

For Judge Ugast, it meant he had to consider that Brooks may have been involved in the Freeway Phantom murders as well as the rapes he had confessed to, though the credibility of the truth-serum testimony was highly questionable. Ugast sentenced Paul Brooks to five life sentences. Almost as a footnote, the US Attorney's Office announced they would be dropping the charges against Melvin Gray due to lack of evidence.

The stunning public testimony about the gang and his own role in it must have prompted Morris Warren to try and distance himself from the crimes…make himself out to be a victim of the US Attorney's Office rather than a perpetrator of gang rapes. It is also possible that he simply wanted more attention than what his former compatriots were receiving in the media. As a result, he gave a lengthy interview to the *Washington Post* from Lorton Prison.

Warren, as the victim, did not come across sincere. He was forced to spend time in the maximum-security section because some of his victims had relatives in the general population, and his life would be at risk. He claimed police had beaten him so badly that he had to be taken to DC General Hospital. The reality was that he had overdosed on drugs, which was why he had been taken there.

Warren dismissed the idea that he was cooperating willingly. The prosecutors had coerced him to testify against John Davis. No doubt Davis's letters to Warren were having their desired affects. In the interview he claimed that he had known Davis his entire life, "and can't imagine him being involved in rapes or murder." This, despite the testimony his other former gang members had given.

According to Warren, it was Ray Banoun who engaged with him for information on the rapes and murders. "I went over there. He asked me if I'd turn state's evidence against Davis, he'd drop any charges that might be coming down on me. I told him I didn't know if Davis ever raped anybody. I didn't think he was that kind of dude, and, to the best of my knowledge, he didn't have to rape anybody. He said am I willing to cooperate with the government or not? I told him no. He told me I'm blowing my chances of getting back out on the street."

After his conviction for the Green Vega rapes in October 1974, Warren said the prosecution stepped up the pressure on him to incriminate Davis in other rapes and murders. This was, of course, contrary to the evidence released days earlier by Judge Ugast, which said that Warren had initiated this cooperation by comments to his parole officer and another inmate.

In the *Post* interview, titled, "Jailed Rapist – 'I'm going through hell.'" Warren attempted to pretend that none of it had ever happened, openly denying that he had cooperated with investigators at all. In fact, Warren was not a bad person at all – he was a victim.

He wanted to be portrayed as a man that could have nothing to do with rape. He said that he, "...never had the feelings of aggression or unrequited sexual needs that would provoke him to rape a woman."

"I always had a young lady. Some of my sister's friends would like me, other people that I knew or people I'd just meet every day," said Warren,

"You have some men must have been hurt in younger years by women, by their mothers, sisters, girlfriends...they seek revenge in the only way that they know best..." he said.

"I never want to be there, to see a man taking advantage of a woman. I don't like it. The way I feel, if you can't get along with a woman then leave her…"

The *Post's* Stephen Green reached out to Banoun for his take on Morris Warren. He said that Warren had described how Brenda Woodard had been kidnapped and that she had been taken to an area near the Pepsi Cola plant there and had been raped and killed there. Then he had led the investigators to where her body had been dumped.

"[Warren] kept himself neatly out of the rape and neatly out of the killing…as they were arriving at the location of the Pepsi Cola plant and the hospital there, he took himself out and said he had to go urinate, so he got out of the car and went next to a pole to urinate, and the others continued, then they came back without the girl. And he just got back into the car."

Banoun went on to relate the nature of the immunity that Warren had been offered. Banoun stated that when he spoke to Ben Wolman, Warren's attorney in Prince George's County, "I indicated to him that the District of Columbia would not accept a total grant of immunity, that PG County could do so if they wished but in the District of Columbia, if Warren wishes to become a witness and continue to cooperate, he would have to plead to some lesser offense than first degree murder in the cases he testifies in."

Three months later, Morris Warren asked the court to allow him to enter the regular prison population. He claimed he was no longer in danger, but Judge Samuel Block questioned whether Warren would be, "committing suicide by wanting to go in the yard with other men." One of the greatest worries was that Leon Williams, the father of Diane Williams, was a guard at Lorton. With Morris Warren being labeled by the US Attorney's Office as one of the "prime suspects" in the Freeway Phantom cases, there was a genuine fear of for his life. Mr. Williams told Warren's lawyer that there were prisoners who wanted to harm him. Eventually, after much wrangling, Morris Warren entered the general population at Lorton.

By January 1976, it was evident that the Freeway Phantom investigation was not moving any closer to prosecution. The Green Vega rape cases were also winding down. The final case came up against John Davis before Judge Silvia Bacon. As Ray Banoun recalls, "Davis goes to trial before Judge Bacon. Silvia Bacon was one of the toughest sentencing judges. Davis started quoting from the Bible, screamed at his attorneys, and insulted prosecutors in open court. He and Warren were in court for a routine hearing on a rape case, and Davis called me a devil and a demon. He said I put him in jail for a crime, he hadn't committed."

Davis did everything he could to disrupt the case. Morris Warren was there to testify against him, and Davis prodded his former friend, telling him to "speak up" and "be a man." His own attorney, Thomas Farquhar, was shut down by his client, at one point telling him to shut up.

Davis barked in court, "I want my freedom, I want to be out of jail. It is as simple as that."

His violent grandstanding made it nearly impossible to get the victims to come to court and testify against him. Many had done what they could with their lives and were trying to move on after their attacks. Ray Banoun ended up dropping the last of the rape charges leveled at the two men due to the unwillingness of victims to testify again. Both Davis and Warren had so many counts against them, it was believed neither would see the light of day as free men.

For the families of the victims, it had been years of information leaking to the press with no tangible progress towards arrests or prosecution of their loved ones' killers. They took to the press, speaking with the *Washington Afro-American* in mid-May. The family-formed, Freeway Phantom Organization demanded answers. "They believe that the prime suspects in the case are in jail. They want someone to tell them yes or no."

They appealed to the justice department for answers.

"...the girl's relatives and friends have a very pressing and personal concern. That is, what is the status of the police investigation? Are the killers actually in prison (as there is a strong reason to believe), if so, why haven't they been convicted so that everyone will know. Or are they still free to strike again? And if so, what effort is being made to catch them?

"If your investigation justifies indictment, we petition you to indict the guilty persons so that we may know that they have been apprehended. This will offer great relief to the parents of the girls who were murdered, and it will further give the larger community a sense of relief at knowing that the Freeway Phantom murderers are serving time on the Green Vega Rape case."

The appeal to the press worked. Ten of the family representatives met with US Attorney Earl Silbert to demand an update on the investigation in late June 1976. They were briefed for two hours about the Green Vega Gang and the tenuous connections to the murders of their family members. Silbert assured them that the investigation was continuing, but rumors abounded that the cases were moving from cold to frigid.

In November 1976, Ray Banoun was transferred to the Fraud Division of the US Attorney's Office. The pit-bull US Attorney was still committed to the pursuit of the Freeway Phantom "I have every intention of continuing the Phantom investigation. ...I will carry the investigation with me." US Attorney Silbert tempered Banoun's dedication in *The Washington Post*, "I can't say how much time he'll be able to take out, but the investigation will not end." He went on to outline the issues facing the work the task force had done, "The sticking point apparently is two camps. One wants to take the investigation to the grand jury. Another feels there is insufficient evidence to do so."

Almost without a whimper, the efforts to find the Freeway Phantom went from a large multijurisdictional task force to boxes of material stuffed in a closet at the Washington Metropolitan Police Department. As far as the majority of the Washington MPD was concerned, they knew who had committed the murders – the Green Vega Gang.

The gang's time in court was far from over. There were numerous appeals filed. Charges by Warren, of a lack of speedy trail fell on deaf ears with the Court of Appeals. Warren claimed that he had suffered from pre-trail prejudice because of media coverage. The judges dismissed that off-hand, pointing out that on numerous occasions he and his family had called their own news conferences and had granted the media with interviews. One of the appeals did stick. It related to the very first convictions of Warren and Davis years earlier. Ironically it was these convictions that had started the investigation into the Freeway Phantom cases.

Warren claimed that by having a joint trial with Davis, he had been unjustly sentenced because more charges had been leveled at Davis, and his association with Davis as a co-defendant had hurt him. The appellate judges agreed on December 30, 1976, and ordered him to have a new trial separately.

There were hurdles with retrying the cases after the passage of several years. One of the victims, Sharon Williams, had died of causes unrelated to the case. Two of the other victims were still emotionally and mentally suffering from the assaults on them, and there was genuine fear that putting them back on the stands and forcing them to relive the events that scarred them might cause even more damage.

The argument made by Banoun was that they should not be required to appear to testify, but that their previous testimonies from the first trial be used. The risk was that Morris Warren could claim that his Constitutional right to face his accusers was denied. At the same time there was legal precedent in such matters. In May 1978, testimony was given on the issue of the witnesses being forced to endure another trail.

Dr. Leon Yochelson testified that Reed was suffering from a severe mixed psychoneurosis with particular emphasis on depressive mood, phobic reaction, and anxiety. He found that the depth of her depression had reached suicidal levels and that suicidal tendencies were still present. In the case of Marilyn Reed, she had changed her name, her religion, and her entire lifestyle. These changes had not successfully blunted the emotional and psychological effects of the violence she had suffered and that the trauma of another court appearance would most likely shatter her fragile adaption to society, possibly leading to permanent psychological injury.

Dr. Sheila Hafter Gray determined that Ms. Reed, who had become Muslim since her attack. "Raised in Mississippi and moved at the age of 12 to DC. Her father died the next year – she was one of seven children and the only one who didn't live up to her mother's expectations. Impulsive, she had already three children before the rape by Warren." She was unable to work. The trial would have, "...aggravated her feelings of personal guilt. And have even caused regression." She exuded, "An individual making an intense effort to maintain an outward picture of calmness and poise. However it soon became increasingly evident that control over deeper emotions, particularly those of anxiety and depression, was tenuous at best."

Dr. Gray's examination of Miss Jenkins, another of the victims, concluded that the attack, "had affected her entire character structure and social adjustment. She was afraid of men and had renounced hope of having a happy marriage. She suffered from repression, denial, and anxiety."

Ultimately Chief Judge Harold Greene sided with the mental welfare of the victims. Judge Greene ruled that the jury would be told why the victims were not attending the trial, and that their previous testimony should be accepted as evidence. Once more Banoun took up the sword of justice against his old adversary, Morris Warren. This time the legal system was swift, and Warren was again sentenced for his crimes.

It would take more years for appeals and protests for Morris Warren to wind through the court system. It would be 1983 before Morris Warren faced final justice. His two prior convictions were vacated, but in 1983 he would finally be convicted of kidnapping while armed and two counts of rape and assault with intent to commit sodomy. He received five concurrent terms of imprisonment, the largest being two sentences of ten years to life on each of the rape charges, followed by consecutive sentences of five to fifteen years on the two kidnapping counts.

So, did the Green Vega Gang commit the Freeway Phantom murders? That is the only question that demands answering. It depends on who you talk to and when. In an August 3, 1980, interview with *The Washington Post*, then-retired detective Louis Richardson strongly affirmed that he believed that the Green Vega Gang and the Freeway Phantom crimes were onc in the same. "No question in my mind: these are the guys. I don't give a damn what anybody says, I know that they showed us when they took us to the scenes. What [evidence] we had couldn't take it to a jury and prove it without a reasonable doubt. But how can a man tell you about a crime, the scene, clothing the girls wore, how she was killed, if he wasn't there.

Richardson elaborated, "[Melvin] Gray was then displayed a photograph of Nenomoshia Yates, a girl who was known to have disappeared from the Safeway store in the Benning Road area and had been one of the Freeway Phantom killings. Gray positively identified her as being the girl they picked up on Benning Road…"

"Melvin Gray was also displayed a photograph of Carol Denise Spinks, the first known victim in the Freeway Phantom killings. Gray positively identified her as being the little girl who was in their company both times they were at his apartment. Gray later withdrew his statements.

"On May 16th [Warren] took us to the areas where Brenda Woodard, a homicide victim, had allegedly been kidnapped, raped, and murdered. On May 17th, he showed us the alleged locations dealing with Darlenia Johnson, although while showing them where her body was abandoned, he took us to the place where Brenda Crockett's body was found."

The words of Louis Richardson, even in retirement, carried weight in the Washington MPD. His record for solving homicides is outstanding. His stand that the Freeway Phantom killers were the Green Vega rapists is deeply embedded to this day in the mindset of many in the Metropolitan Police Department.

Ray Banoun, in 1981, told the *Star Newspaper* in Prince George's County, "It could not have happened with only one person." Again, the hint pointing to the Green Vega suspects as the possible perpetrators.

That same year the Atlanta Child Murders were grasping at the nation's attention. A new phrase was being used for such crimes, serial murders. As with most serial killings, individuals try to find ways to connect them with other such cases. People immediately began to wonder, was the killer stalking in Atlanta akin to the cold cases in Washington DC. "I just don't think there is any similarity between what is happening in Atlanta and what's happening here," said Assistant Chief Maurice Turner of the DC Police to *The Washington Post*. The Freeway Phantom cases became a sad reference point for every serial killing spree in the African American community.

One place to try and mine for the truth is Morris Warren himself. Incarcerated for the last forty-six years, he has made numerous attempts to appeal to appellate judges as his case went up for appeals. His letters to them, a matter of public filings, either show a man who is confessing his lies, or simply adding to them.

In a September 27, 1982, letter to Judge Revercomb, Warren wrote:

> Please be informed that in 1974, Mr. Morris Warren told the United States Attorneys' office that he knew who was responsible for those famous Freeway Phantom rapes and murders. In reality, I really didn't know anything directly or indirectly about those painfully [sic] crimes. The truth is I put those crimes on innocent men out of revenge. I was revenging the fact that my co-defendants were pleading to armed robbery and first degree murder charges in Prince George [sic] County, Maryland, also with the testimony against me. I got this revenge idea from the television that I was watching one day in the old DC jail. If I remember correctly, two ex-policemen were only charged with one of those Freeway Phantom crimes. That left six unsolved. I thought to myself, "Why not put the other six on them?" that way I could kill two birds with one stone.
>
> 1. I could pay them back for snitching; 2. And maybe wind up getting myself out of jail at the same-time.
>
> My common law wife who had been with me every [sic] since I thought out this devilish scheme and tried to get her favoritism on it rejected my plot head over heels. As a matter

of fact she told me to not do this terrible thing because I would only cause more problems but would let whoever is responsible for the crimes get away.

I was deeply rooted in my anger and nothing was going to stop me from paying my codefendants back.

When I decided to take her and conscious advice, I knew I was up to my eyeballs in news publicity and under attack from the United States Attorney's office.

Ever since then I have been subjected to all kinds of inhumane conditions not only from officers but from inmates as well.

I was able to get through to most of the guys at Lorton as to how all of this stuff came about, involving me. They all seem to be able to be so realized [sic] officers and inmates alike. Telling people my truth about what has taken place makes me feel good in my thoughts as well as my heart. I thank God every night for his hand in guiding me to do the right thing.

Some people refuse to let go of the past publicity concerning me because it gave them something to talk about there are still such people here, in the jail, who refuse to let go of the past regardless of how much I tell that about the truth of this matter.

Six days later, he followed up that letter with the following:

"I wrote you a few days ago explaining to you the conditions I was faced with and up under, well, "I'm no longer in those demeaningful [sic] circumstances."

I thought to write you and let you know that everything has been settled in my best interest. I'm really happy that it turned out that way. So I guess you can treat the letter I wrote as a means of letting you and all the world know that my co-defendants and I <u>don't know anything</u> about those Freeway crimes, indirectly or directly. As my letter explains, it was me who started that revengeful scheme, plan, and plot. All in the name of wanting to pay my co-defendants back. I can't undo what I have done your honor, nor will saying I'm sorry probably help in anyway but if I ever get out of this terrible mess, I will atone for every unlawful deed and act I have committed against my fellow human beings.

The author's own attempts to interview Warren have been blunted, less by him and more by prison regulations. His correspondence with these authors is scattered with religious passages. In a February 2018 letter he wrote:

"You and your daughter have been running around on the wrong track, don't believe the hipe [sic] [God knows] you and your daughter are somewhere else or got the wrong title, the both of you have been [MIRAGED] by fake news. DON'T BELIEVE THE HIPE! [sic]"

Was the investigation worth it? It *did* get a group of very dangerous men off the streets. Getting them behind bars spared countless other potential victims harm. While the number of rapes attributed to the Green Vega Gang was always a lofty number, between 500 and 1,000, only around 150 fit their modus operandi enough to be considered viable cases. Of those, only a few ever actually went to trial.

In terms of the Freeway Phantom cases, the investigation did not yield any viable evidence or substance that could link the gang to the murders. It is important to note that a lack of evidence does not equate to innocence. It simply means that there was nothing to corroborate the fanciful stories that were told to the investigators.

There also was a willingness on the part of at least one investigator, Louis Richardson, to look the other way when it came to the gang's errors. When you evaluate the confession of Melvin Gray alone, there are countless discrepancies that would have made it invalid. Richardson was willing to overlook those glaring issues as simple mistakes. The same might be said of the confessions of Morris Warren, but the details of those are still sealed grand jury testimony.

Perhaps one of the more substantive pieces of evidence that the authorities had was the note that was written by Brenda Crockett, dictated or pre-written for her by her killer. Morris Warren never mentions it in his confession. When would the gang have had the time or place for her to write it behind the Pepsi plant before she was killed? Wouldn't John Davis have mentioned it? By his own admission, Warren stepped away to relieve himself.

In 2018, when the question of the note was raised with Ray Banoun, he said, "The only one that would have known anything about that would have been John Davis. Because there's no way that any of these other guys would know that word that was used…what was it…tantamount? They would not know what tantamount was. There's just no way. You would have to see these three guys to appreciate them. They were really totally amazing. Davis was…smart. No question. Even the letters that he wrote to that babysitter, you could really see that guy knew how to write."

The Green Vega Gang used a gun and a knife to control their victims, often beating them. The Freeway Phantom victims, with the exception of Brenda Woodard who was stabbed, were all strangled. That doesn't fit the way that gang operated or worked. None of their other victims spoke about being choked or strangled while prisoners of the gang.

What about the bathing of the victims, the redressing them, the green fiber evidence found on most of the victims? By Warren's own confessions, these crimes were committed in different locations. There was no way to pick up the fibers from a common source. The public, until this book, had no idea that the victims had been bathed. Nor did Morris Warren. Its omission is glaring and brings into question everything he confessed to. Yet strangely enough, Louis Richardson was willing to overlook this physical evidence on the victims in favor of closing the cases.

There are some age variations between the two sets of crimes that don't jibe as well. The Green Vega Gang did rape girls as young as sixteen, but they were the exception. Those victims tended to appear to be much more mature. Most of their victims were between 20 and 24 years old. The Freeway Phantom favored younger girls, with the oldest being eighteen. If the Green Vega Gang was responsible for the murders, why did they change their modus operandi just for the Freeway Phantom victims?

What of the families though? Their high hopes and lofty dreams of closure were to be muddied for decades to come.

Despite the massive amount of publicity regarding the possible connections of the Green Vega Gang to the Freeway Phantom cases, nothing else ever emerged in the form of tips or confirming information that was enough for prosecutors to take the cases to court. Ray Banoun made the right call to concentrate on the rape cases where conviction was assured, rather than pursuing the Freeway Phantom cases in court.

So was the investigation worth it? Yes. They had to be explored, if only to pursue open rape cases in the District. The Green Vega Gang could not be ignored as potential suspects. To do so would have been irresponsible. It would also be irresponsible to openly embrace their confessions in weight of some of the evidence.

John Davis was released from prison on September 13, 2002.

According to documentation we have received, Paul Fletcher was released from prison in 2001, as was Paul Brooks. There is no record of Melvin Gray ever serving a term for his involvement, however minor, in the Green Vega Gang's activities. Morris J. Warren, prisoner 05203-016 remains incarcerated in the Petersburg Federal Correctional Facility in Virginia. He has authored a book of his experiences but has not found a publisher willing to pick it up.

In 2018, Ray Banoun once more confronted his thoughts on the Green Vega/Freeway Phantom connection. "Richardson was convinced they were the same people (the rapists and the Freeway Phantom cases). To this day, I don't know. I really can't tell you that they committed the Freeway Phantom crimes."

One detective disagreed with his colleague Louis Richardson, as to the Green Vega connection to the Freeway Phantom. That was Detective Lloyd Davis. He did not subscribe to Richardson's attempts to simply close the Freeway Phantom cases. In the same 1981 interview where Richardson made his case, Davis offered a rebuttal, a tantalizing hint at someone else.

"The murders were conducted by a long black individual about 50 years old at the time, someone that no one would pay any special attention to. The man's been convicted of sexual offenses before, and is not in custody today, I won't say where, and he's been a former mental patient. I have proof that links all of the cases together...I just don't have enough physical evidence."

So who was this mysterious older man that Davis was hinting at? To get those answers, you must take a trip back in time to 1938...

CHAPTER 12: ROBERT ASKINS – THE SCARLET SISTERS

"Young Mr. Askins's reported story that he wished to save other young men like himself from falling into the hands of wicked and designing women, while a laudatory aim, is hardly justifiable cause for murder in this enlightened day."
—Does the Scarlet Sister Have a Case? *The Washington DC Afro American,* January 14, 1939

Detective Lloyd Davis had a suspect in mind, one he had been investigating for some time, alone, as the Freeway Phantom: Robert Askins. He pursued Askins alone, like a bloodhound in pursuit of a scent. Where the rest of the Washington MPD focused on the Green Vega Gang, Davis went on a different tangent.

The story of Robert Elwood Askins is one that began decades before the first of the Freeway Phantom cases. While it would be a pair of kidnapping and rapes in the 1970s that would put Robert Elwood Askins on the radar of the Washington Metropolitan Police as a possible suspect; in reality he had been a criminal figure in Washington DC for some time, decades in fact. To crawl into the twisted and dark world of Robert Askins, you must first peer into his troubling early years.

His tumble into murder, kidnapping, and rape began with a seemingly random killing. Elizabeth Brown, a 26-year-old resident of the District of Columbia was walking to her home on Freeman Court, near Howard University in the early morning hours on December 21, 1938. She was known to police already as a prostitute who plied her trade near the university. A slender, light skinned colored man strode up to her and stabbed her viciously in the abdomen with several deep thrusts. The man fled but had been witnessed by several other people out in those early morning hours.

Elizabeth Brown was taken to the hospital but died shortly after her arrival. There was no obituary for her, merely a few scant sentences noting the crime in the *Washington Post* and *Star* newspapers. Authorities did not spend much time investigating the case. Violence against "red women" did not merit the attention of the police. It would be another week before a person of interest would emerge.

It would be another week before Robert Askins killed again.

Robert's birth father, Herman Lester Askins, came from Harrisburg, Pennsylvania, and his mother Ethel May Buckner, from Arlington, Virginia. They married young; Ethel was a mere 15 years old at the time. We don't know what drew them to the District of Columbia, but they lived at 1814 First Street NW in a modest row-house. Herman registered for the draft in 1918, but there was no record of him serving. Little is known of Robert's father, where he worked, or the kind of man he was. In the early twentieth century the genealogy records of black families are spotty at best.

Robert was born on January 7, 1919 – his sister, Iris, a year later. Ethel worked as a beautician. At the age of 9, his father died, leaving young Ethel to raise her pair of children alone. She enlisted the help of her sister, Ruth, to help out. It left the impressionable young Robert without a male influence in his life as he was on the verge of puberty. Adding to his home tensions, his mother struggled to keep the family afloat. By his own accounts, from the age of 9 on, he worked odd jobs when possible and was responsible for purchasing his own clothing. Whether his being raised in a tight and tense circle of only females impacted him later in life, we may never know.

When he was 15 years old his mother remarried. Askins objected to the marriage so vehemently it would be three years before his new stepfather moved into their First Avenue home.

As a high school student Askins was not an outstanding student, receiving average grades in every subject except French and Chemistry, in which he demonstrated aptitude. He graduated high school in 1936 and enrolled in Miner Teachers' College, on the grounds now of what now is Howard University. Robert was a student for two years at the highly respected Miner Teachers' College.

In early 1938 he was out of school for a short period of time. While riding a bike, he fell and suffered a head injury that left him unconscious for almost two weeks. He recovered and claimed that he noticed no behavioral changes, but that did not mean he did not suffer them. As it would turn out, 1938 would be a pivotal year for this college student, in ways no one could predict.

Askins, by most accounts, was a slender, bright young man, highly articulate – with a brilliant future ahead of him as a chemist or as a teacher. His grades were not outstanding, he never made the honor roll at the small Miner Teachers College where he went to school. In fact, there was no mention of him in the school newspaper whatsoever. The *Washington Afro American* covered him once before his crimes. He was a member of the "Wanderbirds" a group of science students who visited local museums and laboratories. His photograph appeared with other students on a field trip.

Yet, for a young man of color in an era where opportunities for men of his race were limited, his future seemed filled with hope and promise.

Washington DC was a different place for blacks in the 1930s. Education options were limited. Those that did go on to higher education bore with them responsibility in their community. There were only a handful of colleges that blacks could attend – namely Howard University and Miner Teachers' College. The students who attended these schools were seen as future leaders, regardless of the profession they pursued. There were high expectations put on students to lead by example.

This was what people saw on the surface, a carefully crafted image, for his part. In reality, Askins was involved in relatively seedy activities outside of school. Adjoining building for Miner Teachers' College and Howard University was one of the city's red-light districts. Robert Askins was no stranger to visiting the infamous Freeman's Court, an epicenter of prostitution, one of three in the District at that time.

In his spare time, he secretly acted as a police informant, helping arrest others in his community by taking part in sting operations. This was not uncommon with the Metropolitan police, using others to entrap would-be criminals. It put Askins in a position where he played a role, impersonated someone to mislead others – all under the authority of detectives.

Prostitution was a real problem near the two colleges. In a Ralph Matthews penned editorial in the *Washington DC Afro American* newspaper, he tells a great deal about the neighborhood near Miner Teachers' College and Howard University. "The so-called red light district which borders on the edge of Howard University, Miner Teachers' College, and the Hospital, some of the habitués Mr. Askins sought to exterminate certainly must have some value to have existed all of these years in tranquility and apparent bliss....The presence of the scarlet sisters in Freeman Court, situated hard by the moss-covered halls of dear old Howard, has probably saved many a co-ed from designing fraternity brothers."

On December 28, 1938, Askins left his mother's home on First Street and went to the vicinity of Sixth and M streets where he allegedly "made" several prostitution cases while acting in the role of a police informer. This claim was not substantiated by any police officers, but he maintained this was his activity. The weather was bitter cold, only reaching thirty degrees with a stiff wind blowing in front the north, adding to the biting chill, hardly the kind of weather that would have allowed him to pick up women in the first place.

According to his own account, after assisting police with several arrests, he went to Miners Teachers' College where he returned to his studies. After several hours, he found he could not concentrate and became frustrated. Eventually he returned to his home. According to his mother, he had been suffering for several weeks with insomnia, having a difficult time concentrating on his studies. His appetite had all but disappeared and most of the time he was, "upset." Little did anyone realize that this was a symptom of a greater mental problem.

It was at his small home, in the row house on First Street, where something snapped. Askins' own personal account was that he came to the conclusion that he should kill himself. The suicide excuse was little more than a failed attempt to justify his next actions. In his confession to police, he claimed that he had contracted a social disease from a streetwalker just a few short weeks prior to this dreadful night. In his initial confession, he claimed that it was his intention to, "Kill them all, at one time if he could, and he further stated that he intended, his intention was to kill all the prostitutes in town if possible."

His means of doing this was simple and deadly. He had obtained some roach powder from a neighbor that he knew from his classes was potassium cyanide. Steeling himself for what he was about to do, he took several stiff drinks of the whiskey. "I am not a habitual drinker," he would later tell authorities.

The 20-year old student mixed the rat poison in with the bottle of whiskey, to a concentration of 2.9 percent. Recapping the bottle, he set off for Freeman's Court, the red-light district near his college. He had no intention of killing himself alone…he wanted revenge.

At Freeman's Court, only a few yards from where Elizabeth Brown had been stabbed, Askins met Alice C. Brown Patterson. Patterson said she and Askins went to her Freeman's Court address. Once inside, "She saw the bottle sticking out of my coat pocket and she asked me to give her and her friends a drink. Then she took the bottle out of my coat pocket and went into the next room." There, he met three other prostitutes who lived with Patterson: Ethel Prentiss, Arlene Blackwell, Amanda Powell, and Ruth McDonald. Askins poured everyone a drink of whisky, including himself.

Askins put his wallet on the table, apparently as a ploy to show that he was relaxed. He offered an obscene toast, followed with a claim that he would pay one dollar to whoever could drink the whiskey first. The women took him up on his challenge. At first it appeared that Askins had joined them, he raised the glass up to his lips but did not drink from it.

Three of the women did not consume much – all three recognized that something did not taste right and spit it out. One had slammed the drink back, 31-year-old Ruth McDonald who had consumed her drink, "right down." A few minutes later the women became ill, vomiting – their hearts racing. Ethel Prentiss had taken courses for nursing and immediately threw together an ad hoc, "antidote of milk, eggs, and butter." While far from being a cure, three of the women seemed to not have consumed as much as Ruth McDonald who collapsed and could not be revived.

As the women gathered themselves and called an ambulance to get her to the hospital, Askins left, leaving behind at least one glass filled with both the whiskey and poison. Ruth McDonald never stood a chance, dying at the hospital that was only a short walking distance away.

Detective Sergeant William J. Liverman was called the hospital where all the victims had been admitted. On New Year's Eve, two of them identified Askins as the man who had tried to kill them. When the police arrived the next day, in his coat pocket was the toxic whiskey.

He was taken back to the Thirteenth Precinct and was interrogated. This was long before Miranda rights and warnings, in a day where police questioning could be both mental and physical. Askins did not seem to resist; it was almost as if he wanted to talk. They peppered him with questions as to his motive and why he had chosen such a manner to kill his victims or if there was some other possible excuse for his behavior. "Were you drunk on the night of December 28, 1938, when you went into the house with the girl?"

"I wasn't staggering. I could feel a sensation in my head."

Liverman pressed the logic of the young man. "Why did you pour out several glasses and permit them to drink it in your presence and you know it to be poison?" Askins response was detached. "The only possible explanation I can give for that is that the whiskey I had drank before I went to the house had made me unaware of the danger I was exposing these women to, as I ordinarily do not approve of mistreating women. When the woman made mention of the fact that the whiskey had a peculiar taste, I told them to hold everything." This did not mesh at all with the statements of the victims who said that Askins had done nothing after they had consumed the poison.

Askins' confession took a darker turn when pressed further. His intent, as he told Detective Liverman, was to kill the prostitutes, plain and simple revenge for his venereal disease. He claimed that Washington DC had been ruined by the red-light district and hoped to save fellow students from his own fate. Further, he stated he, "...was going to orchestrate a purge of prostitutes." The poisonings, in other words, were just the start of what he had planned. It was a stunning admission, even for the seasoned detective. The officers took his confession down and a few days later he was charged for the murder of Ruth McDonald.

Was it possible that this was not Askins' first attempt to kill? With his arrest, investigators began to look into other murders near the Freeman Court area. The stabbing of Elizabeth Brown a week before the poisoning stood out. Witnesses were brought to the precinct and identified Askins as the man who had stabbed her. On February 2, 1939, he was charged with Elizabeth Brown's murder as well. The young chemistry student with the world as his oyster was now facing a pair of murder charges and the prospect of dying in the electric chair, called "Sparky" by local residents.

Askins' lawyer was John H. Wilson who faced a daunting task. There was no way to claim his client had been wrongly identified as the purveyor of the poison. On top of that, his client had given a full confession to the police. Undoing it was impossible – so all that left was for him to attempt to paint his client as innocent by reason of insanity. He moved for such a hearing quickly.

Technically, Askins did not go to trial for his murders – instead most of what we know was revealed in pre-trial testimony to determine if he was fit to face the justice he was due. The Prosecution's opening salvo was putting Alice Brown Patterson on the stand, describing for the court the events that had led to the death of Ruth McDonald. The testimony of the poisoning was compelling. Detective Liverman followed with retelling of Askins' confession to the crimes. Chemists told of the poison found at his home, in the glasses of the victims, and the cause of death of Ruth McDonald. Askins sat in his seat, leaning to one side, seemingly detached, if not bored, with the proceedings.

Attorney Wilson did the best he could to try and unravel the confession by putting his client on the stand. Robert Askins' gnarled version of events was twisted into a combination of being intoxicated and wanting to commit suicide. "(I am) not a habitual drinker," he emphasized. He first drank the whiskey to build up the courage to take potassium cyanide mixed with the remaining whiskey himself. While waiting for the whiskey to take effect, he walked around, and at that time encountered Alice Brown and was invited in to share his toxic drink. "I told [Liverman] that it was not my intention when I left the house to harm anyone except myself, but that I had drank quite a bit out of the bottle."

When asked by his attorney, "But you did realize the danger to yourself when you poured yourself a drink and carried it to your mouth and failed to drink, didn't you?" Askins responded, "I did not realize the danger I was in as I was in such a bad condition."

Wilson pressed his questioning, "Didn't you know that the cyanide was still in the whiskey that you offered these girls to drink?"

"It was the whiskey I had drank. I was in such a condition that I didn't realize it." When pressed further, he calmly replied, "It was strictly an accident," that he permitted the women to drink the deadly concoction.

Askins summed up his involvement, "If I was in the state of mind that I am now and knew that the whiskey contained cyanide, I would not have permitted them to drink it, as I think that they should be taught how to work other than by selling themselves. I would not knowingly harm any woman. That's all."

When asked why he wanted to kill himself, his response made little sense. "I felt ashamed and worthless and wanted to kill myself because I had worked as an informer for the police."

While on the stand on February 2, 1939, Askins was asked by Wilson why he had made his original confession, claiming that he wanted to kill prostitutes. Askins claimed police brutality had forced his confession. "I was struck twice, and I heard someone say, 'Let's call in Henry Armstrong' and I thought they meant Henry Armstrong the boxer, and I was afraid he was going to come in and beat me up." He accused William Liverman and Philip Abel, both of the Thirteenth Precinct, of hitting him and forcing him to say that he was out to kill prostitutes.

Askins had tried to shift the blame entirely to the Metropolitan Police Department. Their use of him as an informant had driven him to suicide. They had beaten him, forced him to make a false confession. He had gone from being a murderer to trying to put on the mantle of being a victim.

The prosecutor, Assistant United States Attorney Arthur McLaughlin, had an ace up his sleeve to counter these claims. He called to the stand Detective Sergeant Harold H. Hodge, a retired officer, to the stand. Detective Hodge knew the defendant well, stating that Askins had worked for him in 1938 as an undercover man, helping obtain evidence on numbers lottery operators. Askins had told Hodge that he, "Had developed a hatred of women because he had contracted a venereal disease."

Detective Hodge's words and the attempt to unravel the previous confession painted an image of a young man in mental turmoil. Wilson altered his defense strategy after having Askins on the stand. Wilson asked the court to have his client submitted for professional psychiatric evaluation before rendering a verdict on his state of mind at the time of the crime. The formal request was labeled a "lunacy inquisition."

Askins was admitted to Gallinger Hospital for observation. On February 11, 1939, Askins broke the restraining straps on his bed and attacked and subdued three orderlies with a chair that he used as weapon. The furious young man was re-restrained and sedated. Gone was the image of a shy man who was distraught and only sought to kill himself. *The Washington Star* covered the incident, further eroding the thought that Askins was not a victim, but a vicious man, more than capable of committing murder. After that, he became catatonic, not speaking, unable to appear in court. In some respects, it helped his defense.

The psychiatrists came back with the results on March 31, 1939, that Askins was suffering from dementia praecox of the catatonic type. By today's standards it was more of a case of catatonic schizophrenia, a chronic deterioration, a cognitive disintegration of his ability to function. The testimony of the court-appointed psychiatrists was grim. There was little hope for Robert Askins to return to being a functioning member of society, in their view.

After a series of delays, Judge James Proctor ruled on August 17, 1939, that Robert Askins was declared to be of unsound mind. The charges for the murders of Ruth McDonald and Elizabeth Brown were set aside. Askins was sentenced to St. Elizabeth's Hospital in the District. Less than a month from the start of World War II, Askins was transferred from Gallinger to St. Elizabeth's, "Saint E's" as it was called by the locals, where it was thought he would spend the rest of his life.

When it was built in 1855, St. Elizabeth's was on a broad grassy plain overlooking the Anacostia River with views all the way to the Navy Yard and the White House. Institutions for the treatment of mental illness were rare when St. Elizabeth's was constructed, but by the 1930s it was the premier "Government Hospital for the Insane." With more than 4,600 patients, forty-five physicians, fifty nurses, and 1,700 staff around the time that Robert Askins moved in. The doctor to patient ratio said something about the amount of care given, with each doctor being responsible for 100 patients. St. Elizabeth's was a large campus, much larger than most universities in the District. It had a canteen, an extensive library, greenhouses, even a dance hall. Crops of corn and other vegetables were grown on the grounds, seen as a means to give the patients menial tasks to perform. It had an isolated tuberculosis wing that was constructed as well. St. Elizabeth's was a city within the city of Washington.

Robert Askins' mother took a job in the laundry there, presumably to be closer to her son during his time there. For quite some time he remained unresponsive, catatonic. The staff imposed a treatment known as insulin shock treatment. Also known as insulin coma therapy, Askins was injected with doses of insulin designed to put him into comas for hours and even days at a time. There were few standard guidelines for the treatment. Seizures were common for those undergoing the process. For schizophrenia it was considered a standard procedure at the time, though by the mid-1950s it would disappear entirely as being largely ineffective.

The world went on all around St. Elizabeth's, but for the patients like Robert Askins it was as if time stood still. The Second World War was fought and ended – the atomic age and the cold war became the new realities in Washington DC, but for him, none of that mattered. There was routine, and with it, a certain relative sense of comfort.

He tried several times to press the courts to be released from St. Elizabeth's. In 1946 Justice Henry A Schweinhaut of the District Court granted a rehearing of his case. To his chagrin, he was not allowed his freedom.

In January 1948 his attorney filed a writ of habeas corpus for him to be released from St. Elizabeth's. Justice Schweinhaut said he had reasonable doubt that Askins was still insane. The judge ordered the Mental Health Commission to examine him further. Their results were inconclusive at the time, leaving Askins still at St. Elizabeth's.

Oddly enough, other than his shock treatments, he was not given any medication to address his problems. Gradually, as years passed, he began to communicate more with his doctors. He read books and began to demonstrate basic social skills. On March 11, 1949, he was found to be free of psychotic symptoms, and within a few months thereafter he began to get various types of privileges within the hospital. In 1950 he began to have visiting privileges outside the hospital through February 1952, when he was discharged on Social Recovery, usually a treatment for schizophrenia.

By March of 1952, Askins was back on the streets of Washington DC, discharged as sane. It proved to be a deadly mistake.

On September 1, 1952, Laura Mattie Cook, met a young man while working the streets of the District. The 42-year-old took the man into the Logan Hotel near Logan Circle in the Northwest of the city. The Logan Hotel was known as a "tourist home," and had a seedy reputation. The man working the desk and another regular guest at the hotel that night saw her go up to her room with a young man. The man hurriedly left a short time later. It would be in the mid-morning before her body was discovered. Laura Cook had been manually strangled. In her years in DC, she had become well known by the police – having been arrested under several aliases, Laura Emery, Stevenson and Williams. There weren't a lot of clues other than two witnesses, neither of whom knew the man she had last been seen with. The murder merited only three sentences of coverage in the local newspapers. It was a crime against prostitutes, which garnered little public attention. The two Second Precinct detectives working the case, John A. Jones and William McLaughlin, looked for suspects but eventually moved on.

On March 9, 1953, 23-year-old Mrs. Marie Sweeney had met a young man and had taken him back to the same hotel. The man had tried to strangle her as well, but she had managed to get free. The employee at the desk noticed the man as he fled the hotel and recognized him as the same one who had been with Laura Cook. Sweeney did not report the crime, after all, it would have only drawn attention to her working the streets.

On April 22, Detective Jones and McLaughlin were parked in the 1200 block of 11th Street Northwest when they overheard Sweeney talking with another man about the incident, telling him the tale of a young black man who "almost choked me to death." She was more than willing to describe the man and the officers realized that Sweeney had very narrowly managed to escape the same fate as Cook. It was a simple twist of fate that had brought the two officers and Sweeney together.

On May 1, 1954, the detectives were finally able to spot a man who met the description loitering near the Logan Hotel, and he was brought in speak with detectives of the Homicide Squad. When he was seen again lingering around the Logan Hotel, he was brought in once more. When questioning him about both incidents his stories did not match from each session, adding to the officer's suspicions. They decided to see if any of the witnesses could identify him. In a lineup, both Sweeney and the night clerk at the Logan Hotel identified the man. Robert Askins was once more facing charges of murder...a crime that he had committed only 183 days after being released from St. Elizabeth's.

Askins was held in custody until a grand jury could be convened. All that the prosecution had however was two eyewitnesses who saw him enter the hotel with the victim and leave alone. There was no physical evidence to connect him to the crime, merely circumstance. While they could pursue a case of attempted murder against Marie Sweeney, their goal was to have Askins locked away for a long time to protect the community. So the US Attorney's Office reopened the Ruth McDonald poisoning case, where there was ample evidence and witnesses. Since Askins had not gone to trial years before, he could not claim double jeopardy.

The grand jury heard the testimonies in both cases. In the case of Ruth McDonald, they ruled on November 2, 1954, that Askins should be indicted for her murder again. The deliberations around Laura Cook took eight more days and the indictment was dismissed by Chief Judge Bolitha J. Laws due to lack of evidence. Thirty-five-year-old Askins was readmitted to St Elizabeth's.

Assistant United States Attorney Thomas Flannery had to first prove that indeed a murder had taken place. On the first of February, 1955, Dr. Richard Rosenberg, deputy coroner, took the stand, testifying that Miss McDonald had died from consuming potassium cyanide. The detectives came to the stand and said they had recovered the whiskey bottle from Askins' house, and it was deemed to be the source of the poison. Another bottle was found at Askins' home and the two contained the exact same concentrations of cyanide. Also the glasses in the room where the poisoning took place contained lethal amounts of the poison. The testimony took two days but, when combined with his previous confession, there could be little doubt that Askins had committed the crime.

The prosecutor's case left little room for Askins' defense attorney, George E. C. Hayes to work with. He pushed forward with an insanity defense. Calling Doctor Joseph Gilbert to the stand, he testified that he had examined Askins in early 1939 and found him insane.

Flannery had been expecting this defense. He called a rebuttal witness, Doctor Amino Perretti, a psychiatrist at District General Hospital who testified that he believed Askins was sane at the time he committed the crime. On cross-examination Dr. Perretti stated that this was based on reviewing records, rather than actually examining Askins himself.

Askins' mother, Ethel Young, testified her son and become "upset" in the summer of 1938. Doctor Morris Kleinerman, formerly of St. Elizabeth's Hospital, stated that he had examined Askins in June 1939. In his professional opinion, he was unable to form an opinion of Askins' sanity six months earlier when the crime took place.

On the fifth of February the testimony came to a close. The ten men, two women jury started their deliberations on the eighth, but only for two and a half hours. The next morning they signaled they had come to a verdict. Robert Askins was guilty of the second-degree murder of Ruth McDonald, seventeen years earlier. He is sentenced to fifteen years to life.

His attorney, George Hayes, had one more ace up his sleeve. In Washington DC at that time, the statute of limitations determined that you must be charged for a crime within five years of when the crime was committed. He filed an appeal on behalf of Askins, pointing out that his client had been charged with the murder sixteen years after the murder of Ruth McDonald. On January 17, 1958, the US Court of Appeals ruled that Askins was to be set free. The court ruled that the statute of limitations had lapsed on the crime and removed the power of the lower court to punish him.

Robert Askins was once more loose on the streets of Washington DC.

CHAPTER 13: ROBERT ASKINS – PREDATORY BEHAVIOR

"My main concern is to establish, by the grace of God,
that I did not commit the crimes of which I am accused."
—*Robert Askins*

The evening of July 8, 1976, was a typical July night in the District of Columbia. It was eighty-two degrees with humidity that hung in the air, making every surface seem tacky to the touch. Only a few days before the nation had celebrated its bicentennial, which had brought record numbers of tourists and visitors to the capital to witness the massive fireworks displays and parties. During the summer months, the District is always filled with out-of-towners, but this year there were more than usual.

Twenty-five-year-old Martinia Stewart lived on 749 12th Street, a working-class neighborhood in Washington DC. Tourists rarely wandered into this section of town, and definitely not at night. Martinia was slight of stature and looked younger than her actual age. Ms. Stewart was walking down 8th Street SE heading home as she had done countless times before.

A green car pulled up beside her. The driver –a black man, in his late forties, five foot, seven inches tall, got out of the car and approached her, flashing a badge and telling her he was a police officer. He ordered her into his car, claiming that she was wanted for questioning. Thinking he was a plainclothes policeman, she got into the car and was driven off to a neighborhood near New Bladensburg and Montana Avenues Northeast.

She soon came to realize that this was not a police officer at all. He drove her to a house and threatened her with violence to compel her to go inside. Once inside the home, Ms. Stewart's life was in jeopardy, and she knew it. Her kidnapper ordered her upstairs where she was raped and sodomized. She was a fighter though, and tried to get away, throwing a can opener at him – only to then be, once more, subdued.

Her attacker's behavior in response to her resistance was odd. He gave her a pencil and dictated a note to her, stating she had been aggressive towards him, and that he was absolved of the responsibility of physical abuse she had received.

After one of his sexual assaults he drifted off to sleep. Once more she attempted escape, this time trying to open a window in the bedroom where he held her. Once more, her attacker grabbed her and pulled her back.

The next day, he ordered her into his bathroom. There he drew a bath and bathed with her in the tub, taking the time to dry her off. He asked her to put her clothes back on and at noon, she was allowed to leave the house.

For a time she ran, just to put some distance between her attacker and herself. She flagged a passing police car and explained that she had been kidnapped and raped, but the officers were, "cold and unconcerned." Frustrated, she signaled a passing taxi and went to Washington General Hospital.

There, police officer Arlene Seckel interviewed her and took her statement. Officer Seckel took the matter more seriously, driving around the area where Ms. Steward claimed the assault took place, looking for the house. Later, Martinia admitted that she had seen the house, but was too frightened at the time to tell the officer. Shekel listed the address as "impossible" to determine in her report. It appeared that her brutal rape was one of the hundreds in the District that would go unsolved, let alone be a critical link to the Freeway Phantom case.

Gloria McMillan was young and attractive and lived at 724 3rd Street NW, apartment 402. It was an older building, red brick, low rent at the time. McMillan appeared much younger than her 23-year age. She had been out late and coming home on March 18, 1977, not thinking of any danger in her neighborhood. While waiting for an elevator at her apartment building, at around 1 a.m., she was approached from behind by a black man, in his early fifties, six foot, 220 pounds, long gray sideburns. He put a "big stick" across her throat and started choking her. "Don't move!" he warned her. The "stick" was cold and heavy and would later be identified as a section of iron pipe. She obeyed, nearly petrified with fear. He told her if she screamed, he would kill her. It was the kind of threat that forced her compliance.

Her attacker took her to his green car and blindfolded her. He drove off, driving for somewhere between ten and twenty minutes through the District neighborhoods. When he finally took the blindfold off, she saw a nearby Amoco station across the street from a tan bricked corner row house at 1700 M Street NE and 17th Street NE.

Once inside he made her go upstairs in the house to a small back bedroom. There he tied her hands and ordered her to strip naked and to lay on the bed with him. Her kidnapper-turned-rapist violently assaulted her several times and sodomized her. At one point in his attacks, he also even attempted to use the pipe on her as well, but she resisted. Failing with that, he jammed a piece of paper into her vagina, a bizarre act hinting at a deep level of mental corruption.

Somewhere between 2 a.m. and 3 a.m., she began to fight her assailant, attempting to get free. He took her to the window and tried to throw her through it, but the determined Ms. McMillian hooked her foot under the bed, preventing him from fulfilling his threat. She punched through the glass before he violently flung her back into the room. The shattered glass cut her arms and hands, which were covered in blood. She screamed, but no one came to her aid.

Crying, she pleaded with her attacker to let her call her mother or someone else to take her to the hospital. His response was ice cold. "There is no hope for you. You are going to die anyway." In her words, "He said he was going to kill me. He kept choking me."

Then her assailant's behavior took an even more sinister turn. She would later tell authorities, "Every once in a while, he'd rub his head like he had a headache and he'd laugh. He then said, 'I didn't mean to hurt you.' He seemed like he had a split personality."

Gloria's ordeal was not over. "I passed out for a while. I woke up. He was raping me again, and I was in a lot of pain." Then, in a strange turn, he then gave her a bath, even putting lotion on her, wrapping her injured arms up in sheets. To ease her pain, he gave her three Bayer aspirin, hardly enough to take the edge off the horrific ordeal she had been put through.

Her strange assailant forced her downstairs to the kitchen. When he emerged from the kitchen, he held a large knife and was carrying a big green plastic bag. "He said he was going to take me to Virginia and finish me off."

He moved to the back door of the kitchen and unlatched the door. As he turned she rallied her resolve, kicking him, "…in the dick," and bolted for the back door. She made it to the nearby Amoco gas station where she summoned help, then blacked out.

At 1 a.m. the next morning, Ms. McMillian woke up at DC General Hospital in the emergency room, unaware as to how she had gotten there. Next to her was a McDonald's bag with hamburgers in it. Had it been left by a well-wishing

Samaritan, or had her attacker, in some quirk of his sick personality, left the meal with her? Still weak, she called out for her mother and gave the nurse her name before passing out again. It would be several more hours before she could give a statement to Detective Everett of the Sex Squad.

Her story was so depraved and twisted, it was almost inconceivable. Everett waited until she was strong enough then drove her to the area and identified the house she had been held in. She spotted the home at 1700 M Street NE, and the police determined who the owner was, they even had his photograph on file.

Gloria McMillian identified the photograph of the owner as Robert Askins, the man who had attacked her. Police went to his home and apprehended him without a struggle. He was brought in for a lineup where she positively identified Askins as her assailant. A no-knock search warrant of the house was issued and corroborating evidence in the form of a section of pipe, a knife, and a pistol was found. Askins also owned a green car that was identified by Ms. McMillian.

A mask and women's underwear were also found in his house and taken into evidence. When Askins heard about it, he immediately claimed it was planted evidence, even though it had no bearing on his case. According to him, it was proof that the authorities were conspiring against him.

It would take investigators three months before they noticed that this sounded similar to the Martinia Stewart's case. They located Ms. Stewart and drove her to the neighborhood where she too identified the same house as the one she had been taken to. She too was presented Askins in a lineup and identified him as her attacker.

A grand jury was assembled for the two cases and took little time in leveling ten counts against Robert Askins. More than two and half-pages of sordid details of his crimes were presented. They settled on kidnapping while armed; kidnapping; rape while armed; rape; sodomy; assault with a dangerous weapon; mayhem; and malicious disfigurement.

Prosecutors pushed for and received a ruling that the case would be tried jointly but was sentenced bifurcated, split into two parts – one for each of the victims and the specific charges.

No bond was initially granted given his perceived threat to the community.

Askins' first lawyer, N. Richard Janis, was only able to defend him for a month before filing a motion to withdraw as counsel. While he succeeded in getting Askins bond reduced to $25,000 (including conditions that he would remain gainfully employed), he found himself at odds with his client. As he wrote Askins and copied the court, "As you will recall, I explained to you, your aunt, and your sister prior to my retention as your attorney that I would rather not get involved at all if you felt my fees were burdensome. I also explained that you should understand that, depending on the charges placed against you and the work involved in your defense, my fees could quite possibly be greater than $5,000. Consequently as a result of your letter of April 3, in which you make the extraordinary statement that you signed the agreement, 'due to stress, strain and confusion,' I have very serious doubts about whether I am now willing to continue to represent you under any circumstances. Moreover, at the lineup, which is scheduled for April 15, 1977, the government intends to present complaining witnesses in two other rape cases which you are a suspect." He would be the first in a string of lawyers that Askins struggled with.

Askins was out of jail on bond, but far from out of trouble. He had worked for seven years at the National Science Foundation (NSF) where he worked as a GS 8 Computer Technician, a relatively complex and demanding role in 1977. Askins proved to be an outstanding employee – he received a special achievement award for his "Outstanding dedication to duty and superior technical quality of his work." Askins, however, never bothered to let the NSF know that he had been arrested and was unable to come in for work. When released on bond, he contacted work and was told to not come in for at least a week, a prudent move given his circumstances and charges against him. Subsequently he was fired.

Askins also said that he was working at Thorpe's Excavating and Building Company, but the courts could not find such a company. Efforts by the court to contact Elder O. Thorpe, the alleged owner of the business failed, mostly because his business address was little more than a PO Box.

Without a job, Askins was brought back into custody and his bond was raised to $75,000. He protested, claiming that he had no idea employment was a requirement of his bond. Eventually Elder Thorpe did respond, writing in a letter that Askins did some work for him, starting on June 14, 1977, for $4.00 an hour. Askins helped him on government contract jobs as an electrician and other tasks like pouring concrete and hanging doors. At best, it was part-time employment.

Askins also worked at the Neighborhood Develop Center on First Street NE in Washington DC where he was employed as a "Neighborhood Organizer," which included setting up block parties and coordinating cultural enrichment trips. His manager, Executive Director Edward Nesbitt, spoke highly of him. "Should the opportunity present itself, I would not hesitate to rehire him to work as a member of this staff." Askins lost his position, however, when arrested and the nature of his crimes were made public.

A longtime friend of Askins, Rudolph X. Pitt, owner of the SS TV and Radio Service on H Street NE was willing to offer him a job, despite the charges against him. It was not enough to sway the courts. Unable to afford his elevated bail, Askins remained in jail awaiting trial.

During the summer of 1977, Askins had two other lawyers represent him, each leading to further delays. While his trial had been set for October 18, it was moved as Askins struggled with find someone able and willing to defend him.

For a while, the burden fell on H. T. Alexander. Against his client's wishes, his attorney insisted that the court evaluate Askins' mental condition. For Askins, this was an affront that he would not tolerate. By early 1978, he was sent back to St Elizabeth's for observation and began to search again for a new defense counsel.

Dissatisfied with his defense so far, Askins met with and convinced R. Kenneth Mundy to take up his case. Mundy was well known and respected in the District's legal community. He was a man who would later go on and defend Mayor Marion Barry against drug and perjury charges years later. Considered a bit flamboyant but deeply respected, he was known for his flowery courtroom style, wit, and his flair of loud clothing – he was no slouch. More importantly, at least for the rest of his legal struggles, Askins had one of the best defenders in the city on his side.

Mundy faced challenges both from the prosecution and his client. Both victims were claimed to be prostitutes, and Askins had a history with violence with prostitutes.[1] In a letter to the court, he wrote: "I vigorously object to the introduction in the record of the false, unfounded, and groundless report of some forty years ago that I expressed animosity or ill-will towards prostitutes, as I have never expressed those sentiments. I cannot acquiesce to insanity as a phase of my defense as it is apparent that the productivity report has as its objective the liking of the fraudulent offences of which I am accused with erroneous assumption that I have an antipathy towards prostitutes. I have never had the slightest dislike for prostitutes."

"It is true that I had some substantial mental problems for a consider time prior to my arrest on March 20, 1977,

---

1. Nothing has been found in our research to substantiate those allegations. Records of petty crimes from the 1970s were purged by the DC police after twenty years and have been long ago destroyed.

but those problems had absolutely nothing to do with prostitutes." For Askins, he was attempting to pretend that his prior arrest and confession had never taken place.

In Robert Askins' world, in regard to Martinia Stewart, was that *he* was the victim, not her. As he would later write the judge in his case, "Any indication of the defendant's lack of predisposition toward violence is the fact that although the defendant was severely injured by Miss Martinia Stewart when she struck him with a can opener when he reentered the room and found her rifling his bureau drawer his only reaction was to have her write at note as to why she struck him. She told the defendant that she struck him because she was high off of drugs and she did what her 'high' told her to do."

In fact, in Askin's mind, he was helping his victim. "It is further respectfully submitted to your honor that the defendant demonstrated his sense of social responsibility by taking Miss McMillan to the DC General Hospital and seeing to it she had ample funds to get treatment for her self-inflicted wounds which were caused, as it developed, from her drug problem." He claimed that McMillan was a drug user as well and was high on methadone when he had encountered her, per her own alleged words to him.

Today the defense tactic of painting a rape victim as responsible for her plight would be seen as heinous. This was the 1970s, and it was a more commonplace approach. In other words, both of Askins' victims were drug users, and their version of events were outright lies. To him, they were fair game. There was no evidence of drug use in either victim at the time, however.

What emerges from court documents is that Askins' view of himself was that of a selfless person to a fault, extraordinarily generous. He claimed that in the case of Gloria McMillan he merely took her in under the auspices of wanting to help her. Even his attorney struggled with his explanation. "I have always showed skepticism as to whether a jury would believe that you would give such a large sum of money ($100.00) and spent ten (10) hours doing nothing with a "street walker," that you never knew or met before and simply approached you on the street." Askins was essentially claiming that he had seen two prostitutes and had brought them to his house to help them with their drug abuse – and had even paid them money.

The police, in their search of Askins' house, took with them several photographs of him with other women. Their concern was genuine, was Askins photographed with other rape or murder victims in the District? His version of events was more twisted. "…the Assistant United States Attorney has access to numerous snapshots that were seized illegally from the defendant's residence that tend to show that the defendant had very good relationships with a wide range of females." He exuberantly demanded that the photographs be returned.

While Askins wanted to parade a large number of character witnesses before the court, his lawyer was equally skeptical. He wanted Naomi Clements, a former friend, and her daughters brought in to prove that he had never molested them – thus, in his mind, painting him a kind and gentle person. Mundy told him that the problem was that none of his character witnesses could substantiate parts of his story in regard to the crimes he was charged with. Most of those individuals that he wanted to call to the stand were simply to validate that he was a truthful person or that he had been with their children and had not molested them. Mundy's client did not seem to understand how character witnesses were to be applied, despite being told in writing.

Their biggest struggle came over the use of an insanity defense. Askins wavered, almost daily from the correspondence to the court, as to whether he supported the use of that defense. Mundy was faced with a daunting task of pursuing this defense. Given his client's years in a mental institution, he felt that an insanity defense was Askins' best chance to avoid jail time. In a letter to the judge, Askins seemed to defy his lawyer in his own defense. "After due deliberation, I hereby unequivocally waive, or rather reject *in toto* the insanity aspect of my defense..."

Judge Alfred Burka of the Superior Court of the District of Columbia ordered a psychiatric evaluation of Askins on February 22, 1978, at his old haunt of St Elizabeth's. Three doctors testified at the trial and agreed Askins had been suffering from dementia praecox in 1938-1939 during his initial trial. What followed, however, was testimony that was difficult to pin down for either prosecutors or the defense.

Doctor George Weickhardt detailed his long, painful road of mental disorders that led to his crimes. "As far as I can now determine Mr. Askins was arrested on December 29, 1938 and charged with the murder of two women. At that time Mr. Askins told me that he was a student at Miner Teachers's [sic] College but he declined my request to tell me about the events which led to the charges. "According to his mother, who was interviewed by Dr. Sidney Maughs on April 18, 1938, he had complained of insomnia and difficulty in concentrating on his studies prior to his arrest. She also described him as nervous, and as having little appetite for food. Following his incarceration, he was described by various physicians as unmanageable, violently disturbed, restless, confused, poorly oriented, rigid and mute. At other times it was said he gave incoherent replies, indicated he was dead, and spent a great deal of time masturbating. He was regarded by a number of psychiatrists as catatonic.

"On March 31, 1939, at a lunacy inquisition he was found by a jury to be mentally incapable of standing trial.

"By December 1939, he had shown considerable improvement. By March of 1940, he made further improvement.

"In 1943 the murder charges were dropped. His physicians were reluctant to release him from the hospital and he remained at St. Elizabeth's under a civil commitment.

Justification for keeping him in the hospital was explained in a report by Dr. Edgar Griffin dated November 9, 1944. At that time it appears that Mr. Askins insisted that he had never been mentally ill. He refused to answer the examiner's questions saying the he would only do so in court. He was described as dull, apathetic, paranoid and antagonistic.

"In March 1945 Mr. Askins indicated to Dr. Raymond Ridenour that he had been confused during the early part of his hospitalization but had recovered and ought to be released despite the fact that he had received no treatment in the hospital.

"Following a number of unsuccessful attempts to obtain his release by petitions to the Courts a physician who examined Mr. Askins in 1948 remarked about a definite increase in sociability. Thereafter hospital privileges were gradually extended. Soon Mr. Askins obtained regular employment away from the hospital and eventually he was discharged.

"In summary the record shows that an acute catatonic psychosis which developed in 1939 gradually remitted. Eventually, according to Mr. Askins' statements to me and supported by medical documents, he became regularly employed, self-sufficient and acquired a reputation for reliability and productive work.

"The foremost question which I felt called upon to answer as a result of my examination regarded recurrence of the psychotic episode. I could find nothing to indicate that any such recurrence ever took place. At no time in recent years did he seek or did anyone suggest that he needed psychiatric treatment.

"To what extent then had he recovered from his mental illness in 1976? By that year, according to his own account, he had been performing at a satisfactory level in highly technical work for over five years and had prudently invested his earnings.

"Nevertheless, I found residuals of mental illness as a result of my examination. He was extremely evasive in answering many of my questions. He tended to gloss over much of his past behavior, to minimize the significance of many of the most dramatic incidents in his life history, and to emphasize sometimes to the point of fabrication, events which would shed a favorable light on the outcome of his present predicament.

"I found Mr. Askins to be articulate, perceptive and highly intelligent. His memory particularly for remote events was exceedingly good."

He went on to add, "In my opinion Mr. Askins has only minimal traces of a previously flagrant mental illness. Such residuals were insufficient substantially to impair control over his own behavior in 1976 or 1977."

The final ruling on Robert Askins' mental capability came on August 3, 1978. Dr. Harold M. Boslow, acting chief of the Pre-Trial Branch in the Division of Forensic Programs, sent the court St. Elizabeth's final ruling. "Dr. David L. Shapiro, staff psychologist, recently reexamined Mr. Askins, and the following determinations were made at the medical staff conference. He remains competent for trial by virtue of having a rational as well a factual understanding of the proceedings pending against him and being able to consult with counsel with a reasonable degree of rational understanding. Further, on or about July 9, 1976, and March 19, 1977, the dates of the alleged offenses, he was suffering from a mental disease which substantially impaired his behavioral controls, and the alleged offenses, if committed by him, were the product of his mental disease. Further, as a result of his mental disease he lacked substantial capacity to appreciate the wrongfulness of his conduct and was unable to confirm his conduct to the requirements of the law.

"It should be noted that our opinion is based on a reconstruction of events, rather than any statements made by Mr. Askins. The patient has not been able to discuss anything about his mental state at the time of the alleged offenses. There are indications, however, of a general deterioration in his mental status and some bizarre behavior at the time of his alleged offenses.

"He has been diagnosed as Schizophrenia, chronic and undifferentiated type, and is currently receiving no psychotropic medication."

The prosecutor, Earl J. Silbert, United States Attorney, was frustrated by the diagnosis. On two distinct occasions before the filing of the report finding [the] defendant productive, Dr. Shapiro, the examining psychologist from St. Elizabeth's Hospital, found that he could not determine whether the defendant was productive because the defendant refused to communicate with the psychologist about the allegations in the case. Indeed, in the third and final report from St. Elizabeth's, Dr. [David] Shapiro based his ultimate conclusion that the defendant was productive not on anything that the defendant told him or upon his observations of the defendant in relation to the offenses charged, but upon a rather mystical, "reconstruction of events" in the case.

Essentially his mental state was broken into two components. One was whether he was able to understand the charges against him and work towards his own defense. In this case, Askins was deemed able to stand trial. The second aspect was his productivity – determined by a productivity report. A Productivity Report renders an opinion if the defendant at the time of his alleged criminal offense had a mental disease, or a defect that would substantially impair his behavioral controls and, if so, whether such an alleged criminal act, if committed by the defendant, was a product of a mental disease or defect. Further, it determines if the alleged criminal has a substantial capacity to appreciate the wrongfulness of his conduct or conform his conduct to the requirements of the law. Their summary was that Askins' mental processes were likely inhibited, and he had impaired functioning at the time of the attacks.

A great deal of emphasis in his psychiatric evaluation was placed on his relationship with prostitutes. Doctors Shapiro and Weickhardt referred to statements Askins allegedly made years ago where he had issues with prostitutes and "women in general." Askins vigorously denied that he had ever made such statements.

By the end of his evaluation he seemed to waver on Mundy pushing for an insanity defense, writing Judge John F. Doyle, "Although I am aware I was suffering from a mental disability that substantially impaired the functioning of my mental processes prior to, at, and subsequent to the times of the alleged offenses, I have not had a mental disorder that would cause me to commit the heinous offenses falsely ascribed to me." Essentially he was trying to have his cake and eat it too by claiming that he was impaired but not enough to have committed the crimes.

He tried to sway the judge on his case as well. Askins denied doing anything wrong in regard to the women who accused him. "I have been stupid, naïve, passive gullible, dependent, ignorant, and idealistic but I have never sought to impinge on the mental or physical integrity of anyone in my life." The fact that he had been convicted in the murder of Ruth McDonald was either omitted or, in his mind, a false conviction.

Askins continued to wage a war of words with Mundy over character witnesses, which he saw as the crux of the case. He believed that he could win over the judge with a staggering number of character witnesses who would ascertain that he was a good person, honest, and reliable. None of these seemed to support that he was incapable of the crimes he was accused of, rather that he would not lie about them.

In the bizarre world of Robert Askins, he was a kind and giving person, and the victims had independently fabricated very similar stories as to what he had done – further coordinating their lies with the police. Likewise the psychiatrists at St. Elizabeth's hospital were fabricating things, putting words in his mouth. It was a grand conspiracy. He went so far as to write the judge to complain about his attorney. "…your Honor, none of the witnesses that I feel are vital to my defense may not have been contacted yet. Moreover, my attorney and I have not discussed the trial strategy, fully." Yet paperwork in his files shows they met quite often. The point of contention was that Askins refused to allow his mental capability to be brought forward. As he wrote the court, "…I must say that the crux of my defense to the charges pending against me is not my mental condition at the time I was accused of committing the alleged offenses, but rather that the charges are in fact fraudulent. I was and am physically, mentally, and constitutionally incapable of committing the said offenses or even conceiving them."

In short: The whole world, in his mind, was conspiring against him.

Yet just a few days later, in a bizarre twist, Askins changed his mind again about his mental state as part of his defense. On October 19, 1978, he sent a letter to Judge Doyle. "There is no way I could have been involved in these matters except for the fact that my mental processes were out of synchronization and in disarray. I could not use my memory, knowledge, judgement, and experience to make the necessary adjustment that people ordinarily make as a matter of course. I was passive, permissive, and dependent. Well before my arrest I was trying to make arrangements for mental therapy. While I was in the DC Jail, I felt the need for psychiatric evaluation because I thought I was going to cave in mentally." Whether prompted by his attorney or operating on his own, Askins realized that his only escape from jail was likely the path he had taken before, straight to St. Elizabeth's Hospital.

Despite his client's tenuous grip on reality, Mundy did mount a vigorous defense. He filed a motion to dismiss for lack of a speedy trial on July 10, 1978. This was rebuffed by Prosecutor Silbert, who pointed out that almost all the delays had been because of the actions of Robert Askins, not the prosecution. Judge John F. Doyle agreed, and the trial continued.

The physical evidence was overwhelming and supportive of the two victims' testimony. Photos of Askins' car, maps of his home that matched the victims' descriptions – even the plastic bag and knife he threatened Gloria McMillan with were all presented to the jury.

The trial was almost anticlimactic once rulings on Askins' mental state were resolved. He wrote the judge often during his trial, barraging him with over a dozen letters. Near the end of his trial, he seemed to be grasping at straws. In an attempt to clear himself, Askins asked the court to perform a polygraph test on him. "...as I have told every attorney associated with my case, I am willing to take a lie detector test. If the test indicates I have ever kidnaped or raped anyone, I will plead guilty to all offenses. I would like for the complainants also to submit to such a test administered by a qualified disinterested person (FBI)." Polygraph tests were inadmissible in court, so there is little doubt that Mundy had nothing to do with the letter Askins sent Judge. Doyle.

R. Kenneth Mundy left no stone unturned in his defense. He had scientific analysis done to validate that none of Gloria McMillan's hairs were found on Robert Askins, and none of his hairs were found on her. The fact that he had bathed her, however, might account for the lack of evidence. Still, it was some of the only scientific evidence submitted in the case.

Mundy requested copies of medical records of the two victims, especially any treatment for drug use. He claimed that his client desired copies of photographs of the two women as well, something both eerie and bizarre by today's standards. He attempted to separate the two trials but failed in that effort.

Mundy's client was not alone in court. His sister Iris Jackson, a retired teacher, visited him twice a day during the year plus of his time awaiting trial. She was the one who helped raise his initial bond money. His aunt, Mrs. Ruth Cuffee attended court every day, along with his three nieces. For them it had to be difficult, trying to be supportive while listening to Askins' life being laid bare for the world to hear.

There were more than family members in court. In 1965 Askins had been accused of raping his girlfriend's 16-year-old daughter. While a report was filed, the accuser dropped the case. In Askins' words, it was because of the "rather callous treatment received by the complainant and her mother by the police in the case, [that] the mother ultimately decided not to prosecute." They were present during the trial as well, though Askins was sure they would have not testified if called upon. "The defendant vigorously challenges the Assistant United States Attorney's assertation that a former girlfriend and her daughter were prepared to testify that the mother decided not to encourage her sixteen year old daughter to prosecute for the alleged offense of rape in 1965 because of the callous treatment received by complainant and her mother in contention with the case." In reality his former girlfriend and daughter were prepared to testify against Askins, in rebuttal, if necessary. Silbert came to court prepared for any contingency against anything Mundy could throw in the way of defense.

Askins argued that he was set up during his lineup, that he was the only person that did not have his shirt tails out, making him easy to identify by the victims. A photograph of the lineup show that four of the nine men had their shirts tucked in, including Askins. Robert Askins saw grand conspiracies orchestrated against him throughout the trial, but in reality these were only in his own twisted mind. When confronted with the photograph, he denied it was accurate.

The centerpiece of Robert Askins' final defense was that both women, in his mind, were prostitutes and had approached him for the purposes of plying their trade. He had taken them back to his place where they had attempted to lure him into sexual acts, all of which he rejected. Feeling sorry for them, he paid the women and let them go on their way.

Silbert's summation of the case was captured in a letter during the appeals process that would follow: "The Government respectfully submits that the defendant's lifelong pattern of criminal behavior combined with the vicious and life-threatening nature of the two most recent incidents are clear indicators that the defendant poses a substantial threat to the community at large and to its female members in particular." "We submit that rehabilitation is, at best, a dim hope for this defendant, given his past record and the length of time that he has been engaging in criminal conduct."

On October 19, 1978, a jury of six women and six men led by Foreman James Short, delivered their verdict at 1:55 p.m. Guilty on all counts.

On December 14, 1978, Judge John F. Doyle delivered the final judgement on Robert Askins, delivering his sentence. He was sentenced to jail to between ten and fifteen years to life on the rape charges. The other charges were an array of sentences ranging from two to six years served concurrently. The kidnapping charges alone earned him ten years to life – also to be served concurrently.

Led off to a string of federal prisons, Robert Askins thought his legal problems were behind him. That was not the case. Investigators for the Freeway Phantom cases were viewing him with renewed scrutiny. And one officer, in particular, was determined to find out if he had anything to do with DC's most infamous string of cold cases. And the evidence, while circumstantial, was difficult to ignore.

CHAPTER 14: ROBERT ASKINS – THE FREEWAY PHANTOM?

"Lloyd Davis was a homicide detective that worked the case, and he had Robert Askins as a suspect. He developed Robert Askins as a suspect…to be honest with you, he developed the best suspect [we had]. He and I discussed this suspect, and I didn't like his suspect. I was in Sex Squad at the time he was arrested. And I told him, 'He's too old.' But Davis said everything else fit."
—*Romaine Jenkins in Interview with the Authors*

One of the detectives who interviewed Robert Askins immediately after his identification in the Gloria McMillan was homicide detective Lloyd Davis. He perused the criminal history of Askins as bizarre to say the least. At least four things jumped out at him about the former chemistry student. One, he had allegedly bathed Gloria McMillan (and subsequently, Martinia Stewart, as he would learn later.) This kind of behavior was odd for someone who had taken a woman off the street and from her apartment building. Kidnappers and rapists generally do not spend their time with their victims in such a peculiar way.

Second, he had forced Gloria McMillan to write a note. Both of these were trademarks of the Freeway Phantom, and neither had been made public. The note, left on the body of Brenda Woodard, was something unique in the case files of the DC police. There had been two other murder cases where notes were involved in the time period – according to our research. What made the Woodard message stand out was that it had clearly been crafted by the killer who had made Woodard write it. This was exactly what had happened in the case of Gloria McMillan, who had written a note, word-for-word, under duress. That rightfully stood out to Davis.

Third, Askins kidnapped his victims and was with them for a considerable period before they escaped. Rapists and most murderers tend to perform their heinous acts and immediately put distance between them and their victims. Askins spent time with them – hours. If they had not gotten away, it is hard to know just how many days he would have held them.

Four, Askins used a vehicle to transport his victims from where the victim was first found to the location of the crime. The Freeway Phantom also used a vehicle to perform the same activities, with the addition of using a car to dispose of his victims' remains.

Many in the Metropolitan Police Department felt the cases had been closed. When James Trainum investigated the crimes decades later, the myth prevailed. "I got called by a couple of pissed off detectives bitching at me that, 'We solved those cases.' I said, 'With who?' They said, 'The Green Vega guys.' I said, 'They conned you.' That's the way that jailhouse informers work. And they're really *really* good at it. They are very smart. You want to believe. God knows I've been taken by them a few times. I just learned to be a lot more cynical and do a lot more checking." This reaction was decades later – Davis was dealing with only a few years distance from the gang's implication in the cases. Despite the belief that the Green Vega Gang was responsible for the rapes and killings, Davis began to explore Robert Askins as a suspect in the Freeway Phantom cases.

Detective Davis did the legwork, old fashioned gumshoe detective investigation on Askins. He interviewed neighbors and learned that in the 1971-1972 period, his neighbors had seen him burying something in his back yard. Could it be evidence of these or other crimes?

Askins had his place all to himself. Askins had asked his roommate at 1700 M Street NE to move out in mid-March of 1971 and had lived alone ever since. This was just a mere five weeks before the first victim, Carol Spinks, was kidnapped and killed. Having his roommate move out left him with a place to himself, where he could hold his victims hostage, rape, and eventually kill them.

Davis evaluated his employment records at the National Science Foundation and determined that his timesheets proved that he was not at work during any of the Phantom abduction times. While most of these would have been off his normal work hours anyway, it was far from conclusive – but it was a brick in a potential case he was trying to build.

He crawled through the details of the psychiatric tests that had been administered to Askins as part of his trial for the McMillan and Stewart cases, and what he found was even more disturbing. They revealed that Askins had "...difficulty in interpersonal relationships and possessed a discreet hostility towards the opposite sex." When he was presented finish-the-story tests where subjects were allowed to fabricate endings to stories, Askins stories ended with the female character either dying or committing suicide. His doctors concluded that he was a man that was "psychosexually emotionally immature and should be considered dangerous."

There were other bricks that Davis hoisted and placed in constructing his case against Askins. In the case of Gloria McMillan, Askins had posed as a police officer to get her into his car, flashing a fake badge. In the Freeway Phantom cases one of the prevalent theories is that the killer was a person of authority, either posing as a police officer or an actual policeman. It would have been one of the easiest ways to abduct the victims quickly and discreetly. Unlike today where people might question an officer as to why they were being approached; in the 1970s, young women would have been likely to obey an authority figure such as a policeman without question.

Askins had been a police informant in the 1930s, so he knew the lingo and had been around officers enough to pick up the basic processes to impersonate an officer. While not incriminating on its own, it was, in Davis's mind, another possible connection that could be drawn between Askins and the Freeway Phantom cases.

There were other aspects of Askins that made him attractive as a suspect. Both of his final victims were in their twenties but appeared much younger, perhaps mistaken for girls of the same age as the Freeway Phantom victims. Askins had used strangulation on Laura Cook, Marie Sweeney, and Gloria McMillan. He had used a knife with Gloria McMillan – and Brenda Woodard had been not only strangled but stabbed several times, the only one of the Freeway Phantom victims to have suffered such wounds.

Davis's investigating was trademark detective work. Reviewing the autopsy reports of the victims, he found that in the Yate and Woodard cases, there was evidence pointing to the killer being left-handed. Robert Askins was also left-handed. Another brick was carefully tapped into place in the case that Davis was meticulously building.

Pulling all the physical evidence, he sent it to the FBI for re-analysis. New techniques and analysis provided the first tangible links to the cases. An FBI lab report on September 9, 1977, certifiably linked the cases when it was reported that the green synthetic fibers obtained from the victims were microscopically alike and probably originated from the same source. Synthetic green fibers were found on the victims:

Victim:	Location of the green fibers:
Carol Spinks	Her shorts and panties
Brenda Crockett	Her shorts, blouse, and panties. Black fibers were recovered from the scarf on her neck
Nenomoshia Yates	On her body
Brenda Woodard	Her socks and panties
Diane Williams	Under her brassiere

Only Darlenia Johnson's and Teara Bryant's bodies did not show the evidence of strange green fibers, likely due to the days they had spent exposed to the elements as they lay along the freeway.

The fibers gave a physical link in five of the Freeway Phantom cases for the first time. As Romaine Jenkins, who would later work the cases related, "They were all synthetic fibers, and the fiber-man at the FBI told me that visually they didn't look green, but microscopically they did. The FBI could never tell me the source of the fibers."

At the time, Davis pushed the fiber evidence as far is it would go. At the time the fibers were discovered, the FBI felt that they were likely from the killer's automobile, though there was no indication as to make or model that matched the evidence. This was mostly based on the fact that these were rayon and that was commonly used in the auto industry at the time. Years later, when reexamining the fibers, it was believed that they were too weak to have come from a trunk or car mat, meaning they didn't come from the killer's automobile. Ultimately, the FBI could only tell him what the fiber sources weren't, not where they came from.

Some clues were available in where the fibers were found. Their killer was believed to have bathed and redressed the victims. Detective Romaine Jenkins, who worked the case years later provided some clarity on these points. "He redressed them (the victims). The fibers were all found on their underpants. If the fibers were found under your shorts and whatever else you had on, that means they had been removed. They were found on their bras and their underpants. That means they were undressed." "He made them shower or whatever while they were alive. And Brenda (Crockett) had on knee boots and under the knee boots she had on long socks. The fibers were found on her socks. So the boots had been taken off." This is further substantiated with the finding of a fiber inside the bra of Diane Williams. As Jenkins would later relate, "It looked like it came from a bathrobe mat. Which sounds really reasonable, that if they had to shower or bathe, their clothes were right there." Frustratingly, the fibers could not be linked to Askins.

It is commonly accepted that a high proportion of murderers and a higher proportion of serial killers will take items from their victims as "trophies." They do this to give them a physical reminder of what they did, perhaps to relive the experience they felt when they took a life. A number of items were missing from the Freeway Phantom murders. These items included:

- Carol Spinks was discovered without her blue tennis shoes (size 8 ½)

- Darlenia Johnson was missing her brown lady's loafers – one of which may have been recovered near the body of Nenomoshia Yates

- Brenda Crockett was missing white tennis shoes and several pink plastic and foam hair curlers

- Brenda Woodard was missing three schoolbooks (*Modern Algebra*, *20th Century Typewriting*, and *Gregg Shorthand*) and two buttons were missing from her coat and her skirt.

- Diane Williams, while found fully clothed, was missing her shoelaces.

It was likely the killer would still have these items to allow him to rekindle the memories of his twisted deeds. Davis knew this and was counting on finding these things in Askins' home.

With enough in hand to generate a warrant, Detective Davis asked for them – to search Askins home on M Street NE and his vehicle. Officers with shovels dug into the back yard. His car was searched and indeed a button was found, but it didn't appear to be a match to one of the missing buttons from Brenda Woodard. Detective James Trainum recalled reading the search warrants: "I think Brenda was missing a button off of her coat. They found a button. The button was the same size as the buttonhole on her coat. But it was a different kind of button. It was a different type of button. They were stretching it, trying to match the threads from the button to the coat. Sure, follow up on a lead. But the way it was worded they were trying to shape the evidence to fit their theory. That happened a lot." As it turned out, the button found was not even the same color as that on Brenda Woodard's clothing.

Askins' car drew attention because it was the same make and model as off-duty police cars. Armed with a fake badge and his knowledge of police techniques, it may have allowed Askins to blend into the neighborhoods where he could have operated and added to his potential impersonation of an officer. In the case of Martinia Stewart, an older woman, she had been fooled by this deception into getting into a car with him. It is not entirely inconceivable that the younger Freeway Phantom victims might have felt the same way. For Davis, it was yet another brick in the case he was trying to make – his modus operandi.

Searches were made for any of the possible trophies that he might have kept from his victims, but not a single one was found. It is entirely possible that he had hidden them somewhere else or had committed the crimes in a different house, but nothing ever turned up that ever pointed to a different locale where the evidence might exist.

Digging in the backyard of his small home yielded nothing as well. They searched for fiber evidence, taking samples from everything green in the home and car. All of it was sent to the FBI and came back negative. It is quite possible that in the intervening years between 1972 and 1978 when the warrant was executed, that the source of the fibers had been thrown away. It is also just as possible that it never was in Robert Askins' possession in the first place.

In Askins' desk drawer there was a copy of the final ruling in his appeals case. One footnote in that order read, "To hold otherwise would be tantamount to allowing the prosecuting officer to determine whether or not the statute of limitations should or should not be applicable." The word, "tantamount" stood out with Davis since it appeared in the note the Freeway Phantom had left on the body of Brenda Crockett.

Davis turned his attention to that word. Was it one that Askins used? He went to the National Science Foundation and interviewed Askins' coworkers. Indeed, that word was part of his vocabulary. And, like the person who dictated the note on Brenda Crockett, he did not use the word in the proper grammatical context. Again, another piece of circumstantial evidence that pointed to Askins involvement with the Freeway Phantom cases, but nothing substantial.

There were problems with poking at the word as a link. As James Trainum put it in our interview with him, "They kept running down that word, tantamount. Suddenly, every suspect they were running down was using that word. It's like when you come up on the scene of the robbery and they say they were robbed by a guy wearing a clown outfit. You turn the corner and suddenly everybody has a clown outfit on. That's just the way it is." Just mentioning the word to people might prompt them to say that he used it because that was what the police were looking for.

There were things that worked against Askins as a suspect in the case. One was his age. At the start of the Freeway Phantom spree he would have been fifty-two years old. The profiles for the killer all pointed to a much younger man. As a counter to this, was that why the killer chose young girls – to better exert control? Askins tended to concentrate his crimes on women he believed to be prostitutes, and none of the victims seemed to fit that pattern of behavior with him. None of Askins' known victims were as young as the Freeway Phantom victims. While all circumstantial bits of information, they carry considerable weight given the lack of physical evidence.

For three years Detective Davis pursued Robert Elwood Askins before eventually winding down his investigation. While the top suspect in the Freeway Phantom cases, no physical evidence ever connected him to the cases.

CHAPTER 15: PROFILES OF A SERIAL KILLER

"Consideration must be given as to why this series of murders has stopped. Based upon research conducted by the NCAVC (National Center for the Analysis of Violent Crime), this type of offender does not just stop because he wants to. The offender has either died, been incarcerated in an institution of some kind, or has moved from the area. If the offender has moved, it is likely that the new jurisdiction has experienced similar murders of similar victims."
—*FBI Profile of the Freeway Phantom, 1990*

When the Freeway Phantom cases began in 1971, there was no such thing as professional profiling for serial killers. In fact, it would be several years before the phrase, "serial killer" became widely used. That does not mean that police didn't try to develop profiles of who might be killing young women in the District; it simply means there was nothing to compare these attempts against. Simply put, no one knew how serial killers acted or what to look for...so their opinions were based more on their beliefs than anything related to studies of these kinds of perpetrators.

In the early days of the investigation, psychiatric doctors and institutes were contacted, less for their opinions on the killer, but more to know if they had any patients who might be potential suspects. Regardless of that, many offered their options as to what to look for personality-wise.

The investigators did not reach out to the mental institutions until two weeks after the murder of Brenda Woodard. There was a coordinated effort to contact all the institutions in and around Washington DC, hopefully finding a doctor who knew of a patient who might be capable of committing a string of rapes and strangulations. At the same time, they tapped these professionals for their perspectives as to whom the killer might be.

On November 30, 1971, Dr. Rafi Iqbal, at the Springfield State Hospital in Sykesville, Maryland, was contacted by investigators. Dr. Iqbal was in charge of the Admissions Ward and Forensic Psychiatry Section of the state hospital. Dr. Iqbal did not believe that any of his current patients were responsible for the crimes. At the time more than half of the patients in the hospital were alcoholics and not considered violent.

In discussions with the investigators, he offered that the suspect's activities were characteristic of an extreme mental illness, likely a "sociopathic personality disorder." He believed that the suspect should be considered quite clever. It was, in his opinion, that the suspect was not hospitalized and was likely able to function in society without attracting much attention to himself. In other words, he could appear as a normal individual to everyone except his victims.

What caused this seemingly typical person to snap? Dr. Iqbal suggested that he had a recent traumatic experience – and that alone led to his violent behavior.

Another doctor at that facility, Dr. Sergio Palacio, agreed with his colleague that they had no patients who were likely suspects. He went on to suggest that the likely suspect should be considered extremely dangerous…bordering on psychopathic extremes in behavior, and as such was to be considered very dangerous. Such a person would exhibit paranoid delusions, possibly triggered by phonetic sounds. His belief that sounds may trigger an explosion of violence was tied to the name "Denise" being so common with the victims...though there is no mention of how the killer would know that some of the girls had Denise as part of their names.

On the same day, investigators turned to the Spring Grove State Hospital in Cantonsville, Maryland, in hopes of finding a lead. They met with Dr. Bruno Radauskas, the superintendent of the facility. He asserted that his facility was unlikely to have such patients. The criminally ill were usually transferred to the Perkins State Hospital in Jessup, Maryland. He agreed to undertake a review of the records of his patients, but none came back as viable suspects.

Dr. Radauskas echoed Dr. Iqbal in that he believed the perpetrator of these murders, "likely functioned very well in society." He suggested it was a "personality quirk" that manifested him to opt for strangulation as the means to kill his young victims.

On December 1, 1971, the Freeway Phantom detectives met with retired FBI Special Agent Walter McLaughlin. Agent McLaughlin was a well-respected investigator who had served in Pennsylvania, specializing in sex crimes in an era when the FBI didn't focus on such criminal endeavors. He was short, "built like a tank," and had developed the first ever sexual-crime classification system, much of which is used still today. In the 1950s and '60s, McLaughlin saw this as an emerging field and taught some of the first classes at the FBI on the subject...making him a perfect individual in 1971 to offer his opinion on the Freeway Phantom cases.

According to McLaughlin, he believed that the unsub (police jargon for Unknown Subject) is a young Negro male. This is mostly substantiated with his free and undetected movement in the close-knit neighborhoods. He may have a job or even live in those areas. He definitely has familiarity with the streets he hunted on.

The unsub demonstrated a degree of higher learning, with at least one or two years of college education. The killer had ready access to an automobile. Based on the note left on Brenda Woodard and his actions – he harbors a hatred towards women.

McLaughlin further theorized that the unsub sought out victims who appealed to him in a personal manner, possibly linked to his mother, wife, or girlfriend. He didn't see the victims as children at all – simply as females. The name Denise meant nothing; it was simply coincidental that some of his victims shared this name. He believed that the killer had previous brushes with the law, likely being minor incidents.

His suggestion to the investigators was to contact the high school English teachers in the area to determine whether any students they have had in the past used or misused the word, "tantamount."

The next day the investigators met with a forensic physician in nearby Arlington, Virginia – Dr. Regis Riesenman. He suggested that the suspect felt inadequate and/or insecure, and that this is likely stemming from having a weak or absent male or father figure and a dominant or strong mother. Dr. Riesenman felt that this psychological cocktail of a weak or nonexistent father and a strong mother led the suspect to develop dangerous hostility and cowardly traits.

In his analysis, the suspect is paranoid and schizoid…a likely sadist since he appears to obtain sexual thrills from the use of physical violence. He did not rule out that the suspect practiced necrophilia.

He believed that the suspect may be under the influence of drugs, and he is possibly a megalomaniac, braggart, who labors under a strong compulsion to kill. In his thinking, the likely suspect is clever, with above-average intelligence.

Riesenman's 1971 analysis states that the proximity of the body dumping sites on or near major highways is an indication that he craves publicity and attention, "… much as a pyromaniac does…" As such he may be keeping clippings of the newspaper articles about the murders, using them to provide him with a level of gratification over his "accomplishments."

A week later the investigators returned to Springfield State Hospital and met with Dr. Oscar Prado. This time they were not looking for potential suspects, but his opinion as the Director of Forensic Psychiatry as to the nature of their unsub.

In Dr. Prado's view the common characteristics of the cases was that all the victims were young, slightly built, Negro females who were wearing "revealing clothing." This is a little hard to comprehend, most of the girls were short skirts, but hardly were wearing what would be called mini skirts. Their outfits were, for the most part, what other young girls were wearing at the time.

Dr. Prado felt that the name Denise had no bearing on the case. Despite the lack of physical evidence in three of the cases, he insisted some type of sexual assault had to have occurred with all of the victims.

He believed that the killer was akin to a man, "going on a hunt," choosing an area to operate where he would find a "pool" of potential victims who met his mental criteria. In his mind, this was a white male, based mostly on the fact that his victims were black. Interestingly, he said if all the victims were white, he would have thought it was a black suspect. He said that the killer was likely a "leg man," because all the victims were in skirts or shorts.

The potential suspect would be "typical" looking in appearance, be in his late twenties in terms of age, extremely clever with above-average intelligence. He would likely be an unreliable employee, most likely working in some sort of blue-collar capacity. The murderer had likely not been hospitalized, but if he had, it would have been for a crime related to violence rather than sex.

Dr. Prado suggested that the person they should be looking for was potentially suffering from a "superman complex," with grandiose delusions. He was complex and consumed with a severe hatred of women.

The investigators then met with Dr. Ernest Williams, the assistant director of Psychiatry at the Freemans Hospital at Howard University in Washington DC. Dr. Williams felt that the victims' age was a driving factor with their killer. He hypothesized that the killer chose to "experiment" with younger victims because he could not sexually satisfy himself with older females. He killed his victims because after he had sex with them, he was humiliated and embarrassed because of their ages.

Dr. Williams also felt that the name "Denise" was significant, that the killer had been jilted by someone with that name and that he had to have a positon with access to public records that helped him identify his target-victims. In this age before the internet and social media, there are very few potential sources for this kind of information. While Dr. Williams does not say this specifically, it also means that the killer would have targeted and stalked specific victims for his crimes.

Just prior to Christmas in 1971, the investigators visited the University of Maryland in Baltimore and met with the Medical Services Evaluation team of Dr. Jonas Rappaport: James Smith, Boyleston Smith, James Olsen, Irving Douglas Poole, and Mr. Nick Conti. This group evaluated the information provided to them by the investigators and formed a profile of the Freeway Phantom.

To them, the killer was not a very strong student, probably not successful in school but considers himself to be an intellectual. This is best evidenced by the misuse of the word "tantamount" in the note left on the body of Brenda Woodard. He was seen as falling into the category of a "rapist-displaced aggression type" sex offender – one who selects his victims at random and derives pleasure more from the violence of his actions than through any sexual activity with his victims. This type of rapist takes out his violence on his victims, not because they have done something to him, but because someone else has…as such he is displacing his rage, turning it on innocent victims rather than the source.

This group said the killer likely possessed a tendency towards pedophilia and that these stemmed from him having feelings of "sexual incompetence" with older women.

Who should the police be looking for? The group said that he was likely a Negro male, described by others as "a loner," withdrawn to others. He would likely have a good paying job and had ready access to transportation. People who knew him would not see him as openly aggressive…in fact he would appear quite normal in his daily interactions with others. A wolf in sheep's clothing, as it were.

How did he operate? The team said it was probable he was employed as, "a deliveryman of sorts, wearing a uniform in his daily work." This conclusion was arrived at because three of the Freeway Phantom victims were abducted near grocery stores, and one worked in a laundry.

The next time that a glimpse into any attempt to profile the killer or killers comes from Louis Richardson in the true crime magazine, *True Detective Stories*, in May 1973. While such seedy magazines tended to sensationalize these crimes, especially sex crimes, it was not unusual for detectives working cases to grant interviews or even write the articles published in them.

Detective Richardson did not rely on psychiatrists but more on his own gut instinct in creating a profile. It is important to note that he does so in the middle of the Green Vega Gang cases, where he believes the gang was responsible for the Freeway Phantom killings.

Richardson believed in what he called the "sweet talk" theory. Under the guise of this theory, the killer does not use force to get the victims in his control but convinces them with words. To substantiate this, he points out that in the case of Brenda Crockett's phone calls home, she does not say that she had been taken by force, only that she had been, "picked up."

In the article he says that he had recently changed his mind about the killer. In 1973 he believed that the killer had lived in the Washington area for a long time. "Some event in his recent personal life may have triggered the killing and those killings which followed."

Richardson believed the killer dumped his victims along expressways for specific reasons. The highways in DC at that time were lightly traveled and because of their long flat nature, the murderer could see headlights coming at great distances, giving him the time needed to remove the bodies from his vehicle. "Also, motorists avoid stopping because of the high speeds at which they drive, especially at night."

The police theory in 1973 was, "…that the Phantom is from the middle-class because strangulation is associated with middle-class and upper-class slayers. However, it may be that the physical act of strangulation is a source of pleasure – probably sexual – to this maniac, and he may get his thrills in this fashion."

"Such a man (a sweet-talker) would have to be articulate and not frighten girls from middle-class homes. Yet, the killer could be just the opposite, ordering girls into his car at gunpoint."

"The Phantom could be, for example, the son of a woman who knows of her boy's fiendish tendencies and keeps him locked up at home. The mother may not connect her son with the Phantom crimes, even though the Phantom could only strike after he had slipped his locks at home." While pure speculation – it is an intriguing theory with little to back it up.

By 1973, Richardson had dropped the speculation that the name, "Denise," had anything to do with the crimes. "Do you think some guy is going around saying, 'Hey, little girl, what's your middle name?' Of course not.

"We believe someone has seen something but doesn't want to become involved. This may have [been] confided to a relative or friend," Richardson added.

The Washington Post elicited the insights of Dr. William Dobbs, the acting director of forensic programs at John Howard Pavilion, for his insights as to the killer during the peak of the Green Vega Gang trials.

Dobbs firmly believed the killer had some relationship or attachment to St. Elizabeth's Hospital. His own private digging had narrowed the patients there to a list of three possible subjects. When he approached the families, he found himself facing a detective of the Washington MPD. The message was clear, outside investigators looking into the killer's identity were not invited or desired.

In 1990 the FBI provided an analysis and profile of the Freeway Phantom cases. This is significant because this is the first time a profile had been done when there was solid statistical information on serial killers in the FBI's databases to compare against. In other words, it was the first profile done in the modern era of profiling, and as such is probably one of the more reliable sources.

The FBI analysis was broken into sections dealing with the victimology, the medical examiners reports and crime scene analyses, building up to the final section on offender characteristics and traits. While it is tempting to simply publish the entire file, unedited, we did obtain this through confidential sources, so we will limit our direct quotes and avoid some sections that might put any investigation in peril. It is important to note, as well, that since the FBI's profile in 1990, we have a more in-depth understanding of serial killers, so some of their analysis may be outdated.

Also of significance is that the FBI considers Teara Ann Bryant to be part of the Freeway Phantom case overall.

Whether this is a result of the Green Vega Gang investigation or a completely independent conclusion, we do not know.

Victimology

It is clear the FBI was not working with consistent information on the victim's habits, sexual histories, etc., in their analysis. Some of that is that the victims were so young in some cases. In others, it can be attributed to reporting by different officers and an overall lack of depth in some of the questions that might have been asked. Furthermore, the age of the victims proves challenging. Some were so young that it is difficult to know all their potential behaviors.

The FBI's conclusion was that the victims were essentially at low risk of being the targets of violent crimes. What may have made them more susceptible was their age and naiveté. Combined with being alone at night and outdoors increased their risk factors. The lowest at risk was Teara Bryant who was walking home from the hospital on a heavily traveled roadway.

Their common denominator was being adolescent, black females, alone at the time of initial contact with their killer in highly populated areas. The FBI concluded that their killer was not someone they knew but a stranger.

Medical Examiner's Reports

The causes of death on all but two of the victims was asphyxia due to strangulation. Darlena Johnson's cause of death could not be determined due to her advanced state of decomposition. Brenda Crocket was strangled with a ligature. Nenoshia Yates showed signs of both ligature and manual strangulation, and there was a hint of that as well with Dianne Williams. Teara Bryant died of strangulation, but it was impossible to determine the nature of it – manual or ligature.

Brenda Woodward stands out because she was killed as a result of a stab wound to her right breast and had two additional wounds to her abdomen and a superficial wound to her head and both hands. The hand wounds were a strong indication that they were defensive in nature. Brenda had put up a fight.

Even so there was no evidence of "overkill" or excessive trauma.

All the victims with the exception of Darlena Johnson are believed to have been sexually molested with an inconclusive determination with Teara Bryant.

Green synthetic fibers were found with the following victims:

Victim	Location of the Fibers
Carol Spinks	Shorts and panties
Brenda Crockett	Blouse, shorts and panties
Nenomoshia Yates	Shoes, sweater, bra and panties
Brenda Woodard	Socks and panties
Dianne Williams	Brassire

These fibers physically linked five of the Freeway Phantom victims.

Crime Scene Analysis

The FBI looked at the totality of the crime scenes, which were comprised of three distinct locations. Where the victim and the offender first had contact; where the victims were assaulted and killed; and where the final location of their bodies were disposed.

The FBI determined that the nature by which the victims were killed, the depositing of the bodies and the fact they had no relation to their attacker, all point to "…our conclusion that these homicides were perpetrated by the same assailant."

Their killer chose them because they were young. "The offender offset his risk somewhat by approaching the older victims later at night." His approach to his prey was to not apply immediate physical force. The lack of defensive wounds, other that Brenda Woodard, "seem to suggest that at least for a time the victims were willing to be in the company of the offender. Either they did not perceive him to be an immediate threat or he was able to gain complete control of his victims by fear and the threat of immediate and serious bodily harm. More likely, it is suggested that the offender used a combination of the two. His approach to the victims may not even have been perceived by them as an immediate threat. Yet, once he had the victims alone, he was able to dominate and control them by the display and threat of a weapon (possibly a knife). With younger victims, the display of the weapon may not have been necessary as they could have been intimidated by the offender's age, size, and/or verbal threats."

While all the victims' remains were disposed of within the Washington DC Metropolitan area, some of these locations were close to the areas where they were last seen/abducted from. Because of this, and the wide variance of his areas of operation, they believed that the killer was, "probably familiar and quite comfortable with both the areas of abduction and disposal."

There was one case that stood out, that of Teara Bryant. Investigators believe she had been attacked, killed, and deposited in the water upstream from where her body was found. This made her the only possible Freeway Phantom victim to share where she was attacked, and her body deposited.

The FBI profile indicates that the murderer's contact with his victims was "opportunistic." The victims were out alone, at night, walking…not necessarily following a standard pattern. Some were known to accept rides from strangers. The killer had to have used an automobile to abduct his victims. He may have simply used his car and an offer of a ride as part of his initial contact with them. "This does not preclude the possibility that he was driving around looking for potential victims," the profile highlights.

This was a killer who spent considerable time with his victims, in some cases, days. Oddly enough the FBI profile doesn't explore this beyond a few short references. After he sexually assaulted them, he moved the bodies to his vehicle and deposited them along major roadways. He made no effort to conceal their remains; they were left in plain sight. The FBI concluded that by depositing the bodies on such heavily traveled roadways, "the offender reduced his risk of having the bodies connected to him. If confronted near the disposal areas, he could have the same 'alibi" as thousands of other travelers, 'I was just driving down the road.' This procedure also offset the offender's risk of being seen in the short amount of time it took him to 'dump' the bodies." Because he used highways, he may have hoped that the depositing of the bodies could be blamed on someone passing through the area, such as a transient. If anything, his use of such public places seems to be brazen.

Perhaps the most chilling thought was that the killer had no hesitation about being in the vehicles with the dead bodies of his victims and not being detected.

The mortal remains of his victims were the only way the killer could possibly be connected to his victims...the only way they could identify him to the authorities. "He, essentially, removed any chance of being identified by killing the only witnesses he believed to exist, the victims."

The analysis of the crime scenes indicated that this serial killer was rational in his thinking. Rationality meant that he understood fully that what he was doing was wrong. There were two distinct instances of this in the Freeway Phantom cases. Brenda Crockett made two phone calls to her home after her abduction. The first call was answered by a 7-year-old sibling...and the killer was not able to obtain the information he desired from that call. The second call was answered by an adult. No doubt, at the killer's behest,

Brenda asked, "Did my mother see me?" To the FBI this was significant. "This question demonstrates the offender's concern with possibly having been observed with the victim, either at the point of abduction or during the transportation of the victim."

Brenda's statement that, "I'm in a white man's house in Virginia," was seen for what it was, a deliberate attempt by the killer to mislead the investigation. First he was telling Brenda to tell the family friend that he was Caucasian, and secondly, he was misleading them to believe he was in Virginia. Further, these calls did not appear to come from a public pay phone, which means that the killer had taken Brenda to his residence and made those calls from the safety and comfort of his own home.

The second example of a rational killer came in the note discovered on Brenda Woodard's body. The handwriting was Brenda's, but the wording in the note didn't conform to the language that she would have used. The note had been dictated in some manner by the killer. He had done it in a place where she could not be seen or helped, again most likely in his residence.

The FBI profile points out that out of all the victims, Brenda Woodard's death was unique. "Realizing that her situation was grave may explain why Woodard's cause of death was different from the other victims. Simply, the victim physically resisted, and the offender overcame her resistance with his knife." The FBI profile further dove into her case. "The tears to the victim's inside-out sweater with the corresponding stab wounds suggest Woodard had been sexually assaulted by the offender, allowed to redress then was murdered. Further justification for this conclusion stems from the fact that the green synthetic fibers found on her socks and panties likely became affixed during sexual interaction prior to the killing."

In reviewing the crime scenes, the FBI noted that matching green synthetic fibers had been found on five of the seven victims. Black Negroid head hairs were found on the bodies of Spinks, Crockett, Yates, Woodard, and Williams. The analysis also pointed out some of the flaws in how investigators had managed the crime scenes. In the case of Woodard and Williams, brown Caucasian head hairs were also found. In their humane desire to show respect to the victims, police had used blankets from the trunk of their cruisers – possibly being the source of the Caucasian hairs. In other words, they may not have come from the killer at all but had been simply cross contaminated with the blankets.

The FBI's review of the crime scenes indicated that: "Overall, many aspects of these homicides reveal that the offender utilized only the amount of force necessary for him to maintain physical control of the victims, yet he demonstrated he was willing to escalate his control over any victim who resisted him by using more force himself. Evidence of excessive force on his part in most of the killings was not apparent nor were their indications that the offender expressed an unreasonable amount of anger or range towards any of his victims. Sexual motivation [and] desire to exert control and dominance over women appear to be the offender's primary stimuli. His transportation of his victims' bodies suggests a degree of confidence and emotion control on his part."

Offender Characteristics and Traits

What characteristics does this killer exhibit? The FBI's review of the totality of the investigative material believes that investigators are dealing with a black male suspect. This is substantiated by the finding of Negroid head hair on many of the victims and the racial make-up of the neighborhoods where the victims were first approached and abducted.

The killer was likely to be between 27 and 32 years of age. This was arrived at by examining the ages of the victims, the degree of trauma inflicted, the amount of control the killer had to use over his victims and, to a lesser degree, the willingness of the victims to initially be in the presence of their killer during their first contact. The FBI admits though that the age of the killer was difficult to access. It proved difficult for them to compare the chronological and emotional age of the Freeway Phantom. "This estimate relates to a suspected chronological age, however, no suspect should be eliminated based on age alone."

The murderer was smart – possessing a high school education and likely a higher education such as college.

The Freeway Phantom is able to have relationships with people, even women but likely does not have the skills to maintain "healthy" relationships. The FBI believes he is single and either lives alone or with an older, significant female.

Control is the watchword for this killer. He desires to maintain control at all times and is probably confident outwardly to others – which is how he can engage with his victims. Having Brenda Crockett make two phone calls home to determine if he had been spotted is validation of his degree of confidence. His control with Brenda Woodard was such that he was able to make her write a note that he had either prepared or dictated to her.

The killer follows the media coverage of his crimes, going so far as to have Brenda Woodard sign the note he left on her body as coming from the Freeway Phantom. There is another possible clue in the note. By having the victim write it, he knew it would be difficult to trace to him. Was this a sign that he was familiar with police investigation techniques? According to the FBI it was possible. In having Brenda Crockett tell the family friend that she was in Virginia being held by a white male certainly was an attempt to manipulate the investigators directly. He would possibly have kept newspaper clippings about his crimes…informal trophies of his accomplishments.

The killer knew Washington DC, especially the areas where he initially engaged the victims and where he deposited their bodies. His concern over possibly being spotted by Mrs. Crockett may be a hint that he even lived, worked, or frequented the areas where he kidnapped his victims. "Being from that area, the offender would not necessarily be considered a total stranger. Certain victims may have recognized him, not necessarily from any personal relationship, but rather as someone they'd seen around."

The killer most likely held down a full-time job. All his victims were confronted after what would be considered normal working hours. Their bodies were all disposed of late at night or early in the morning. The killer never demonstrated a desire to rob his victims, everyone he picked was too young to have any money of consequence on them. The FBI believed he could be working as a delivery man, postal worker, medical assistant, a role in security, the military or possibly in recreation. The bureau believed at the time he had a way of blending into the communities where he stalked his prey.

The FBI acknowledged that the killer owned his own vehicle – a late model car and kept it well maintained. The green synthetic fibers may have originated from a carpet in such a vehicle, or so the FBI believed at the time. It was not ruled out that he may own a van or some sort of larger vehicle where he could have been afforded time alone with his victims.

The Freeway Phantom was not a drinker or drug user, at least during the times of his crimes. His control obsession would not have allowed it. The use of such substances would have lowered his inhibitions and possibly ruined the experience he felt.

The killer had issues with women, that was supported throughout by his choice of victims and the note left on Brenda Woodard's body. In his own words he had little regard for women in general. He was, in the profiler's minds, most likely intimidated by women his own age or older. That was why he chose younger women as targets.

They were easier to control and allowed him to act on his disdain for the opposite sex.

If the murderer did have an arrest record, it would probably include, "…vice-related offenses, such as solicitation for prostitution or assault on women."

As to the killer's mental state, "The offender feels no remorse or guilt, as to him killing the victims had no consequence. His only concern was that he may have been seen with the victims. Once he became assured he was not a suspect, he would have felt safe."

When done with the murders and disposing of his victims, he went home or to another "safe place." There was little on him physically in the way of evidence that linked him to the crimes, with the exception of the case of Brenda Woodard – where he would have had blood stains from his assault on her with a knife.

There was a gap of ten months from the time he struggled with Brenda Woodard and his next victim, Dianne Williams. She was the only victim who seemed to have fought back in a significant way. For him, this was a loss of his dominance, his control – she had forced him to stab her. There were two possibilities for the gap to the FBI profilers. One, after the resistance he experienced with Brenda Woodard, he may have had, "some difficulty and retreated into his fantasies of past killings," rather than return to his hunting patterns. In other words, her fighting back ruined the experience for him or even scared him that he could not maintain control.

The other possibility was that he had moved on, been institutionalized/jailed, or left the area. When he was trolling for Dianne Williams, he returned to the same area where Spinks and Johnson had lived – returning to his old stalking grounds.

The media coverage likely bothered him up to the time of Brenda Woodard's disappearance. Police, when pressed in the media as to the links to the crimes, said, "No comment." He rectified that with the note, saying, "yes," he had killed those girls. In other words, he was taunting the authorities, challenging them.

Despite this wealth of potential information from the FBI, the profile alone would not bring this serial killer to justice. Profiles don't solve crimes; they are tools in the hands of the authorities to help them evaluate suspects.

This profile is dated in some respects. We now have a broader understanding of serial killers. Not all killers stop their murder sprees because they are jailed, move on, or are institutionalized. Some experience life changing events that force them to change. In the case of the BTK (Bind, Torture and Kill) Killer, he simply got a new job. The Green River Killer got married and stopped. Others cease because they have a close call with police, and it frightens them with the reality that they might be caught.

Regardless of why the Freeway Phantom may have stopped – he did. While for the betterment of the city and the surrounding communities, it also left the authorities with no new sources of evidence or information.

CHAPTER 16: KEEPING THE FIRES BURNING

"Are either of you squeamish?"
—*Former Detective Romaine Jenkins to the authors.*

To follow the trail of the Freeway Phantom investigation after Robert Askins, the next phase of the investigation passed to the caring hands of Detective Romaine Jenkins. Her house is pristine, and as you sit with her, the eyes of a dozen or more large children's dolls seem to stare at you from numerous angles in the room. The dolls are a reminder of her love of children and how she dedicated her life's work. While she never says it out loud, it seems that each has a special purpose, if only to remind her of the many cases she has worked. They are silent sentinels to the lives she has impacted.

Romaine's mannerisms and voice are stately…with an air of dignity that has been well earned. She is ever the detective still, even in retirement from the Washington Metropolitan Police Department. An interview with her is a class, a lesson, where she asks as many questions as the interviewer. You cannot help but walk away deeply impressed and wiser for the visit.

Detective Jenkins has several boxes of material tucked away at her home, including yellow, legal notepads filled with her handwriting. When she speaks, she doesn't refer to the notes often – she doesn't have to. The former detective has files with the crime scene photographs and autopsy photos as well. The images are chilling as the eyes of the victims stare at you across the decades that have passed.

If you are given the honor of meeting with her, you don't realize it at the time, but you are sitting on the edge of your seat, hanging off every word she gives you.

And Romaine Jenkins has a story to tell.

"I graduated from Howard University in 1965. I joined the police department June 25, 1965. I was assigned to the Woman's Bureau that's because at the time you had to have a college degree in Psychology or Sociology, and I had a degree in Sociology. I spent about two years at the Women's Bureau, and then they disbanded the Women's Bureau, and it became The Youth Division. I think I stayed there a year. At that time I found out that Homicide was looking for a female because they didn't have any female investigators. So I applied for the position. At the Women's Bureau I handled a lot of babies' deaths and infant/child crimes. That's how I got to know the guys in Homicide. Sometimes if a child died, Homicide took over the investigation, so I knew some of the guys from Homicide and I applied. I was the first female detective in homicide.

"At that time females had to have a college degree to join the force whereas males did not. They could come in with a GED.

"I worked shift work. Basically what they wanted me to do was to handle all of the infant deaths and the abortions – because at that time, abortions was unlawful in the District of Columbia. I handled abortion cases mainly. After a period of time, you know, I started working regular homicides. Let me see, I was in homicide for four years, four years of investigating cases. And during that time, that's when, you know, that's when the Freeway Phantom cases took place.

"I never investigated those cases directly; I was promoted to sergeant in homicide at that time and I did supervision over Yates and I was working nights providing plans. I supervised the detectives that worked on that.

"I spent around four years in homicide then I went to the Sex Squad/Branch where they investigated all of the rapes… any type of sexual assault with women and young children. I was a supervisor there. I spent ten years in Sex Squad. When I left there I went to the US Attorney's office where I was the supervisor for the career criminals unit. I supervised seven detectives who handled the career criminal cases. We were housed in the US Attorney's office, and we did investigations with them. At that point in time, I decided to reopen the Freeway Phantom cases because I had seven detectives, and they had more experience than the entire homicide squad because they all had all been homicide detectives. They had been there at least ten years or more. They had quite a lot of experience, and the US Attorney's office relied on us to make sure the cases, for instance the homicide cases, and career criminal cases were properly prepared so they could get a conviction. So we did witness interviews, everything involved in case preparation so those cases could go to trial, and they could get a conviction. So that's what we did.

"That's when I decided I was going to reopen the Freeway cases. What spearheaded it was, one day, when I was in Sex Squad, I came across a very thick folder on the Freeway cases, and it said that, the preliminary report was, that the prevailing thought was that the Green Vega guys were culpable. And the public was left with the impression that they were the ones that had actually done the cases. However they couldn't prosecute them for some reason, but they were going to get lots of time in jail, and it all turned out to be a big hoax.

"That always remained with me. When I got to Career Criminals, when I had all of the investigators' experiences, I said, 'Let *me* reopen the cases, and let me make sure every i was dotted, every t was crossed, that could be done." That's when I started gathering information…what files I could come up with.

"DC had destroyed the evidence in their cases. I talked to a lot of the detectives who had retired, and they gave me their notebooks and their notes and so forth. I was able to regenerate a lot of the information. PG County gave me their files and Maryland State Police had one case, Diane Williams, and they gave me their information. I VICAPed (entered the victim/crime scene information into VICAP[2] database) the cases for the FBI because that had never been done.

"Before I VICAPed the cases I was able to get into the FBI files. They assigned a case agent to me, and I spent months down at Buzzard Point at their office going through all the files that the FBI had.

"The first thing was to gather all of the information that I could. A lot of the information that I gathered was on the Green Vega guys. This was one of the most expensive criminal investigations or homicide investigations that had ever taken place in the city. I think that they had over a hundred people working on this investigation. Hoover gave all kinds of agents. There were lots of tips, and they covered everything, but in some ways they got sidetracked on the Green Vega guys, to the exclusion of everything else.

"A lot of work was done on the Green Vega guys. However, it didn't stop them from checking out all other tips. Everybody was a suspect in those cases. Congressmen, four-star generals, everyone was a suspect at one time from a tip coming from the public. The impression left was that the Green Vega guys were the ones. They said they were, but it was a hoax. They were just pulling their legs. They [the investigators] couldn't prove it. The guy [Warren] eventually

---

2. VICAP - - Violent Criminal Apprehension Program. This database collects a wide range of standardized information about cases to allow investigators the ability to document and compare similar crimes around the country.

admitted it was a hoax. I think that one newspaper article did express that.

"There was nothing about the cases that would make you think that it was a group of guys like this. Nothing. These girls wouldn't have gotten in a car with these bunch of guys. These guys had done a lot of rapes. They were in jail for what they did. Oh yeah, they are capable."

Several of the crimes stick out to her as a seasoned investigator. Brenda Woodard's struggle resonated with Romaine. "She put up a fight. When she realized that her time was up, she put up a fight. She was strangled as well as stabbed. This was a *fight*.

"Another reason she [Brenda Woodard] stood out… I kind of suspect that she knew the suspect, and he had to know something about her. Someone kidnaps you off the street, and you don't get to know your family's history. Where her body was left was where her mother works. When her mother got off work that morning, if the police were not on the scene with her body – they had to reroute the buses where her mother had to go another way. Her mother would have walked down the hill to get to the bus right past her daughter's body. Her mother did see the wig and she said, 'My daughter did have a wig like that.' She didn't know at the time that all of that was…you know.

"That is *not* a coincidence. It was someone that knew her. I can't say that it was a friend of hers, or a close friend, but it was someone that she recognized and someone that she did not fear."

That was not the only instance where the killer seemed to be depositing his victims where someone they knew might find them. "Another anomaly was Diane Williams who was found on 295. Her father was a guard at Lorton and the way home he took 295. …she's found on I-295 the same 295 where Spinks and Johnson are found, she's found on the *other* side of the road, further down. So that tells me that possibly she's gone there because her daddy's got to come from the Lorton, and that he's going to be going to be on the other side and going to see the police over there because her father didn't know that she was missing." Again, no small coincidence in Romaine's trained eyes.

"Spinks, victim number one. At one point he [her father] said it was a phone call and another person [in the family] says she got a note. But she [her mother] was directed to go to PG County Hospital in reference to her Carol. She went out there and looking for Carol in PG County Hospital, the same hospital where Woodard is found, you know. But whether it's a coincidence or not...but she did. Mrs. Spinks went to PG County Hospital to inquire about her daughter because she was told to." Who it was that had told her to go there remains a mystery to this day.

Detective Jenkins studied the cases intently, and there were things she noticed about the neighborhoods where the victims lived. "This covers all potential quads of the city. The first two girls, Spinks and Johnson, they came from the same neighborhood. Their bodies arc found fifteen feet apart on 295. The third young lady, Brenda Crockett, was 14th and U Street Northwest, which at that time was the red-light district. That's where all the drugs came from.

"If someone had grabbed her, people would have seen it. She's the one that called home and wanted to know if her mother saw her. So if she was with whoever, they saw her mother.

"Brenda Woodard and I pretty much grew up in the same neighborhood. I had just moved from that neighborhood about a month before she was killed. I know no other neighborhood like I know that one. Nothing goes on in that neighborhood with somebody not seeing. I know it. That's why she felt at ease walking home from school. Usually she got a ride from Sherman Mitchell, I think that was his name, his car broke down, so that's when they caught the bus from night school that particular night. But there was no reason for her to really fear him."

The politics of the Vietnam War and of Nixon's Watergate scandal tugged at the resources that could be put into investigating the murders. "Those were tumultuous times because I remember when we were going to work on Carol Spinks when it first happened, the division commander stopped us and said, this is the May Day demonstration. Everybody is all-in on that detail. So you know, we didn't go, we were turned around from doing it, even though the case was investigated, but I remember when three of us were going over there and work on the case, we were stopped because it was May Day, it was so much going on in in the city, you know, so much chaos."

With the Vietnam War protests, hundreds of thousands of people came to Washington DC, if only for a day or two. Some investigators suggested that the killer may have been one of the protestors, so someone simply passing through the city. Ms. Jenkins disagrees with that theory of the day. "I don't think it was an outsider of who just came to town, a transient person could not have been the killer." The complexities of DC's road system would have worked against someone that did not know the area well. This killer did, he operated in neighborhoods where he could easily blend it with the bustle of the city.

Romaine notes that there are three distinct phases to the crime. There was where the girls were picked up by their killer, where they were raped and murdered, and where the bodies were dumped. This was a killer that kept his victims, in some cases, for prolonged periods of time. In the case of Carol Spinks, he not only kept her, but fed her.

"How do you keep her in your apartment for almost a week? Because she's disappeared on April the 25th and she's not found until like May 30th." There were no tie marks on her wrists, no indication that she had been gagged for days at a time. "How do you keep somebody, a young girl like that? If it was an apartment, you know, you'd hear it. This person who's got to have a house. He wouldn't have taken her to a room." Was it a basement perhaps? "Yeah. If you live with your elderly mother, and she's upstairs on the top level, and you're in the basement, maybe." But her thinking is simpler – the killer lived alone, and he had the means to keep Carol Spinks prisoner for a prolonged period of time without the neighbors hearing or seeing anything. "Do you [as a killer] have a job then? I don't think so. How could you leave her? What did you do with her while you're working?"

Carol Spinks showed signs of some struggle, being hit in the face. "She was the only one that was not raped, she was sodomized. They said her hyman was not intact, but it didn't show signs that she had been raped, but she had been sodomized because her rectum had been forced." It begs the question, why was she treated so differently? Did her appearance in some way elicit a reaction with the killer, perhaps reminding him of a loved one?

Detective Jenkins picks apart the cases meticulously, methodically going, trying to get a better glimpse of the Freeway Phantom. "How is he getting them into the vehicles? In describing all these victims, everybody says that same thing about all of them, they were very quiet and shy. Now Darlenia Johnson was probably a lot more outgoing than the others. But her family describes her as being a quiet person.

"A 10-year-old is not going to do it [climb in car] because her mother sent her. Especially because her mother saw her [Carol Spinks] and asked, 'Why are you away from the house? I told you not to leave.' She said that her sister, I think it was Valerie, wanted her to go to the store for some TV dinners. She said, 'Get your dinners and go back home. I will deal with you when I get home.' So she [Spinks] *knew* to go straight back home. She was not going to dilly-dally around.

"Nenomoshia Yates was the same thing. Crockett was the same thing. They wouldn't dilly-dally, they would, you know, they were told to go to the store, and they were coming back, from the store. Apparently they all made it to the store. On the way back, they encountered him.

"Then you have to ask yourself, 'Who knows the city that well to travel all over the city?'

"I don't think it's somebody just driving around. Why are you in the area? That's the question I can come up with. A cab driver would go to different places. If these young ladies…if you pulled a gun up and said, 'Get in the car,' they would do it."

The case of Brenda Crockett calling to her family tells Detective Jenkins more about her killer. "When she first called her sister, she was crying. Then when she talks to Mr. Cadwell, he says she's not crying. And she says, 'Mr. Ted, I'll see you.' That's how she ended the conversation. So she wasn't upset. Can you imagine a 10-year-old snatched off the street, by some strange man? And she calls home twice, and she is not boo-hooing and whooping and hollering? Why is she not afraid?"

To Jenkins, Brenda's calm speaks volumes. "It was somebody who she trusted. And they saw her mother…let me say this…he had to know that was her mother. If she said, 'There goes my mother,' that doesn't mean anything to him unless he knew it was her mother. And that's why he let her make them phone calls. *He* recognized that was her mother. He didn't just take her word for it. He recognized her mother. That's what he wanted to know. Did the mother see them? But if the mother saw them, maybe the mother would recognize him.

"Think about it. 'A white man have picked me up, we're in Virginia.' A little girl doesn't talk like that. 'Now he's going to send me home in a cab.'" To Romaine, it points to someone who clearly knew not only Brenda, but her mother.

For an organized serial killer, one that abducts, rapes, kills, then moves the bodies to another location to deposit them – control over his victims is everything. At any point when he is with the victims, if he loses control, he is going to risk being arrested. Romaine Jenkins analyzed that as well during her time investigating the cases. "Oh, he had *massive* control over them. Yes, their shoes were missing. On the scene of Yates, a lady's loafer is found. So whoever took her out of the vehicle, the loafer came out too. And Darlene Johnson was wearing loafers, and she was found without shoes. It was assumed it might have been hers, but they never took it to her family and asked them." The lack of shoes is one way that serial killers prevent their victims from potentially fleeing.

The fiber evidence was important to Romaine as she hypothesized what happened to the victims while in the killer's control. "I didn't know about the fibers until I reopened the investigation. I think it was 1978 when the fiber evidence in these cases came out. See, Crocket, Yates, Woodard, and Williams all had the same or very similar fibers. And they were all synthetic fibers, and the fiber-man at the FBI told me that visually they didn't look green, but microscopically they did. So the FBI could never tell me the source of the fibers."

The fibers led to one of the most fascinating insights that Detective Jenkins exposed is that the killer most likely didn't just kill his victims after he raped them, he also bathed or showered them. "When Carol Spinks left home, she was wearing two pairs of shorts. When her body was found, she was only wearing one pair on and her tennis shoes were missing. Crockett went to the store, she didn't have shoes on…however the soles of her feet were clean. Here's the thing, she went to the store without shoes on. The soles of her feet should've been dirty. Right? It tells me that she, and the rest of these girls, were bathed. As a woman, when I looked at the autopsy photos, and so forth, it seemed that these women had been in water. Because you wash away the evidence, after they were killed.

"And he redressed them. The fibers were all found on their underpants. If the fibers were found under your shorts and whatever else you had on, that means they had been removed. They were found on their bras and their underpants. That means they were [completely] undressed."

It is unknown if the Freeway Phantom bathed his victims when they were alive, or after they were already dead. It is believed that they were dead when he redressed them though, thanks to the sloppy way that the clothing was put on and the location of the fiber evidence. Perhaps the bathtub was where he strangled them…it is impossible to know for sure.

"Brenda Denise Woodard had on knee boots, and under the knee boots she had on long socks. The fibers were found on her socks. So the boots had been taken off.

"He redressed them. The fibers were all found on their underpants. If the fibers were found under your shorts and whatever else you had on, that means they had been removed. They were found on their bras and their underpants. That means they were undressed."

"Whatever they touched, the fibers generally came in contact with whatever it was. At one point the FBI said that the fibers, the rayon fibers, were used for autos. That was Lloyd Davis talked to someone about fibers, and they said this type of fiber, it was too weak to be a car mat fiber. It looked like it came from a bathrobe mat. Which sounds really reasonable, that if they had to shower, their clothes were right there."

It casts an eerie image of a man, having raped his victims, having them strip naked, tossing their clothing on a bathmat with green fibers. He washes them, removing what he believes is any trace evidence – or perhaps exercising some strange ritual in his own mind. Then he kills them, dries them off, and redresses them. In doing so he gets the bathmat fibers in places where they might never have normally been.

"This is somebody who is in *control*; he is in full control of his victims, and he's exerting that control with the police.

He says in the note, 'I will admit the others when you catch me, *if* you can.'

"The fact, that he strangles them with the ligature and manual. That tells you something else about him too, because he gets to, he has to exert control. It takes a long time to strangle or something. Most of them were ligature and manual strangulation."

Were mistakes made by the Washington Metropolitan Police Department? It is always a sensitive subject to bring up with anyone in law enforcement. Romaine does not hesitate in raising some of the mistakes that were made. "He wanted the bodies to be found. He wasn't trying to secrete anybody. The only thing is that Darlena Johnson, the Metropolitan Police were so sloppy, the body was found on the 12th and it wasn't recovered until like the 18th of the 19th.

"She was *so* badly decomposed. The police couldn't find the body. The guy found the body, called the police. I was in homicide at the time, and I thought somebody should be written up for dereliction of duty, you know? Every scout car that went…nothing found. Finally, one of the highwaymen went to his neighbor, who happened to be a sergeant in the traffic division and said, 'There's a body out on 295. We've called the department.' It would not have been this bad if she had not laid out there that long. Well what happened is they kept getting called into dispatch and, I have copies of transcripts, the dispatcher was sending the police out there and they went, and they kept coming back…10-8, 'nothing found.' Will let me say to you is if you run down 295 when the scout car right, and you don't stop to get out and look how you suppose to find."

Darlena Johnson's body was so badly decomposed from spending almost a week on I-295 that no formal cause of death could be determined, nor could any trace evidence be recovered. For a long time the MPD never discussed their failure to find a dead body alongside a major highway and even today, they do not admit the horrific error.

Hair samples were recovered from the bodies of some of the victims, but these could have been cross contaminated as a result of the police attempting to provide the young women some dignity. "Most of the hair fragments found on the victims were black, maybe two of them compared to Caucasian hair. But they could've been transferred. Because in the case of Diane Williams, as soon as that Park Policeman pulled up the scene, he went back to his trunk and got a blanket out of the trunk of his car throwing it over top of her, which was not necessary. So you know, so any, any Caucasian hairs on her could have come from that blanket. Brenda Woodard, there were some Caucasian hairs I think something one of them were dyed red or something, but it's hard to say." So while hair was recovered from the scenes, there is no way to prove that the hair had anything to do with the killer.

The biggest mistake made by the MPD was the pursuit of the Green Vega Gang. The Green Vega rape cases drew a great deal of resources and attention to the Freeway Phantom cases. While many officers still hold the belief that the gang was responsible for the crimes, Romaine Jenkins has deep-seated reservations. "They used this system, this system allowed itself to be used. If you read the papers, it in this state's attorney in PG county was up for reelection, so he wanted the say these cases were closed, you know it, and they knew who did it and that pissed Morris Warren off. So he decided to take back everything he had said. All of this was in the news articles at the time. But you know what, it was an embarrassment because so much time and manpower. That was such a massive investigation, and they wasted so much time even though they did uncover other things, everything that Lloyd Davis did, he did himself. He didn't pay him a task force, and he covered everything.

"Morris Warren was trying to put all of it on John Davis and I'm telling you, they did so much background, I think they almost went back to the time they were born. ...that's how extensive the background they did on these guys, so he knew everything about any job they can to tell you when they clocked in when clocked out, they can tell you everything about these guys.

"Let me say this. The things that we just discussed and how we bounced around, all that went out the window when they got with the Green Vega guys. They never asked any of these questions because obviously they did it, because they think if they had bounced it all they wouldn't have been taken for that ride.

"One of the guys said in the FBI interview, 'I don't know where those bodies were dumped'...but I can tell you by the look on the detectives face that we were not even close – right there. They said, 'No, that's not it, that's not it.'" [Warren] could tell by their reaction.

"But people can, they can read you in, you have to be so careful, especially with criminals.

"I know people who were in Lorton with them. They would have died. They said if these guys had killed those little girls, they never would have made it. I know some people that were locked up with them. Criminals don't like folks messing with children. Rapists catch hell in jail too." Ultimately the Green Vega case, in her mind, drew resources that might have been better spent on pursuing other potential leads.

Romaine reveals another chilling find from one of the autopsies of the victims. "In one of the victims, inside her vagina was found debris. The FBI report only says debris is found. In this report the debris that is found human tissue. And this is found in her vagina and that has puzzled me for the longest time. Why would *human* tissue be found inside of her vagina? The person who explained to me is a friend of mine, he said it was a male who entered her was uncircumcised, foreskin, but nobody thought about that at the time. Nobody. Nobody never questioned this, and I saw that in the autopsy report. If they had it, they could've gotten deep DNA."

Despite its missteps, the Washington Metropolitan Police Department did try at least one tool that had never been tried before. In the case of Brenda Woodard, the police had a mannequin made that resembled the victim in terms of build and stature. The mannequin was dressed in the clothing of the victim and was photographed with copies provided to the media. Two of the DC papers printed the image in hopes that someone would recognize Brenda and provide new tips. For the time, it was out-of-the-box thinking. Unfortunately it did not generate truly actionable tips for the investigators.

Other potential leads consumed considerable resources but led to little results. Such was the instance of a search for a Volkswagen Beetle thought to be the killer's car. "Another thing about Yates. There was a young man who claimed he saw her get into a car that looked like her mother's when her father came home from the hospital.... His second wife, just had a baby and he went to visit the baby and visited his wife [either wife number] one and two and he said, 'Where was NiMi?' [Nenomoisha], because they called her NiMi, and the little boy said, 'Oh, she's gone with her mother. She got her mother's car.' But when he called her mother and she said, 'I hadn't been over there,' but the little boy said she was with her mother. That's because that's the car her mom picks her up in, in a blue, in a Volkswagen.

"On the scene, the guy who found the body says that there was a car, a Volkswagen, parked on the side of the road, and there were two people in it. And there were other cars on the road, and he described the other cars, and they announced it over the radio

"And what it was, it was some young kid, some young white kids who had been to a party, and they were going home. I think they lived in Suitland, and they also said this car they thought it was a small car, possibly Volkswagen, and there were two people in it. Well, if this has anything to do with it or not, nobody knows. But the Volkswagen was *near* the scene. According to the boy who found the body. The Volkswagen was near where the body was found. He described the people in the other cars, and remember, it's pitch black out there, but he was able to. But he was able to describe them, and he described the people in the Volkswagen.

"There were people in the area, there were people in there, and they identified those kids. PG County took statements from them and so did the DC police.

"They don't remember seeing anything. The only thing they admit that there was a car, some said they thought it was a Volkswagen, but they saw silhouettes of two people in it. One had a bush cut and straight hair. It was two males, one had straight hair. Which made you think from the report that one was white, and one was a black man. That's kind of what, you know, they, they alluded to and the guy who found the body, he, you know, that's what he alluded to. But they saw this car, and they found the tracks as a small car, like a Volkswagen or something similar.

"Of course, that's like a really common car time at the time. Then you have the kid who says that she got into a Volkswagen, you know. This kid thought it was her mother's car because her mother had Volkswagen, but her mother was known to come pick her up from time to time."

There was physical proof of a Volkswagen near the body, a tire track in the dirt. The police took a photograph of it because the imprint was too faint to be cast in plaster. Articles were run in the DC newspapers and searches were made for cars that were owned in the area that matched the description. After hours of digging and running down potential cars, nothing came back from the effort. Whoever had been near her body that night has not come forward or been identified to this date.

The press quickly descended on the theory that the name, 'Denise,' may have been a vital clue that somehow connected the victims. Was it a coincidence? Romaine recounts her thoughts on that matter. "That a *very* common middle. Everybody was looking for an angle with it, and I remember the police department got so many calls. Everybody named Denise got a call saying 'You're next,' or 'I'm coming after you,' or something like that. Those calls were rampant, these are the things that kind of throw investigation off all off kilter. You know, you want the public to help. Sometimes their help gets in your way of it."

There were other honest mistakes that were made. The inclusion of Angela Barnes as one of the victims of the Freeway Phantom is a common one. Initially her death was seen as part of the string of crimes, despite some of the obvious differences. When her killers were caught, policemen, it was clear that her case was separate from the others. And the murders continued after her killers had been identified. Resources were spent initially to tie the Barnes case the other Freeway Phantom crimes, but they proved to be unnecessary.

Ms. Jenkins recounts, "Angela Denise Barnes's name is brought up because they thought they were all connected at the time. We didn't know the term 'serial killer.' That term wasn't even applied. We didn't use the term 'serial cases' because there was some confusion as to whether these cases were really connected or not.

"But once the note was left, he said, 'I'll admit the others, catch me if you can.' That was a direct hint to the police. I believe that if they ever caught the right person, he probably would have admitted that he was the one that did the case.

"The one thing I do recall, that we were sworn to secrecy, that we would never divulge, the contents of the note.

Because it was all we knew. We were told to not divulge the contents of the note."

The note found on the body of Brenda Woodard was a chilling and startling moment in the investigation. For the first time, the killer was communicating, to the police and the public at large.

> this is tantamount to my
> insensititivity (sp) to people
> especially women.
> I will admit the others
> when you catch me if you can! (sic)
> <u>Free-way Phantom!</u>

Notes had shown up in the period in a number of cases. One was Robert Askins, in a note he had Martinia Stewart write. Two others had been left with murder victims as well in the same years. Naturally those had to be investigated, but none were directly connected to the Freeway Phantom cases.

To Romaine Jenkins the note is the core of the case, the one time the killer provided his voice to the investigators – taunting them. "Brenda Woodard was an average student. If she was writing something, and she was with someone, and she knows that she is going to die, or she'd been kidnapped, why did she write the note like she does? That note was *copied*. I don't think he dictated that note to her.

"If you see it, it is double spaced, and it had punctuation in it. Who puts punctuation in notes? Same thing with the notes left in the other two murder cases [at the time]. Punctuation was used. If you are writing a quick little note, why do you put punctuation in it?

"Look how each line, each thing is lined up, because she copied it. Put a period in, an exclamation point. Who puts the exclamation point in a note?

"He said, 'Write this, write this,' and that's what she did. Because if somebody is dictating, she couldn't spell tantamount. Come on, give me a break. I might not have been able to spell it because I'm not familiar with." Romaine's insights create a chilling scenario of the time that Brenda Woodard and her kidnapper spent together.

"I believe that the note was given in her case because the police were saying that they thought it was more than one person. Some people have suggested that this was his way of letting me know, uh uh, it was just one person."

To her thinking, the killer prepared the text that Brenda was going to copy before he had kidnapped her. It would have been difficult to do once he had her in his control. He planned on her copying the note before she become his target. And the note tells Romaine a great deal in a mere two dozen words.

"Also, they're *not* all females; his victims. That's why I was looking at the other cases with the notes were found because this guy has a thing about women, but he'll kill anybody. The other notes [in other cases], even though they're very racial in message, however, they are written on manila paper, notebook paper, lined paper, and also they have punctuation marks, exclamation points and periods. People who write notes to the police don't do that, but I noticed that in both in all three of these cases."

The premeditation still gnaws at the retired detective. "He claimed he planned this. Somebody else was going to copy that note. When she's writing the note, do you think that she realized what she was writing? It is underlined and has exclamation points. You mean he's gonna dictate something and say put a period here, you put an exclamation mark here?"

Her reference to the check mark at the end of the note bears some scrutiny on its own. "Yeah, that is odd. So it was almost like he went down, and I think that was the one mark he made, that's his signature. Right. There's no reason for her to have done that.

"That was his signature. That was his contribution after that. 'Yes. You did well.' That's what he told her here, you did well, that's just what he told her to do. Remember, she still doesn't know she's going to be a victim because remember at this point where she's written that note, she had not been raped, and she has not been strangled. Because if she had been raped and strangled that note wouldn't have looked like that. So, she wrote the note clearly thinking that everything was all right. But once she finished it, and he said you did good. That's when everything changed…everything went south then."

Almost all the investigators focused on the word, "tantamount," but to Jenkins, that isn't as important as the rest of the note itself. "I never use the word and was not familiar with it until the case came up. Okay, so tantamount is used. So you know, it's, while it's not a common word, it has some meaning, and he didn't use it properly. I don't care what they say, I'm not familiar with the word, but what does it mean? Equal in value to, you know? So this is, this is equal to my, my insensitivity of people killing these girls is equal to how I feel about people, especially women. So he'll kill *anybody*, he's done it."

The Washington Metropolitan Police engaged language resources outside their normal realm of operations to try and decipher everything they could about the note. "Someone at the FBI and in Naval Intelligence felt that note was military. Whoever wrote that note was in the military. Because of the way it was phrased. Now that is what they told me. I kind of agree if the guys at the FBI and Naval investigation services say that this was someone who was in the military, and he got and he was court marshaled and put out on the article 15. That's what they see there [in the note].

"If you look at the note, and this is strictly off the cuff with me, all of the psychiatrists all said that the word was used improperly. It says that this is tantamount to my insensitivity to people, especially women. What is the "this" he's talking about? Murder is tantamount. And this person is a murderer. Whoever did these cases didn't just grab these ladies and rape her and got killed. This person killed folks. That was his main objective. That's all.

"Even though they said the note was military, you don't call yourself 'insensitive,' nobody calls themselves insensitive. Somebody *else* said he was insensitive. Some directive that said that. I spoke with a couple of psychiatrists over at Saint E but you know, they didn't come up with anything substantial. Everybody was guessing. Everybody got hooked on the word 'tantamount,' they tried to equate that with how intelligent, or lack of intelligence, the person had. And that didn't mean anything."

Detective Jenkins attempts to use the note to recreate the crime scene in her mind, hoping it will give insights as to the killer's identity. "He was the invisible man. He is truly invisible. But she had enough light to see to write that note. She didn't write that note in the dark. She had a good hard surface to write on. A desk maybe.

"She had pencils. A pencil was found in her pocket. Remember, she's coming home from school. So she had pencils. The note was written in pencil."

Perhaps one of the most chilling things about the note is something not on the written page, but about the page itself. The edge of the notebook paper has not been torn from the notebook. It has been cut out. "But here's the thing. Then you're in somebody's house who has a hard surface, a writing surface. You don't carry scissors around.

"He did not want the police to be able to trace where that note came from because it was in a notebook where they have some impressions. If you found the notebook where you would find the impressions. So that's why that note is cut out from the middle of a notebook. I don't know if that's something that would be key to closing this investigation or not. The reason why I say cause that's the only thing that we even know about the note. Nobody's ever talked about the note being cut. I noticed it when I saw it."

It is a hint of intelligence in the Freeway Phantom, a person who knew something about police investigative techniques. Did he cut the blank page out at the same time he composed the note, before he had kidnapped Brenda Woodard?

To her the note is everything; it's the voice of the killer communicating to the authorities. "That is *him*. And tantamount has nothing to do with him. Right? And it's just, it shows you the connection between his actions and what you have laying on the ground. That's all that word means."

Serial killing cases all have one thing in common, a tendency for people (and investigators) to try and explore connections to other, seemingly disconnected murders. There were two that stood out for Romaine Jenkins that were worthy of potential exploration. One was the murder of Teara Ann Bryant and the other was the Suitland Slayings.

In the case of Teara Ann Bryant, found November 30, 1972, in the Anacostia River, Detective Jenkins believes there are links to the Freeway Phantom cases. "When I reopened this investigation, one of my men had worked this task force. He said, 'You know there was a seventh victim.' I said, 'I don't know about another.' He said, there was seven – there could be eight, depending on how you count. I said, 'Another victim?' He said, 'Yeah. Teara Ann Bryant. I included her...'

"Here's the unique thing, the weird thing about her case. Some of the guys that were working this investigation, one of them told me, 'You know, what happened?' I said, 'no.' He said, 'We went to a psychic. And the psychic told us that the next victim was going to be found in the water, face down. They said that Teara Ann Bryant was found that way, just like that.'"

While somewhat strange that investigators might be turning to psychics in their desperation to solve the Freeway Phantom case, Jenkins believes that there are some elements of Bryant's death that links her to the other victims. "I say yes, she is one [of the victims.] And some of my men said yes. Because she's young, black, female, on her way home. She fits the mold. She had stopped at Dunkin Donuts to get some donuts and where she was attacked – well they can't say she was raped, but she was strangled. But if you toss her in the water you eliminate any fiber evidence. When she was attacked, she had on a teddy, and that was open. And her underwear was found on the embankment, and her body had floated down the other side of the bridge. So I say yes."

Other cases had potential connections. The Suitland Slayings, for example, occurred several years later, but remain unsolved to this day. "They were all from DC, most them from Southeast. They were like between nineteen and maybe early twenties. And I think they believe they were strangled. A couple of them were so badly decomposed, they didn't know. But the interesting thing, and I don't know this for fact, but the dump site where these girls have been found is the opposite side of where Yates is found at the gates on Pennsylvania Avenue. The gates at the cemetery and that, that, that's amazing. But you have five black females from southeast DC."

So who is the Freeway Phantom in the eyes of Romaine Jenkins? "Someone who might have been in the military. Probably in the military. At that time we had a lot of people here. It was during the demonstrations against the Vietnam War. There were a lot of people from the military living here. A lot of military bases are around the city, and we had a lot of guys coming back from the war."

There was a brazen aspect to the killer, a strange lack of concern about being caught with the bodies as he dumped them. "He has no fear of traffic. Where the bodies are found, those are busy roads."

Romaine wonders if the civil rights tensions, only a few years after the DC riots in 1968, may have been a contributing factor. "You know, this person is, was, also very, very shrewd. And, and I was wondering if he was trying to stir up racial animosity by having a 10-year-old child, saying that a *white* man picked her up and took her to Virginia.

"The press called him the Freeway Phantom before the note. He was following the case in the press. Yes. He kept up with the cases. He did. He did. He certainly did, he kept up with them, no doubt about it."

Detective Jenkins points out to the fact that the killer may have actually reached out to the victims' families after their loved ones were discovered. In an era before caller-ID, tracing of such calls was unheard of. Romaine reveals that the killer may have taunted at least one family, that of Diane Williams. "You know, because he's so sadistic and insensitive that he is putting the families through. The Williams got strange phone calls. I think one or two calls that I killed your daughter or something like that."

Was the killer necessarily a black man? Wouldn't a white person have stood out in these neighborhoods? "No. That's a common misperception. No, no one would have thought that because growing up in the neighborhood, who came to the black neighborhood all the time? It was the insurance man. He came every week, collected his money and nobody ever robbed him or anything else. Nobody paid any attention to. Who were some of the workers who worked on the apartment complexes? They were white companies and their white workers who came in."

As she reflects on the cases, under the cool, silent gazes from her doll collection, she wishes she had the tools that the investigators had today back in the 1970s. "Oh, it's a mind-blower. But you know the irony of it all, can it, can it ever come to fruition? I don't know, it looks awfully hard. It's hard now because you have a generation of police officers who see investigations differently. They have DNA, they have computers. We were using carbon paper and typewriters when this stuff was going down. We didn't have computers…carbon paper and typewriters, that's what we used. And you were a gumshoe detective because you went out and knocked on doors and got information. Now you press a button and some computer will tell you what you wanted. We didn't have all of those things."

CHAPTER 17: ROCKING THE BOAT

"Geographic profiling determines the most probable area of the offender residence through an analysis of crime locations. The process focuses on the hunting behavior of the offender within the context of the crime sites and their special relationships. For a crime to occur there must be an intersection in both time and place between offender and victim. How did this happen? What led to the criminal encounter? What do the geographic elements of the crime tell us about the offender?"
—From *Geographic Profile of the Freeway Phantom*, March 2005, D. Kim Rossmo, Center for Geospatial Intelligence and Investigation, Texas State University

When you first meet former MPD Detective Jim Trainum, you are greeted with a smile and the kind of rugged expression that makes you instantly know what his lifelong profession is. He has that "cop look," about him, friendly, warm, but backed with grit. It is the look of a man that has put up with a lot of shit in his life, and who has a low tolerance for idiocy. Trainum is the kind of law enforcement officer you should want in your department. He doesn't just go along with the crowd, but constantly challenges authority to make things better – and right. He is not seeking to win any popularity contest, that isn't his style. If that rubs some people the wrong way, he shoulders that burden without complaint.

"I left the department under kind of a cloud. I bucked the system. I did some things, pissed a bunch of people off. I dealt with a lot of police reform issues. As a result, I'm considered a traitor. My nickname for several years was 'Benedict Trainum.' It's because I supported things like the video taping of interrogations, identification reform, other best practices." While many of these things now are considered standard best practices, it is clear that the Washington Metropolitan Police Department preferred the more old-school approach to law enforcement.

His track record stands for itself. Detective Trainum started his career as a firefighter in Arlington County, Virginia. He hired into the Washington DC MPD in 1983 and rose to the rank of Detective in 1992. He worked in the Homicide Branch, the Major Case/Cold Case Unit, the Violent Criminal Apprehension Program (VICAP), and finally the Violent Crime Case Review Project as its director. He even appeared on the TV documentary: Chandra Levy: An American Murder Mystery, having worked the famous case while with the Washington MPD. He's also authored a book, *How the Police Generate False Confessions: An Inside Look at the Interrogation Room*. Now he is private consultant, helping review and reverse wrongful confessions and assisting law enforcement agencies on a wide range of issues.

Jim Trainum was the last known public figure to attempt to crack the proverbial nut on the Freeway Phantom case. His story is as simple as the former detective himself.

"What we had in the District of Columbia, was a serial killer that was working in DC in the late 90s. Name was Darryl Turner. It was a bunch of girls being found murdered up in Petworth [neighborhood]. Of course when you have something like that happen, you have a lot of media attention, the *Washington Post* did a huge article on 100 dead women in the last ten years. Murders…suspicious deaths…that sort of thing. So what do we do if there is media attention?

We form a task force. So they formed what they called the Female Analytical Project. Two washed up detectives came in and started to go through all of the case files. And that's pretty much all they did.

"I was just coming off that Starbucks triple murder case[3] at that time, and I was pretty fried. After the media went away, because Darryl Turner got arrested...the detectives on that task force, they went away.

"This was at the advent of DNA. We had CODIS DNA, but we didn't have a database. I'm going, 'Why don't we see what we can do with these cases? Let's start looking at them and see if there's anything that we can do with DNA?' That sort of stuff. Then I extended it out to, what I call predator murders. Because most of those are stranger-on-stranger cases; robberies are usually stranger-on-stranger, and you have to investigate them the same way. Where, with other murders, you look for associations, with these you look for forensics, that sort of thing. I was trying to come up with a system, putting all of these cases into VICAP database, we were building our own databases, we were trying to find the evidence. And the Freeway Phantom case came up. People mentioned it...I remembered hearing about it years ago."

Detective Trainum faced an uphill battle against the myth of the Green Vega Gang that still permeated the Washington MPD. Most detectives thought looking into the Freeway Phantom cases was a wasted effort given the prevailing thought that the Green Vega Gang had committed the crimes.

Trainum explained how such jailhouse confessions worked. "Well their angle was, 'You've got me, but if I give you this information, you'll give me a break.' You'll get my sentenced reduced, things like that. That's how they

---

3. The July 1997 murders of Mary Caitrin Mahoney and Emory Allen Evans, at a Starbucks north of Georgetown in the District of Columbia. Carl D. Cooper was sentenced to life for these killings in April of 2000.

play it. They're very good at it. They know there are certain things that they can't say. They can't say, 'If I give you this, then you'll do something for me.' They will say up-front, 'No, I'm doing this just out of the goodness of my heart.' 'I feel bad for the families.' Afterwards, after they testify, after they say that bullshit on the stand, then they'll write the prosecutor. Then they'll get the break. They know enough not to bring it up beforehand. Because if there's nothing like that beforehand, they come across better as a witness. But afterwards the prosecutor will go back and give them all kinds of breaks."

Searching for the case files for the murders proved to be a daunting task, given the mismanagement of the evidence and files over the years by the MPD. "When we first started looking at the Freeway Phantom case, we only had a file that was about this thick [1/2 inch]. Jack. Nothing. We started making phone calls. PG County had some stuff. So we were just trying to summarize the cases, search for the evidence – we couldn't find the evidence. I was doing this out of the FBI field office, and one of the things I did was I asked the FBI if they had any of the files, and low and behold they had a file shelf full."

The FBI involvement in the Freeway Phantom came one primary point of entry, the case of Brenda Woodward. Her body had been found on what was deemed to be national park property. That made it in the jurisdiction of the FBI, and their involvement resulted in copies of the case files being somewhat preserved. For such a string of cold cases, it was a wellspring of material.

"We were trying to summarize the cases, get it into the database. First, we had to get it organized. Whose names are in the files? If they come up some other place can you link them to the file? We had a case management system back then that really sucked, of course, but you could at least link names. I had a really good intern, Maya Long, she's really smart …she took that file and really organized it…really did a wonderful write up on it."

What was different about Trainum's look into the Freeway Phantom cases was that he did so with the idea of applying new investigative techniques. One of those was to employ geographic profiling. "We brought in Kim Rossmo – have you ever heard of him? Ken is one of the smartest detectives and people you will ever meet.

"Kim was a detective in the Vancouver Columbia Police Department. He developed geographic profiling. You don't look at the offender behavior, you look at the crime scene. You can basically ask, 'Why here?' He came up with some algorithms where he's able to plot multiple crime scenes; the more crime scenes the better.

"Let's say you have a serial killer. You have an abduction site, the dump site, all of these different crime scenes. He's able to give you a map to see where the person's focus points or anchor points are. He kind of follows how animals hunt. An animal will look for a choke point, like a watering hole, and that's where they'll hunt for their prey.

"Let's, as an example, say you are a burglar. You don't want to burgle too close to your house, right? Because people know you. So you go outside of that one zone. This is the zone where people don't know you, but you know the area. You're comfortable. You can't go too far out, because you don't know the area, you don't know the escape routes and all of that. So the center is the focal point. Very simplistically, that's how it works. He worked on the Chandra Levy case. He came in and did a geographic profile."

Geographic profiling is a relatively new investigative method. It evaluates the location of connected crimes, using mathematical calculations, to help determine a probable location geographically where a serial killer lives or has strong connections to. Those not familiar with the behind-the-scenes tools and techniques, tend to think of it as Venn Diagrams drawn on maps. There is much more to the methodology than that. It considers a wide variety of analytical factors including such things as traffic patterns, population density, and the hunter behavior of serial killers. It evaluates not just where the bodies are found, but where the victims lived, and where they were last seen.

This investigative field is best used where there is a set of data rather than a single instance. As such, it is often applied to serial rapes and murders, where the perpetrator strikes more than once.

Serial killers are categorized by their behavioral patterns – how they search for a victim and their method of attack. One methodology categorizes them in one of four perspectives.

- Hunter – a killer who uses his home as a base of operations and sets out from there to search for a victim.

- Poacher – a killer who uses another activity site, other than his residence, to search for his victim. These tend to be killers who roam to other cities or along many miles of highway in search of victims.

- Troller – a killer who is involved with some everyday activity that strikes at his prey when the opportunity presents itself.

- Trapper – this kind of serial killer has an occupation where the victims come to him, or he has the ability to lure them in for the kill.

The majority of serial killers fall into the hunter category, which is believed to be what the Freeway Phantom was. Depending on the criminology study you embrace, serial killers often have three zones where they are predators, hunting their victims. It is best to think of these as concentric rings that can be overlaid on a map. The first, most center ring is anchored on where they live and the immediate neighborhood they frequent. It is here that the murderer is most comfortable, they know the area inside and out. It is rarer for a killer to engage his victims in this first ring because there is a significantly higher probability of them being spotted or recognized outright when luring in their prey.

The next zone out is where the serial killer has a high degree of familiarity with the neighborhoods, roadways, etc., but is not where they work or live. This concentric zone is one where the murderer is comfortable, knows where to hunt his victims, how to get out of the area quickly - but not where they will be recognized. This is the predatory hunting fields where a serial killer is most likely to engage, kidnap, or kill his victims.

The third concentric zone is where the killer only has tacit knowledge of the terrain and road networks. He is less familiar with the people there, the neighborhoods, etc. The probability is lower that the killer will seek his victims here because he is not as comfortable with the geography as he is in the other two zones.

In conducting geographic profiling other factors form "mental maps" for a serial killer in terms of the areas where they operate. These mental maps explain the distribution of their crimes. This can include the attractiveness of the locales to them engaging with victims; the number of types of barriers to a particular neighborhood; the familiarity with routes, traffic patterns, and distances to travel to and from these areas. All of these contribute to form an activity space where they operate out of. Within that activity space, there can be anchor points such as their residence, work sites, a home of a close friend, favorite bars...the places of routine where the killer freely visits.

Geographic profiling factors this type of zone pattern into its algorithms. It layers in perspectives of the victims of serial killers as well. It looks at variables such as where they live, where they work or go to school, and where they were last seen. These aspects of the victimology are all crucial in developing a geographic profile. They develop a visual pattern on a map, to identify where the killer may live or reside, and, of equal importance, where he is likely to not be found. When there are no suspects, this map may provide investigators with areas where they should concentrate their efforts.

When suspects do exist, geographic profiling can provide an additional layer of analysis by factoring in where the suspects live, where they work, and where they frequent. Combined with the details of the crime scenes and victimology, this technique can be used to further refine the suspect list.

Additional information comes into play during the analysis, especially around the type of murderer the serial killer is. The FBI, starting in the late 1990s, identified serial killers into two classifications; organized and disorganized. Organized murderers plan out their crimes, think through where they are going to go and what they are going to do before they do it. They have access to transportation that allows them to intercept their victims in one location, take them to another to kill them, then carry their bodies to where they are dumped. They tend to have stable working histories and can fit in socially when needed. Many organized killers are of average or above average intelligence. They follow their crimes in the media and can remain calm, almost rational when committing their horrific acts. With organized serial killers there is more often than not, a separation of where the crimes take place and where the bodies are deposited. An organized killer may have a significant other in their life who is unaware of the crimes they are committing. Organized killers exert control over their victims, in fact it is all about control.

Disorganized serial killers are impulsive. They strike when the opportunity presents itself, rather than plan in advance. In many cases they struggle to hold down a full-time job, are awkward socially, and immature sexually. There is often no separation from where the killer encounters his victim and where the murder takes place - or even where the body is left. David Berkowitz, the infamous Son of Sam, was a disorganized killer...he randomly chose his victims, shot them in their car, leaving them there with no plan or effort made to cover up his crime. Disorganized killers leave messy crime scenes and often residual evidence as a result.

Since geographic profiling is a data driven model, the more data it has, the more accurate it is. As such it is better suited for use with organized killers because there are multiple locations that can be plugged into their computer model. In this case it is important because the Freeway Phantom was an organized killer. He encountered and kidnapped his victims in one location, raped and killed in another, and left them in yet another. The Freeway Phantom planned his crimes in advance, such as preparing or dictating the note for Brenda Woodard. He removed their shoes in some cases to prevent them from running away, exerting control over his victims to the point where they were forced to bathe for him. As such, the use of this tool was an excellent choice for the Freeway Phantom cases.

Geographic profiling is far from being a perfect science. There are notable exceptions where the analysis does not work. It can be complicated if there is more than one killer, for example. Multiple killers can complicate the analysis dramatically. In some instances the serial killer may be a roving murderer, a roamer, someone who travels and kills along the way or travels long distances. Ted Bundy struck in multiple states across the country, for example. Aileen Wuornos was quite transient (a Poacher) in terms of her range of operation. These poachers tend to be the exception to the rules, however. Most serial killers, while they have access to the means of travel, tend to be more predatory and operate in an area of relative comfort and familiarity.

Another factor that can be deceptive in such analysis is that the area where a serial killer stalks his victims may not be relative to where he lives now, but instead be an area where he lived or worked in the past. If a killer has moved from a particular neighborhood, he may still have a high degree of comfort with it, even though he lives miles away. So when thinking of geographic profiling, one must view the results with an open mind - that this area of hunting or location may not be reflective of the killer now, but tied to him in his past.

D. Kim Rossmo's geographic profile for the Freeway Phantom has been locked away in police files and kept from the public. He applied it to the traditional list of victims, plotting the coordinates of their homes, their abduction sites, and where their bodies were found. Omitted from the list was Teara Ann Bryant, despite the fact that the FBI considered her one of the Freeway Phantom victims.

There are plenty of cautions in the analysis which set expectations. "Internal and external influences influence a criminal's hunting process. Serial offenders gain knowledge with each new crime and often learn from their experiences. Media disclosures and certain investigative strategies, such as patrol saturation tactics, may create special displacement, which might hinder or delay apprehension."

The purpose of the report was to identify, "a base or anchor point – the single most important place in a person's spatial life. For the vast majority of people this is their residence, therefore, the terms anchor point and residence are sometimes used interchangeably. But in certain cases the offender's anchor point is their wok site or immediate past residence. And some street criminals do not have a permanent residence, but rather employ a bar, drug corner, or similar location as the base for their activities."

Rossmo used a criminal geographic targeting (CGT) software program called Rigel that produced a three-dimensional probability graph, known as a jeopardy surface, which shows the areas of probability for an offender's anchor point. This could be overlaid on a street map to show where investigators could focus their efforts.

The results were stunning. The epicenter for the Freeway Phantom was at 2700 Martin Luther King Ave, SE, Washington DC. Longitude 76.996 W, Latitude 38.849 N.

St Elizabeth's Hospital.

The analysis of the results was both encouraging and chilling. "The confidence level of this analysis is relatively sound- with an average of 16 crime locations, the confidence level approaches 70% with a small, 3% peak profile area. Six crime locations, however, can only give 70% confidence levels when the peak profile area is increased to 10%. In other words, the more crimes there are to analyze, the more accurate the analysis is at pinpointing offender residence. Eleven crime sites were utilized in this analysis.

"St. Elizabeth's Hospital was the peak location identified, and the surrounding areas of Congress Heights were given a high likelihood of residence as well."

Thus armed with new statistical data, Jim Trainum had a daunting task ahead of him. "What we were trying to do at one point was very labor intensive, we were trying to reconstruct the neighborhood back then by going to the DC public library, the Martin Luther King library, they have all of the old phone directories, all of the Haynes crisscross directories, just trying to go street by street and see if we had anything. It was so labor intensive, we didn't get very far with it." Still, it added one more piece of the puzzle and allowed Trainum to do something that his predecessors had never done – tie St. Elizabeth's Hospital directly to the Freeway Phantom.

The last big breaks in the case came from an unlikely place – the *Washington Post.* Del Wilbur, an award-winning reporter, began to look into the Freeway Phantom case in

2006. He connected with Louis Richardson who had kept copies of his material in boxes. Wilbur had crawled around his attic recovering the old copies, to present the most in-depth article ever on the cases.

Jim Trainum did something the Washington MPD had never done, he openly embraced the media in the case. For the first time, the contents of the note left with Brenda Woodard were made public, as was the name of Robert Askins. "What Del Wilbur wanted to do with the story in the Post, I shared my files with him. My philosophy was to get the information out there. I caught a lot of shit for him putting the contents of the letter out there. They said that was hold-back stuff. At this stage, we don't have anything."

Wilbur tracked down Askins in prison, but he was uncooperative and denied any involvement in the Freeway Phantom case. While for the reporter that may have been the end of the story, but for Jim Trainum, the case still was unwinding, and Askins still was as viable a suspect as any – especially given his long-term connection with St. Elizabeth's. More importantly, the recovery of many of the old case files, courtesy of Wilbur and the *Washington Post*, Trainum had new data to work with.

"Del was able to get copies of all of this stuff and bring it back and so we were able to build our case files. When Del's article ran, I had given a presentation to the Mid-Atlantic Cold Case Homicide Detectives Association summer seminar. And this guy in the back from the Maryland State Police said, 'That last one, that's our case! What's her name? Williams. We have the case file and some of the evidence. Holy shit, we didn't know that was linked to anything.' We went and traded stuff. They did have a box with some of her clothing. They turned it over to us for us to turn over to the FBI. The FBI sat on it forever. So they just took it back. They tested it and it was my understanding, and some additional work was done after I retired, that there all of these questions about her boyfriend and whether he had sex with her. There was semen in her underwear which the boyfriend denied was his. Then I found a report with the Maryland State police where he denied having sex with her. However they found out he did through the testing. It is my understanding that it was his."

Wilbur's article spurred additional activity on the part of the MPD. Now that Askins had been outed as a suspect, detectives decided to try to engage him. As Jim Trainum remembers, "Well it's kind of funny. Several detectives went and talked to Askins. They thought they might have some DNA. There were two detectives that were really into this. They were going down for something else, and I said, 'Would you mind going and talking to Askins?' I gave them a briefing on it. They go down and talk to Askins and Askins is very defensive and doesn't want to say too much and doesn't want to give up his DNA. They're going, 'It's got to be him, it's got to be him!' And I'm going, 'No, he's just smart.' Just because he's paranoid, doesn't make him the guy."

Trainum's own digging surfaced a new suspect in the case as well, one with ties to St. Elizabeth's Hospital. The geographic profiling proved to be a powerful tool.

When asked whether race played a favor in the case being solved, Jim Trainum is pragmatic in his response. "Well, look at Chandra Levy. A *white* girl goes missing...*unprecedented* response by this department. The family has total access to the chief of police. Anytime they come into town they get an audience with the chief of police. I'm getting phone calls from family members of missing and dead women, saying, 'I've been trying to talk to the chief for years, and he or she won't talk to me.' And I go, 'Do you need me to tell you why?' and they go, 'No.' Sure it does."

How solvable are the Freeway Phantom cases in the eyes of one of the last detectives to probe into them? "It may very well not be. Not all cases are. The other rule of thumb is that the suspect's name is somewhere in the case files. Somebody has been interviewed by the cops and was set aside or something like that. A lot of times, the name is already in there.

"On [the television show] MASH, they called it 'Meatball Surgery.' Well for detectives, it's 'Meatball Investigation.' That's all it is. You do the bare minimum and move on. "Unfortunately, that's where a lot of cases get screwed up. There's this pressure to get the case to a point where you can close it and move onto the next one. And so unfortunately you take a lot of short cuts and you don't do a lot of follow-up."

CHAPTER 18: ECHOES OF THE PHANTOM - THE SUITLAND SLAYINGS

"In the last case of multiple homicides in Prince George's – the Freeway Phantom cases, in 1971 and 1972, in which seven young women from the District were killed and their bodies left near freeways in the county – investigators said that the killings stopped after the persons they believed were responsible were convicted in one of the slayings."
—January 25, 1987. Keith Harriston, Washington Post – *Sorting Out the Jumbled Pieces of the Suitland Slayings.*

There is an assumption by law enforcement that the Freeway Phantom stopped killing in 1972, either with Teara Ann Bryant or Diane Williams, depending on your perspective. No more notes, no more young girls strangled to death with tell-tale evidence linking them to the Freeway Phantom. Bodies rarely showed up on the highways of the District of Columbia that fit the profile of the killer. On the surface, it appeared that the murderer had moved on, was in prison, or had been killed.

But what if that wasn't the case? What if the killer had simply paused in his murderous spree, entering a long cooling off period, then resumed several years later? Certainly that was something contemplated by Detective Romaine Jenkins during her tenure on the cases. "You don't know about the Suitland Murders? Well, five black females were found in

Suitland, Maryland, and it was like a grave site. All these bodies were found there.

"But there you had a dumpsite, that's what made these different. I remember seeing it on television. They said this is a dumpsite. They found one body, then they kept looking and here's another one here."

The Suitland Murders, as the cases became known as courtesy of a *Washington Post* headline, technically remain open to this day with only one, potentially not connected to the others, considered truly closed. To explore these connections, you have to fast-forward from 1972 to 1986…

A group of young children were playing in the dense wooded park at the Bradbury Recreation Center in Suitland, Maryland, on December 13, 1986. The park was one of many in Prince George's County and was just over the invisible dividing line between Washington DC and Maryland. There is a large apartment complex there, the Whitehall Square Apartments. In the 1980s they were middle class housing. The average family income in the neighborhood was around $28,000. The cars that filled the parking lots were not old beat up clunkers, but newer model Hondas.

The recreational complex was wedged in between the recreation center and over three-hundred acres of cemetery land, Cedar Hill, Lincoln Memorial, and Washington National cemeteries. The thick overgrowth in the twenty-six-acre park made it a place for kids to explore and play in.

Like most kids playing in the shelter of the woods on a cold day, they were out to have fun. One of them spotted something that looked out of place…perhaps a mannequin. When they got closer, they found a mostly nude female body. They ran and informed their parents who contacted Prince George's County Police.

Her name was Dorothy Miller. She had lived in the 500 block of Newcomb Street in Washington DC's Southeast. The autopsy showed signs of drugs and her death was ruled as an apparent drug overdose, despite that her clothing had clearly been removed, and there were signs of sexual assault.

Dorothy was unemployed and lived with two roommates. They had become late on their rent and federal marshals had been sent to evict them the day after she was found. It is likely that the investigators gave her case a low priority... chalking it up as a drug user who may have overdosed and was dumped from her source of her demise.

Then the body of Juanita Marie Walls was found two days after Christmas, in the same tangled underbrush in the park, less than a mile from where Dorothy Miller had been found. She had been missing from her SE Washington apartment since October 30 in the previous year. She had been preparing for a gathering of friends and family to celebrate her twenty-sixth birthday. Always a meticulous dresser, she had put on a checkered flannel jacket and wore dark wool slacks. When she left, she flashed her big smile and said she would be back later.

Walls' father owned a barber shop on 15th Street NW, only two blocks from the White House. It was an old-school establishment, no hair styling, strictly haircuts. Her upbringing had been solid. But there were indications that Juanita Walls had problems in life. She had recently been fired from her job as a cashier at the JH Burton and Sons Nursery and Garden Center in Hyattsville, Maryland. Her manager had accused her of selling plants for half price. Her response was violent; she allegedly attacked him with "sharp hand tools." The charge for her assault was still outstanding at the time of her disappearance.

There was a potential link with Dorothy Miller, and that was drugs. Walls allegedly used drugs, specifically PCP. Financially strapped, she had recently moved in with a sister and her niece, 18-year-old Donna Blackeney. Her father had served in the Air Force in 1946, assigned to the 332nd Fighter Group (The Tuskegee Airmen), and she had hoped to pursue a similar career. Her attempt on the Air

Force entrance exam was a failure though. When she simply disappeared, Blackeney assumed her aunt had run off to another city to enlist. "She was looking for a job desperately – she wanted to travel."

Her mostly nude body had been badly decomposed by the time it had been found but given her victimology, there was a sense that drugs were a contributing factor. There was a difference though. Dorothy had stab wounds. Despite two bodies being discovered, the Washington MPD showed little in the way of concern.

On January 11, 1987, 16-year-old James Brannan and friends lived in the Whitehall Square Apartments and went to play, as they had many of times before, in the Bradbury Recreation Center. Everyone knew that the police had been in the park and that bodies had been found there recently, but there was a feeling that the Prince George's County Police had the matter well-in-hand, that they had done a thorough search for other human remains.

While moving through the brush, young Brannan initially spotted some articles of clothing and stockings hanging on limbs…out of place in the middle of the woods. As he got closer, he saw the body of a partially clad female on the ground.

Twenty-five-year-old Pamela Maria Malcom of Suitland, had finally been located, less than a mile from where she lived in the 2500 block of Darel Drive SE. Malcom had been a clerk at the US Patent Office in Arlington, Virginia, earning a respectable annual salary of $14,149 as a clerk since 1979. Her attendance record was solid, and she had had received positive performance evaluations.

She had been missing longer than Juanita Walls, since October 22, 1986. Pamela had been last seen by her mother around 7:30 p.m. that night when she left to walk to a local liquor store to purchase a pack of cigarettes. It was a stroll that should have only taken a few minutes, but Malcom had never returned.

Pamela did not have a history of drug use or trouble with law enforcement. She had been stabbed, which was presumed to be the cause of death. Her discovery by James Brannan caused a stir. There was a new phrase in the vocabulary of the United States that seemed to apply to the cases, "serial killer." That was what this was, the locals had no doubt of that. Someone was killing women in the area and hiding their bodies in the Bradbury Recreation Center. Moreover, the Prince George's County Police had not done an in-depth search of the park. The question was out in the media – were there more bodies yet to be discovered?

The Prince George's County Police scrambled to get in front of the public relations nightmare that the cases were suddenly generating. They brought in fifty police recruits to start going through the recreation center, yard-by-yard. The next day, two more bodies were found, confirming the worst fears of the community.

Twenty-two-year-old Cynthia Westbury of Southeast Washington DC lived in the Stanton Hill Apartments in the 3000 block of Stanton Road. She had graduated from H. D. Woodson Senior High School and had worked for the Washington traffic control board as a file clerk as well as a hotel housekeeper. She had taken the US Postal Service exam in hopes of securing a job there and had taken classes in computer processing. Sadly, by the time the call had come through with the job offer, she had already gone missing.

"I'll be right back," Cynthia Westbury had told her sister on November 9, 1986, as she walked out of the apartment they shared, on her way to visit a friend. Westbury was last seen by a witness, just a few doors down from her apartment building. Wearing a matching denim jacket and jeans, Westbury was known to keep her clothing coordinated and kept her hair well-styled. Cynthia had been seen by a neighbor getting into a gold colored automobile with a driver who was wearing a dress hat. It was not a car known in the neighborhood.

Westbury was not a casual person; she knew the risks of living in a major metropolitan area and was careful. Jacques Chevalier had gone on dates with Cynthia three times in the year before she disappeared. He told *The Washington Post* that he doubted that she would, "go off with any strangers. She was very cautious. I was dressed in a suit and tie, driving a BMW, and she would hardly touch the car. She said, 'I don't get into cars with strangers.'"

When her body was found it had been badly decomposed. She wore two distinct silver rings on her right hand – one with a turquoise stone, the other with a large clear stone. Given the state of her body, her initial identification by relatives was by the rings she wore.

The second body found by the police recruits on January 13, 1987, was that of 22-year-old Angela Maria Wilkerson. She lived in the District in the 2400 block of Hartford Street, Southeast. Her parents had seen a news broadcast on TV and had reached out to authorities, only to identify their daughter's remains. The cause of her death was stabbing.

There were two chilling details about the discovery of her body. First was that she was the most recent of the victims. Wilkerson had last been seen on January 5, only a week before her remains had been found. Second, the medical examiner revealed that she had been dead for only two days at the time her body had been found. What this meant was that her killer had potentially held her as a prisoner for days before she was murdered.

While not a great deal has been made public about her background other than a report in *The Washington Post* that she had been arrested on December 21, 1986, at Zayre's Department Store in Temple Hills, Maryland. The shoplifting charge had not yet been adjudicated at the time of her disappearance. Like the other victims, she didn't seem to have enemies who might lead to her being murdered.

A command post was set up at the police office in a windowless room in Forestville, Maryland. To their credit, the Prince George's County Police mobilized twenty-five detectives to work the cases of the five women. Many of the officers were working sixteen-hour shifts, trying to find the common threads among the women – if any. All had shown signs of stabbing with the exception of the first discovered victim. All five had been sodomized before or after their deaths. What really tied them together was where they were found.

The investigators did surface some possible connections. According to reports at least two if not four of the five women frequented Clancy's, a nightclub in Southeast Washington DC. It was a seedy establishment featuring exotic dancing. It was a dive, the kind of place with placards on the posts warning patrons, "Do not touch the dancers." The Prince George's County Police claimed it was a "straight shot" to the Whitehall Square Apartments three miles away, but in reality it was more of a twisting and turning drive on streets to get there. How tangible the tips were about the women's visiting Clancy's seemed sketchy at best.

In a press briefing, Prince George's County Police Spokesman Corporal Bruce Gentile laid out the problems facing investigators. "We have five points from which we can start. It's like trying to solve a puzzle, but we've got to go out and find the pieces before we can put it together."

Major James Rose, head of the Criminal Investigations Division said that detectives have "strong indicators" that all five deaths were linked. All small stature women, light skinned, all sexually assaulted.

The police tried to reassure citizens. Major Robert Phillips told a gathering of citizens on February 3, 1987, "I wish I could tell you we've solved the murder[s]. I wish I could assure you it won't happen again…I can't." Worse yet they made matters more confused by trying to explain that the victims had not been discovered in the order that they had been killed. So victim number one was not recovered body number one. For a public that was hanging off every word the police offered, it seemed confusing and that did not help the nervousness of the community.

When the police can't reassure your safety, you turn to anyone that offers a sense of security. The group, the New York-based Guardian Angels, came to Suitland to patrol the Whitehall Square neighborhood starting on January 25, 1987. The police were cordial about their offer to patrol the neighborhood but claimed they had the matter well in-hand.

On January 15, the focus of the investigation shifted away from Maryland to the District of Columbia. A nude victim was found in an alley near 62nd Street and Eastern Avenue, two and a half miles from the other bodies in the District of Columbia. The victim had been found at 11 a.m. As the Washington MPD scoured the neighborhood, someone saw her being pulled out of the back of a black van with Virginia license plates at around 8 a.m. The witness got enough information to enable police to begin to search for the van.

The victim was Janice Elaine Morton, a 20-year-old resident of the District. The medical examiner had determined she had been killed only a few hours earlier, most likely near 3 a.m. Ms. Morton had been beaten, sodomized, and ultimately strangled to death. Her death was more heinous because she was twelve-to-fourteen weeks pregnant.

The media drew connections to the victims dumped in the Bradbury Recreation Center – either prompted by Prince George's County Police or on their own. Yes, there were similarities – the same age and complexion of the other victims; her body being left nude. At least one report indicated Ms. Morton had traces of narcotics in her system, which could, if one stretched it, point to the demise of Dorothy Miller. As a counterpoint, none of the Suitland Slayings victims showed signs of being sodomized. The connections seemed thin at best, but by the evening news Janice Morton was being called the "sixth victim."

With the eyewitness of the black van, the police were able to track the owner as William Armah, a Washington

Metropolitan police officer. Armah admitted that the van was his, but he had loaned it to his uncle, Alton Alfonso Best. Even more bizarre, he had helped Best clean blood out of the van. His uncle had claimed that an injured friend had bled in the back.

There was more…Alton Best had been charged previously with kidnapping two women, tying them up in the back of the same van. They had managed to get away and the charges against Best had been dropped, but it was clear that the police were on the trail of someone who was a clear suspect in the murder of Janice Morton. The 31-year-old National Park Service employee was arrested on January 30, 1987, without incident, for her murder. A grand jury indicted him for first-degree murder for Morton's death on April 9, 1987.

Did Best have any connections with the Suitland Slayings victims? Best was thirty-one years old at the time of his arrest. He is said to have been acquainted with two or three of the Suitland victims. According to the police investigations, Alton Best allegedly purchased drugs from the same dealer in Southeast Washington DC that one of the Suitland Slayings victims did. The only other connection made public was that another Suitland victim lived on the same street as the mother of Best's children. These were thin connections even under the best circumstances.

In January the following year, Alton Best, pleaded guilty to Morton's slaying and was sentenced to eighteen and a third years to life. As part of his confession in District of Columbia Superior Court to second-degree murder and sodomy, he admitted in court that he beat the victim with his fists and strangled her with her own brassiere after a night of using cocaine with Ms. Morton and two other people.

While he admitted having a drug problem, he never provided the authorities with any possible connections to the Suitland Slayings. And given his age, he would have been a mere 15 years old at the time of the first of the Freeway

Phantom murders – thus effectively ruling him out as a suspect in those cases.

The Prince George's County Police artfully planted the image in the public's mind that the killing of Morton was somehow tied to the bodies found in Suitland. Paul Leder, Best's attorney, talked to the press on the one-year anniversary of the Suitland Slayings and highlighted that point, "In the press, Mr. Best became the Suitland murderer and that is horrible for him and his family." While there was no sympathy for the brutal Best, it did leave the Suitland Slayings unresolved and relegated to cold case status. No more bodies turned up in the wooded recreation center…no group of young women went missing over time.

That isn't to say that all killings stopped, but those attributed to the Suitland Slayings seemed to. A few women were killed from Southeast DC; on April 5, 1987, an unidentified victim was found dumped in a Washington alleyway and on June 24, Cheryl Henderson, 21, was discovered murdered in a wooded area in the city, her throat slashed. An unnamed victim was found in an apartment complex on September 21. Whether any of those were the work of the Suitland killer, forced to change his modus operandi because of the discovery of his dump site – we will never know.

Ultimately there is one outstanding question: Were the Suitland Slayings connected in any way with the Freeway Phantom cases? Did the killer take a fourteen-year hiatus? It was certainly enough for Detective Jenkins to look into the cases.

There are similarities. Geographically, the killers worked the same neighborhoods. Dorothy Miller, Cynthia Westbury, Angela Wilkerson, and Juanita Walls all live within one-and-a-half miles from St. Elizabeth's Hospital, considered the geographic epicenter of the Freeway Phantom cases. In the case of Cynthia Westbury, she lived only 2,400 feet from the hospital grounds.

The same victims all lived within two-and-a-half miles where Diane Williams and Darlene Johnson lived. It is nearly the same proximity to where Carol Spinks and Darlina Johnson's bodies were left and four miles from where Diane Williams and Nenomoshia Yates were found. The Suitland Slayer and the Freeway Phantom worked the same streets and the victims came from the very same neighborhoods. While separated by over a decade, the odds of two serial killers operating in the same narrow geography is astronomical.

There are other similarities that cannot be ignored. Both the Freeway Phantom and the Suitland Slayer were known to keep at least one of their victims as a prisoner for several days. The Freeway Phantom used a knife once, in the case of Brenda Woodard. The Suitland Slayer used a knife in four of the five cases, but some of victims showed signs of strangulation – the primary means of killing for the Freeway Phantom. Was this a case of the same killer improving his mode of operations?

While both killers operated in the same geography, the Suitland Slayings victims were all deposited in one location - what is often coldly termed as a dumping ground, at the Bradbury Recreation Center. The Freeway Phantom used a pubic highway or street to leave the remains of most of his victims. One sought to conceal his victims, the other put them out where he knew they would be found. Perhaps the Freeway Phantom changed his behaviors after so many years, and the fact that I-295 traffic increased so much that using it as a place to leave his victims was no longer an option. Serial killers usually learn, evolve, and grow. Such could be the case here.

There is no mention of the Suitland Slaying victims being bathed to wash away evidence, nor is there any hint of the telltale green fibers found on the Freeway Phantom victims being found on the Suitland Slaying victims. With more than a decade passing, perhaps the source of those fibers had been tossed out by the killer. We also don't know if the Prince George's County Police were able to check or validate if any of their victims had been bathed and possibly redressed. They clearly didn't bother trying to connect these cases to the Freeway Phantom murders.

The Suitland Slayings stopped, seemingly with the arrest of Alton Best, as did the investigation. That does not mean that Best had *anything* to do with the bodies found in Suitland. The authorities implied that he had a connection with some of the victims, but it was tenuous. The vehicle Cynthia Westbury was seen to be getting into was a distinctly gold car. We know that Best used his nephews' black van. Was this a case of the police making the right connection between alleged perpetrator and the victims, or was Best simply a means for Prince George's County to declare victory while the real killer moved on or stopped?

It is worth noting that in mind that the authorities had found the body of Angela Wilkerson only a week after she had been last seen, and she had only been dead for two days before her discovery. This meant the killer had been dangerously close to being seen in the area. With his dumping grounds exposed and made public, coupled with increased media attention, it is possible that he entered a prolonged cooling off period or stopped altogether. That, or he changed his pattern and stopped using a single dumping ground for his victims.

While the victims of the Suitland Slayer were older than the Freeway Phantom victims, they were mostly from Washington DC. The Freeway Phantom did cluster two of his victims, Carol Spinks and Darlenia Johnson. The Suitland Slayer put all his victims in one relatively small geographic locale.

Is it possible that the Suitland Slayings and the Freeway Phantom cases are directly related? Yes. The possibility does not necessarily mean it is true. It is hard to believe that two serial killers were independently operating in the same neighborhoods fifteen years apart. Since both serial killing sprees remain unsolved to this day, we do not know for sure.

Romaine Jenkins tried to thaw the cases to see if a fresh set of eyes could uncover other possible connections. She was met with a blue wall of silence. "Well, I talked to the detective in PG County because I called when I was redoing the Freeway cases, and I asked him about and he said, 'Oh, you know that guy that DC locked up for murdering that girl? Well, we're pretty certain he's the one who did it, so they didn't go any further.'" It is clear that in the minds of investigators that Alton Best was responsible for the death of *all* of the victims. Despite this perspective shared with a Washington MPD detective, our requests for information on these cases was met with a stony, "These are cold cases that we are actively investigating. Your request for information is hereby denied."

That is little solace to the families that have never been granted closure. This is evidenced by a small personal ad run a half-decade after the murders in *The Washington Post*: "In loving memory of my daughter, Pamela Malcom, who departed this life five years ago today, January 23, 1987. Clouds hide the sunshine, smiles hid the tears, your memories will still keep close, despite the passing years. Mother, Jacqueline M. George-Karar."

If Alton Best was responsible for the Suitland Slayings, then why wasn't he prosecuted for them? Was he simply an easy excuse to close out the murder cases? What evidence, if any, links Best to these crimes? Even if these cases have nothing to do with the Freeway Phantom cases, why haven't they received the same level of attention and public scrutiny?

Are the Prince George's County police simply sweeping these under the proverbial rug?

CHAPTER 19: OTHER CASES THAT MAY BE RELATED

"As with any high-profile murder investigation, detectives working the Freeway Phantom case were inundated with calls from citizens claiming to know the Phantom or have had a brush with the Phantom. Prank phone calls, strange cars moving slowly down the street- people were certain this meant the Phantom was living down the street and targeting them as his next victim. One woman called the FBI in California to claim that the Phantom was actually the Zodiac Killer. Investigators looked into the plethora of leads and determined most of them to be unsubstantiated."
—*Confidential Police Report, The Freeway Phantom Case*

One thing investigators do is cast a virtual net to other jurisdictions to see if there are cases with the same modus operandi as the unsub they are looking for. The Washington MPD and the FBI did this with the Freeway Phantom, and as a result, found several other cases that could possibly be tied in, though all have been ruled out over time. Yet exploring these cases may yet yield new information that could help authorities.

The authors obtained most of these from a confidential police report and are presenting them for the first time to the public.

Angela Denise Barnes

Angela Denise Barnes is a name that is typically always clumped together with the other Freeway Phantom victims. Indeed, in most of the early lists of Phantom victims, her name features prominently. The biggest difference between her crime and the other young girls is that Angela's killers were both brought to justice. She was an unfortunate young black girl killed the same time the Freeway Phantom operated.

Angela was called "Denise" by her family. July 11, 1971, was a typical day for Denise. She was assigned chores for the day, including caring for her 4-year-old little sister as her mother left for work. When her mother returned that evening around 6:30 p.m., all the chores were completed and dinner was prepared. Denise asked if she could visit friends at 8th and Barnaby streets that evening and was given permission by her parents She took a shower, got dressed, and said "bye" to her family with rollers still in her hair. Her mother watched as Denise walked across Martin Luther King Avenue, not knowing it would be the last time she would see her daughter alive.

Later that night, her mother waited for Denise to call to say she was taking a cab home or if she needed to be picked up. Denise called around 10:30 p.m. to say she was at her friend, Marcina Williams' house and on her way home. Her mother waited for her to knock on the door to get her cab fare. When she didn't arrive home, she started to worry and attempted to contact Denise's friends. The next morning, she called the police and filed a missing persons report.

As she explained to *The Washington Post*, "That morning was one I can never express. I was angry, hurt, scared, emotional, and nearly out of my mind after waiting several hours without hearing anything," said Annette Canady, Denise's mother. She decided it was best for her to go to work that morning. She called her husband, Charles Canady, to tell him she still hadn't heard from Denise but was going onto her job at a post office. "I explained to him that the waiting was just too great for me to take and probably working would relieve some of the agony."

On July 13, 1971, in the midst of the Freeway Phantom murders, 14-year-old Angela Barnes' battered body was found near Route 228 at 6:35 a,m. She had lying by the roadside west of Waldorf about seven hours after leaving her friend's home, just ten blocks away from her own home. Her cause of death was a bullet wound to her head from a .38 caliber bullet. Evidence suggested that she was most likely killed in Prince George's County and her body later dumped near Waldorf. Unlike the Freeway Phantom murders, Angela had not been raped.

Charles Canady was called and told that a body had been found that may fit Denise's description. He called his wife at work and said, "Can you come home now?" without an explanation. She rushed home, speeding the entire way, all while praying that everything was all right. Police cars were parking outside the home when she arrived. "Only God knows the part of me that was destroyed when the detectives showed me the picture of my daughter, with her face demolished, rollers still in her hair and a scarf around her head," recalled Marcina.

The family's home on Martin Luther Avenue was in the Southeast section of the city, in a fairly residential area. Marcina had divorced Denise's father and remarried Charles Canady. Eerily, Angela Denise Barnes attended the same school as Diane Williams, one of the last victims of the Freeway Phantom; it's unknown if they knew each other.

Protests and meetings of citizens groups following Denise's murder caused the District of Colombia government to install high intensity street lighting in Anacostia areas. Police patrols were increased, and helicopters were assigned to Anacostia and Congress Heights patrols during the day.

Initially, Angela Denise Barnes case was grouped together with the other Freeway Phantom cases. At the time it made perfect sense, a young black girl murdered and dumped elsewhere. The investigation of her death yielded very little clues and no witnesses were found to her disappearance. Three long years ticked by, until a major break in the case caused major headlines.

Two former District of Colombia police officers were arrested and charged in Angela's death in 1974. Edward Leon Sellman and Tommie Bernard Simmons both joined the police force in 1970 until early 1971; neither completed the yearlong probationary period. Simmons, who was 23 at the time of Barnes' murder, had been assigned to the Sixth District before he resigned from the force. Sellman, who was 27 at the time of the murder, had been assigned to the Fifth District. Both districts adjoin in the Northeast part of the District, where Angela lived. Both men had resigned from the department in early 1971 following an internal investigation when both men allegedly lost their .38 caliber service revolvers. Both Sellman and Simmons reported their revolvers missing during a burglary at Simmons' Temple Hills home when they left the revolvers on a living room table before going out. There were no signs of forced entry at Simmons' apartment and no other valuables were missing. When there was talk of a possible disciplinary action against the men for the missing revolvers, Simmons' weapon was found in the front seat of an unattended police car on 14th Street.

At the time of his arrest, Simmons was married with a 2-year-old daughter. He had been the "ideal tenant" of a two-bedroom apartment for the past two years. Neighbors described him as a quiet man who typically kept to himself. Steve Campbell, Simmons' best friend, described him as "discreet, articulate—his level of consciousness always appeared to be normal."

Sellman, also married with a 6-month-old daughter, also lived in a two-bedroom apartment. Sellman had attended the University of Maryland but was drafted during his sophomore year. He was honorably discharged in 1970 as a staff sergeant.

Leon Williams, father of Denise and head of the Freeway Phantom Committee, praised the arrests of the former police officers at the time. "If they continue a thorough job, I feel they'll solve all of them," he said to *The Washington Post.*

Barnes' case sat alongside the other Freeway Phantom cases until Edward Sellman's ex-wife turned him in. Dorothy Sellman had believed that her former husband was involved in Angela's death and was asked by the FBI to call Edward at the realty office he was working at to let him know that police had asked her about his role in the young girl's murder. "Wow, you gotta help me," Sellman said to her over the phone, adding that she would have to help him come up with an alibi of the time of the murder. Sellman went on to say "If he (Simmons) goes, I'm going with him…I was there when she was killed. I know the chance I'm taking; I knew it then." Sellman was arrested following the taped conversation, and Simmons was arrested the following day. Simmons confessed to the crime, saying both himself and Sellman were involved.

Simmons' confession explained how the crime had occurred, how he had kidnapped and assaulted Angela – and how he had shot her in the head. He and Sellman forced Angela into Sellman's car at gunpoint on the night of July 12, 1971.

Dorothy Sellman testified that she had found blood on her husband's shirt the same day he brought a revolver home in a brown bag. He hit the revolver with a hammer, attempting to break it into pieces. After the odd outburst, he left with the gun and didn't return home until 1 a.m. She testified that when Sellman had finally returned home he was nervous and walking around the apartment in his underwear. When Dorothy got into his car to go shopping, she noticed blood on the backseat and the car had an odor of bleach. Human blood was found in the back of Sellman's vehicle, but the FBI in 1971 could not match it to Angela Barnes.

The following day, July 14, Dorothy testified that she washed the car at a car wash. "On the left side of the car, behind the driver's seat, I could see that the mat on the floor had been torn up," she said. Lifting the mat up, maggots and blood were on the floorboard along with "fibers that looked like hairs."

Tommie Simmons was convicted in Angela Denise Barnes death and sentenced to twenty years to life in prison for her murder. He also pled guilty to assault with intent to commit rape on a 29-year-old woman that occurred on June 28, 1971, in Southeast.

Denise New and Harold Nabors

The FBI's Detroit Field Office reported a crime that may have been related to the Freeway Phantom cases. The crime itself was shockingly violent and remains unsolved to this day.

The first anyone knew of the brutal events was when a wet, bloody young black girl showed up at the doorstep of South Bend, Indiana, farmer Danial Nowicki. Sobbing and bleeding from a gunshot wound to her head, she told the farmer that her boyfriend was dead nearby…that she had been kidnapped.

St. Joseph County Sheriff Elmer Sokol showed up along with local firemen. In nearby Grapevine Creek they found the beaten body of a young black man. The girl, Denise New, was taken to the hospital and slowly her story of terror began to emerge.

On July 26, 1970, Denise New and her boyfriend, Harold Nabors, went to a movie in Detroit, Michigan. After the movie was out, the young black couple were confronted by two armed white males and forced into Nabors' car, which they had appropriated. For forty-minutes the kidnappers made Nabors drive the car, then they swapped seats, putting their victims in the back while they took over the driving of Nabors' 1964 tan Dodge convertible. Their kidnappers drove them all night, arriving in South Bend, Indiana, near dawn.

They stopped in a secluded wooded area and Harold Nabors was tied up by his captors. One of the men repeatedly raped young Denise New. Harold erupted in rage and one of his kidnappers took out a tire iron and beat him to death, tossing his body into Grapevine Creek, where the unconscious youth slowly drowned. With the stark realization that Denise New was a witness to their horrible crime, they used a .22 caliber pistol and shot her in the back of the head. Her body was dumped next to her boyfriend along the bank of the creek. Her kidnappers drove to Gary, Indiana, where their car was abandoned and later found by the authorities. They did not realize that the small bullet had not penetrated her skull and, while stunned, she was still miraculously alive.

Denise New defiantly beat the odds. She should have died, but her gunshot would leave her only with some minor vision loss. Nothing could erase the terror and physical abuse she had endured at the hands of her captors. The FBI became involved because the kidnapping went over state lines. Denise was able to provide a sketch artist with a description of the men, including one she heard referred to as "Bill." Her damaged eyesight made it impossible for her to identify any police photographs presented to her.

The FBI looked into the case as part of the Freeway Phantom murders because it took place just before the events in Washington DC; it involved men kidnapping a black woman, and rape was involved. Aside from the temporal connection – there were a lot of things that made the case a fringe consideration. Strangulation – one of the hallmarks of the Freeway Phantom, was not present in the attack on Denise New. The use of a gun also pointed away from the Washington DC cases. The race of the kidnappers also did not fit the profile of what was expected for the Freeway Phantom, and there was considerable distance between DC and Detroit. As such, there was no aggressive pursuit to tie in these cases.

Carman Colon

The nightmare of the Double-Initial Murders began for the public on November 18, 1971, when two teenage boys biking on Sterns Road in Riga, New York, saw a body in a ditch. They stopped, thinking at first it was a doll. It was not. It was the body of 9-year-old Carmen Guica Colon, clad only in a shirt, socks, and sneakers, who had disappeared two days earlier.

The young Puerto Rican girl had been seen on November 16, at 4:30 p.m., near Jack's Drugstore on West Main Street where she had been going at the behest of her grandfather to pick up a prescription. When the prescription wasn't ready, she left to go the two blocks back to her home but never arrived.

The next reports of her came a half an hour later from motorists driving on I-490. While not confirmed as Carmen at that time, several motorists saw a young girl nude from the waist down, running along the highway. A car was seen backing towards her on the shoulder. In an age where there were no cell phones, the speeding motorists simply drove on by, never realizing the peril the young girl faced.

Carmen Colon had been sexually assaulted and manually strangled from the front. Her pants and underwear were found on I-490 about a half mile from where she had been seen running along the highway shoulder.

The local authorities contacted the DC Metropolitan Police Department thinking there may be a link between her death and the Freeway Phantom victims. The basis of this was that she was a nonwhite female who had been raped, strangled, and left on a roadway. Carmen was Puerto Rican, not black, but the similarities did not end there. She had been running an errand to a local store, much in the same way Carol Spinks had gone to the store to get TV dinners and Brenda Crockett had gone to the grocery store to get some sundries. There was an interstate highway involved. The biggest difference was that the Freeway Phantom did not leave his victims nude, they were all redressed. The FBI concurred that the case was worth exploring further but could not find any other connections.

In March of 1972 the New York authorities received a tip that a man had told his relatives that he had raped a 10-year-old girl in November of the previous year and did not know if she was alive or dead. The suspect named in the letter was Cecelio Colon Pagan, a Puerto Rican man with a laundry list of prior arrests in New York and Florida including two rape convictions involving underage females. In November of 1971 he had returned to Puerto Rico. The FBI checked and could not find any evidence of Pagan having been to Washington DC, so he was dropped as a suspect in the Freeway Phantom cases – but still pursued by the New York authorities for the death of Carmen Colon.

The San Juan police tracked him down, interviewed him, and transferred him to New York for further interrogation. He denied being involved in the murder of Colon, claiming that he believed a former girlfriend had raised him as a suspect because he had been allegedly "playing around" with her daughter.

Pagan was a man with many issues, fearing arrest on narcotics charges and illegally cashing his wife's welfare checks. It speaks a great deal about his personality and demeanor that when he was brought to New York to be questioned, none of his family or friends would take him in because they feared him and believed that he would have charges leveled against him for rape.

Pagan claimed he had made the sudden flight back to Puerto Rico because he had read about the murder of

Carmen Colon and feared that the authorities would attempt to pin it on him.

While he was never charged in the murder of Colon, the investigators took a dramatically different tact in their investigation when two more young girls, Michelle Maenza and Wanda Walkowicz, were found murdered. Because of their identical first and last initials, they were called the "Double Initial" murders, i.e., WW for Wanda Walkowicz, CC for Carman Colon. And given where they lived, Churchville for Carmen, Macedon for Michelle, and Webster, New York, for Walkowicz – there were technically three initials in play. Later, these would be called the Alphabet Murders. Oddly enough this thinking seems to parallel the Freeway Phantom and his supposed targeting of girls with Denise in their name.

Both Michelle and Wanda were not persons of color – which points away from them being tied to the Freeway Phantom. It is of interest that the dates of the three young girls killed in New York state do not conflict with the Freeway Phantom cases. Michelle Maenza disappeared on November 26, 1973, and Wanda Walkowicz on April 2, 1973. Technically it would have been possible for the same killer to have driven between the two distinct areas to commit these crimes.

While there have been several possible suspects and connections with crimes in California, no one has been charged in any of these three murders. Pursuit of Cecelio Pagan is no longer a viable avenue unless DNA evidence can connect him – he died in 1996.

Judy Ann Garrison – One That Got Away?

The investigators believed they got a possible lead in the form of Judy Ann Garrison. The 20-year-old, black female was walking in Washington DC on September 30, 1971, when a black driver pulled alongside her and forced her into his vehicle. He drove her out of the District to Prince George's County, where he attempted to sexually assault her.

Judy Garrison proved to be resourceful and determined, however. While in the car she had removed one of her boots when her captor was focusing on the road. When he attempted to force himself on her, she used the boot heel as a weapon and escaped. Hiding in a ditch, her kidnapper tried to find her, eventually leaving. Judy fled to a nearby drugstore and not only provided a detailed description of her assailant, but, also, the license plate number of his car.

Her assailant, whom she identified in a police lineup, was Jessie Tobin. He lived in Washington DC and had been hospitalized as a mental patient at St. Elizabeth's Hospital. According to hospital records he had been diagnosed as a schizophrenic. Certainly the connection to St. Elizabeth's made him a person of interest. Police investigated her case as possibly the girl who somehow had escaped the Freeway Phantom.

Jessie Tobin had other indicators in his background that seemed to make him a viable suspect. His wife, Kate, had a restraining order out against him, charging both physical and sexual abuse. A grand jury indicted him in the attack on Judy Garrison in April of 1972. The Washington MPD also looked at other open rapes where he fit the description, and found one more, Priscilla Peak.

For a short time Jessie Tobin had to have been a top suspect in the authorities' minds. The problem was that while he was under arrest and psychiatric evaluation, other confirmed Freeway Phantom murders took place. There were other mitigating factors that contributed to the Washington MPD dropping him as a suspect, but those details have been lost over the years.

While police thought, for a short time, that Judy Garrison might have escaped the Freeway Phantom and could be the key to solve the cases, her case was disassociated from the others. Jessie Tobin died on July 31, 1989.

Emily Maria Allen

On April 12, 1972, 9-year-old Emily Maria Allen was approached by someone she knew – Reginald Jackson. Jackson was a seemingly friendly man who lived in her Washington DC neighborhood and worked for her father. As she was coming home from school, he pulled up beside her and commanded her to get into his car, "...or I'll do something to you." She complied, thus starting a two-day odyssey across the US.

Jackson's interactions with Emily Allen were twisted and confused. As the police report on the case described it, Jackson drifted between being "parental to hostile" with her. At one point he gave her $100 and promised to take her on a "fun trip" to New York. He attempted to molest her, but Emily refused to undress for him, and he backed away from his attempt. Jackson told her to work with him to fabricate a story about her kidnapping, forcing her to repeat over-and-over the fictional details that he instructed her on. The story he wove was that two black men had taken her. He insisted that she tell the police and her family the story he crafted.

Jackson had driven her to Baltimore, Maryland, then down to South Carolina. When he learned over the radio that he was the prime suspect in Emily's kidnapping, he panicked and decided to take her to London, Ohio, where her grandmother lived.

Two days later, exhausted, Jackson pulled over on the side of the I-70 to sleep. An alert Ohio State trooper approached the Chevy Vega and ran the plates, only to determine it was stolen. He apprehended the 23-year-old Jackson and his captive without a struggle.

The investigators on the Freeway Phantom case were drawn to the Allen kidnapping because it involved a young black female taken from DC by a man with a history of indecent acts against children. While no sexual abuse had taken place with Emily Allen, the investigators came to believe that he was not their elusive Freeway Phantom.

If Emily Allen had resisted and that was enough to stop Jackson, there was no doubt that the Freeway Phantom victims would have done the same – and they had been assaulted. Also, the Freeway Phantom operated in the DC metro area, where Jackson took Allen across state lines.

For the Freeway Phantom investigators, it proved to be another disappointing lead and suspect. There would be others over the years, all of which ended in the same place – the cold case files related to the cases. None seemed hot enough to thaw their status.

The Oakland County Child Killer

While not part of the official police files as a related case, one cannot ignore the Oakland County Child Killer cases as sharing similarities with the Freeway Phantom. Over a period of thirteen months in 1976-77, four children (boys and girls) were kidnapped, sexually assaulted, and murdered in Oakland County, Michigan, a suburb of Detroit. The victims, for the most part, were strangled, smothered/suffocated, and shot. Two of the victims had been held for hours or even days by their killer – and were fed meals, similar to Carol Spinks. The ages of the victims were between 10 and 12, within the same range the Freeway Phantom selected for his targets. Their bodies were, for the most part, dumped alongside roads – again a hallmark of the Phantom.

The timing of these crimes took place after the Freeway Phantom. Was it possible that the killer simply moved to the Detroit area and modified his MO?

The biggest differences in these terrible murders and the Freeway Phantom cases are the mix of boys and girls as victims. The Freeway Phantom, to the best of anyone's knowledge, did not kill young boys. The use of a firearm to kill a victim also does not fit the modus operandi of the Freeway Phantom.

Recent developments in the Oakland County Child Killer case do not seem to connect with Washington DC but are focused on more Michigan-centric connections. At present the murderer of Mark Stebbins, Jill Robinson, Kristine Mihelich, and Timothy King remains unknown and possibly at large.

The VICAP system used by law enforcement is designed to provide a standardized way to enter crime information so that trends can be analyzed to see if a criminal has moved to a different locale. The Freeway Phantom cases all have very distinct elements related to the victims and the MO of the killer. There is no indication in the historical information that the Freeway Phantom moved on to a different location to continue his killing. If he did, he dramatically changed his modus operandi and choice of victims enough to escape the clutches of law enforcement.

CHAPTER 20 - THE OTHER SUSPECTS

"This is the Freeway Phantom...I
will strike again tonight..."
—Phone call to the Phantom Hot Line. *The
Washington Daily News*, November 19, 1971

In a string of murders as complicated as the Freeway Phantom case, there are countless potential suspects. Some come from confidential sources, others from other law enforcement agencies. The following individuals have, at one point or another, been considered suspects in the case.

It is important to note several things. One, in the 1970s there was no investigative category of "person of interest." Many of these individuals would have easily fallen into and out of that category. Two, almost all these individuals have been cleared by the authorities by the 21st century. That does not mean that they are innocent or guilty, but that, barring new evidence coming forward, further investigation into their involvement has stopped (unless otherwise stated).

As the authors, we are by no means implying that these individuals are responsible for the Freeway Phantom killings. The individuals named may very well have found their way into the investigation by some random tip, a hunch, or the whim of some detective. They remain, in many cases, because no one was able to prove or disprove their involvement – or in some cases, were cleared.

In some cases, names have been changed where the individuals have been completely cleared or their families may have been unaware of their circumstance. These are signified with an asterisk *. The other names remain unchanged, because the public may yet have information that about them that could prove useful for investigators.

Alfred Holmes

Sometimes individuals are drawn into investigations because of supposed eyewitness accounts. Such is the case with Alfred Holmes. Holmes was drawn into the investigation of Darlenia Johnson's death after several individuals said they witnessed Darlenia with him on July 7 and 9. Darlenia had left the recreation center on July 8, 1971. Her body was discovered on July 12. If Holmes had indeed been with her, he may have been able to fill in an important gap of time when she was unaccounted for. At least that was what investigators hoped.

In his interview, Holmes claimed that the last time he had seen Darlenia was on July 4, 1971 – despite numerous witnesses placing them together. This discrepancy drew the attention of investigators. To his credit, Holmes agreed to be interviewed by investigators several times and had a sodium pentothal test administered to him and appeared to have answered honestly, though such tests are notably unreliable and inadmissible in court. After the test, digging into Holmes' story seemed to have run its distance, and he was dropped from further investigation, despite any surviving documentation for exactly why.

George Bullock

Several telephone calls came into the FBI's Washington Field Office in January 1972 from an anonymous source stated that George Bullock (AKA George Bridges and Clarence Fanniel) was the Freeway Phantom. The calls all came from a woman who identified herself as a former girlfriend of Bullock. She further claimed that she had observed Bullock with Brenda Woodard leaving the Miles Long Sandwich Shop on the night of November 15, 1971, the night of her abduction by the Phantom.

While Bullock lived in New York City, police learned that he was in Washington DC at the time of the crimes. Further, they learned that Bullock did not own or have access to a car. He was known to carry a seven-inch knife.

His friends provided investigators with information on Bullock's former girlfriend, Florence Willis. She was tracked down and admitted to being the anonymous tipster. Further Willis admitted to making up the entire story about seeing Brenda Woodard with Bullock. She had lied to have him arrested, so he would no longer pose any threat to her. Willis alleged that Bullock had tried to kill her, and she had filed charges against him for assault. She further alleged that he had smothered a young girl in North Carolina two-to-three years earlier. The Charlotte Field Office of the FBI could find no crime that matched what was described by Willis however.

Willis further claimed that Bullock had a long string of violent behaviors. He often beat, choked, and whipped his sexual partners, though this could not be substantiated. Further, Willis asserted that Bullock carried an arsenal of knives and commonly threatened to kill females. How much of this was true is impossible to ascertain given she had lied to tie him to the Freeway Phantom murders.

This was a case of a woman battered and scorned, someone who was using the Freeway Phantom case to attempt to achieve her own goal? Sadly on such murder cases this happens, people exploiting a crime to their own twisted benefit. At that point, a tip of this sort is normally dropped. The FBI had other compelling reasons to keep George Bullock on their radar.

There had been a US Marine, Corporal Christopher S. Brady, killed at the Washington Navy Yard on September 1,

1971, and Bullock matched the description of the suspect. He was known to carry a stiletto, which was identical to the knife used in the Marine's murder. Another murder, that of Ritchie H. Reed, a government economist, had taken place in the fifth-floor men's room of the New Executive Office Building on October 1, 1971, where he fit the description of the killer.

More importantly handwritten notes were left at each crime scene, riddled with racial undertones. The note left with Reed's body referenced the note left with Brady, linking the crimes. "The Pigs must get out of our community Now." In another line it read, "No European will be safe in our (black people's) city again. If you don't live here, stay out and let us black people have our jobs to support our families. The revolution is now...all power to the people," were among some of the inflammatory comments. The presence of notes, which the FBI confirmed were connected, tied to the crimes ran warning sirens with investigators given the Freeway Phantom's use of a note with Brenda Woodard.

George Bullock's troubled past did not help matters either. He had confessed to participating in a gang rape in NE Washington. The victim was Caucasian, but despite this, the rape connection was attractive to investigators. Bullock worked in DC as a trash collector, working the same neighborhood where Brenda Woodard had been last seen. The final link that made investigators consider him in part of their Freeway Phantom case was that he matched the description given by a guard at Prince George's Hospital, Tillman Roseberry, of an individual driving a red Camaro who had been seen stopped near the site where Brenda Woodard's body had been located the night she had been found.

The Bureau met with Bullock's employer in the city and was told that he was considered untrustworthy and unstable...a person who was "no way a dependable worker." Bullock was known to have a cocaine addiction during the time. One of his bail bondsmen relayed to investigators that he was a female impersonator and carried a .38 revolver. As they probed deeper into his background, they learned he had a reputation for stealing money from employers and considered himself a smooth-talking lady's man who regularly propositioned women.

The FBI brought in Bullock for questioning on January 13, 1972. He provided them with samples of his head and body hairs to compare against those gathered at the Freeway Phantom scenes. He also provided fingerprints. Analysis showed that these were not a match. Bullock's discussions of his whereabouts during the times of the crimes proved to be contradictory. When presented with the contradictions, he refused to change his story.

To his credit, Bullock did agree to a polygraph test, though one was not administered. According to the scant information available, it appears he was cleared of involvement in the Freeway Phantom cases based on his fingerprints, but there are no records of fingerprints having been recovered as part of the evidence from any of the crime scenes. So either that information has been lost over time, or he was cleared as a suspect at the time based on other factors as well. Despite suspicions, he was never charged in the murders of Ritchie H. Reed or Christopher S. Brady, either. Both of those crimes remain unsolved but would surface again during the investigation of other suspects.

Deaton Anthony Caesar*

A well-known figure in Washington DC's home construction business, Deaton Caesar*, was targeted by investigators in the MPD who received a report of a white man in a red Camaro attempting to pick up a young black girl near Benning Road NE. Caesar, a middle-aged white male, was identified as the owner of the vehicle.

According to the police accounts, he matched the vague description given by a guard from Prince George's Hospital of the driver of a Camaro who had been seen near the site where Brenda Woodard's body had been left. Ironically, it was this same description that police had used to target George Bullock. Given that both men were different heights, races, and appearances, begs one to question the validity of the guard's description.

The FBI and Maryland State Police began to tail Caesar. They noticed that he had reddish-brown hair, similar to the Caucasian hairs found on Brenda Woodard's body. As another reason to gravitate towards him, they cited that Brenda Crockett had said in her phone call to her home that she was with a white man in Virginia, so to investigators, Caesar looked as viable as anyone else. When Brenda Crockett stopped speaking on the phone, the line went dead. The FBI learned that Caesar had a switch in his home that could allow him to turn off the phones and switch to an office phone. That might account for someone not hanging up the line.

Mr. Caesar owned six different cars and as they trailed him, he often traveled along I-295, giving him familiarity with where the bodies were left. The Maryland State Police used helicopters to study the movements out of the Caesar home, routinely tracking cars and drivers. Their hope was to catch Deaton Caesar attempting to lure in another victim, if he was the Freeway Phantom. They had no success, however.

Caesar's neighbors said that his 20-year-old son, Markus*, often drove the Camaro as well, so he too was placed under surveillance. The FBI interviewed his teachers and was told that he was "hot tempered," making him intriguing as a suspect as well.

The FBI and MPD brought in Caesar for questioning on January 4, 1972. He admitted to picking up black girls to perform sex but was ardent that he had not had intercourse with them. He would pick them up, park in an alley, engage with them for oral sex, then let them go on their way. He admitted to engaging with prostitutes and hanging around in the District's strip clubs but claimed he had nothing to do with the Freeway Phantom cases.

Nervous that his family would find out his nocturnal habits, he readily provided hair samples to the investigators. None of his hairs matched those found on Brenda Woodard's body, only solidifying the thought that they may have been transferred to her via the blanket she had been covered up with.

Caesar was cleared by his hair samples as being a suspect.

Dennis Allen Dixon

The Freeway Phantom investigators asked doctors at St. Elizabeth's and other local institutions for possible suspects, former patients who might have the mental state that would indicate them to be a serial killer. One of those identified was Dennis Dixon.

Pinpointed by Dr. Samuel Yochelson, the chief of the Behavioral Studies Group, as a person whom authorities should look into, Dixon had a violent past with young women. In 1961 he had tried to assault a 21-year-old woman. As a result of that attack he had spent time in St. Elizabeth's getting psychiatric treatment for more than a year.

Apparently his counseling sessions didn't take hold. In 1963, the then 18-year-old Dixon had lured 9-year-old Beatrice A. Gordon to his apartment. He fixed her a snack of eggs then the two of them retired to his bedroom under the premise of listening to some records. For about an hour they listened to records then the matters turned grim. The pimply-faced Dixon sexually assaulted Beatrice. She fought back and this only seemed to escalate the violence. Pulling off a venetian blind cord, he bound her hands and feet. Dixon filled his bathtub with hot water and drowned her in the tub, leaving her body floating there for his mother to find hours later.

Dixon fled to the Chesapeake Beach area where he got employment as a slot machine repairman. The man who hired him noticed his photograph in the newspaper and turned him in.

Dixon went on trial in June 1963 for the slaying. He claimed that he did not remember her fighting as much as he did drowning her. Her stepfather, John Thomas, lunged from his seat and punched Dixon in the jaw for his callous attitude. The blow did not seem to faze the young man in the least.

Dixon once more was incarcerated at St. Elizabeth's and like Robert Askins before him, had eventually gotten permission to leave the hospital during the day. He had access to a car and a place to stay in Virginia.

When investigators looked into Dixon, he fit the bill of being the Freeway Phantom on several accounts. With Brenda Crockett, she claimed she was with a white man in Virginia, which could apply to Dixon if she was, indeed, relaying accurate information in her call home. He was cold-hearted to the core. Those that knew him said he never expressed any remorse for the murder of Beatrice Gordon.

There were problems with him as a suspect, however. St. Elizabeth's records showed that he had no indication of tardiness during the periods of the Freeway Phantom killings and was back at the hospital by 10 p.m. This would ultimately exclude him in several of the murders with a strong alibi

They met with Dixon and obtained hair samples from him – none of which matched those found on Brenda Woodard. He was eventually cleared as an immediate suspect as a result of the investigation.

James Francis Fletch*

Tips can be the lifeblood of an investigation, but many take investigators down blind, dead-end alleys. Such was the case of James Fletch*. When an article ran in the Waterloo, Iowa, newspaper about the murders in the District, a police informant contacted the Iowa detectives saying that James

Fletch, a local communist, was known to sign letters to an ex-girlfriend named Diane with the signature "The Phantom." He was said to be living in the Washington DC area at the time of the Freeway Phantom crimes.

Fletch did have a history in Iowa of having a violent temper and had assaulted more than one former girlfriend. The Iowa detectives said there was a rumor he was working as a dishwasher at the Russian Embassy in Washington DC.

There wasn't much to go on – a name and a rumor. By mid-April of 1972, Fletch had dropped off as a potential suspect, with no indication that he had ever been located or interrogated on the Freeway Phantom cases.

Colonel Peter Alfred Kapow*

A highly decorated colonel in the US Air Force, Colonel Peter Kapow* worked at the Pentagon and lived nearby in Virginia at the time of the Freeway Phantom murders. Like others, he was identified as a driver of a red Camaro, who had been seen with a black female passenger, "propped up" in the passenger seat. The tipster turned in a license plate number, which the investigators tracked to Colonel Kapow, who had been reassigned from his post only days before and had moved to Georgia.

He willingly met with authorities in 1972 but denied being involved with the Freeway Phantom cases. His son James* frequently borrowed his car and frequently traveled I-295. Kapow allowed for a search of his car and several items of interest were found including a hair roller, barbettes and pins, pieces of tape with hair attached, and a jackknife.

Tillman Roseberry, the guard from the Prince George's Hospital who witnessed the red Camaro was shown pictures of Kapow, his son, and the vehicle. He claimed that it was not the same car, explaining that the vehicle he saw had a different tail-light style, a different tone of red paint, and a different colored top. He also failed to identify Kapow as the man driving the car he saw that night.

None of the items recovered from the car matched any of the victims or their missing possessions. Kapow and his son were removed as Freeway Phantom suspects as a result of the investigators probing.

Ameil Johnson

There were a lot of colorful, if not dangerous characters roaming the streets of the District in the 1970s. One of those was Ameil Johnson. He frequented the area in the neighborhood where Brenda Woodard had been abducted, often loitering near the Miles Long Sandwich Shop. He was known to annoy women in the area, attempting to pick them up, which brought him to police attention.

There were a number of reasons why Johnson appeared initially as a viable suspect. One woman said Johnson had given a ride to a sandwich shop employee that had resulted in his beating, raping, and choking her. He was a drug user, by his own admission, having enrolled in a methadone program. He had bragged to one female that he had shot and killed someone – offering her no details. When found on the street, he often appeared high, either as part of an act to gain sympathy from passersby or in reality. His attempts to gain pity of women included a tale that he had been abandoned as a child and raised in an orphanage.

Police began to probe into Johnson's background, interviewing his former girlfriends. One said he frequently beat and slapped her, often threatening to kill her if she left him. Another said that he liked to stroke her throat during foreplay but never actually choked her. The words to describe Ameil Johnson were "common," "no-good," and "crazy."

A grandmother of one of his girlfriend's told authorities that her granddaughter, who had had a child by Johnson, lived in fear of the man. She claimed that Johnson would inject his five-year-old son "full of dope" and take him around the neighborhood to fight with other children. The child had been hospitalized because of his injuries.

As the investigators continued to peel the onion that was Johnson's life, they discovered that he had been arrested before for rape, assault, and fraud.

Investigators interviewed Johnson on November 26, 1971. He stated unequivocally that he did not want to talk about the Freeway Phantom victims and attempted to dodge questions about the crimes. He did eventually admit that he knew at least three of the victims and had seen Brenda Woodard before in the area around 8th and H streets SE.

Investigators learned he did have a car, a 1965 Ford Falcon convertible. It had been in the shop for repairs on Monday November 15, in the early afternoon and had been in the custody of the garage for a week. This meant that he would not have had a vehicle to kidnap and transport Brenda Woodard at the time of her abduction. The investigators confirmed this with the garage owner. Based on this evidence, Ameil Johnson was ruled out as a suspect in the Freeway Phantom murders.

Donald Nathan Tyler

Donald Tyler had been on the Washington Metropolitan Police Department's radar for some time. In February of 1952, he had been arrested for robbery and rape charges against a Navy Department employee. In April of 1952, the then 22-year-old Tyler had been charged with the murder of Janet Ellen King, choking then shooting her in the head, shoulders, and neck, leaving her body in the gutter of the 1200 block of 19th Street NE. When apprehended he claimed that that shooting was "accidental." She had, according to him, taken the gun from a glove compartment of a friend's car, and it had gone off but could not explain away multiple head shots. He was sentenced to ten-to-thirty years in jail. The judge, Alexander Holtzoff, said that his actions warranted the electric chair, but his mental state had been called into question by his defense team.

As a result, for two months, Tyler was sent to St. Elizabeth's hospital for evaluation. The staff said he was not legally insane but had deep emotional and personality problems.

Eventually Tyler was paroled in 1970 and in February of 1972 he was arrested again, this time for the rape of Alicia Johnson in Pennsylvania. During his assault with a razor on her, he repeatedly told her he had killed other girls or had dumped some victims on the parkway. According to Johnson, Tyler said that none of his previous victims had ever gotten away. Tyler had choked her to the point of unconsciousness several times, telling her he would throw her body on the parkway and would be long gone by the time the authorities found her.

Aside from his incriminating comments, the investigators were drawn to the fact that his earlier victim, Janet King, was 19 years old but looked much younger. Did Tyler have a thing for younger girls?

Tyler met with the investigators and provided hair and writing samples, (to be compared with those found in the notes recovered from the murders of Christopher Brady and Ritchie Reed.) His hair samples alone eliminated him as a suspect in the Freeway Phantom cases.

Roger Allen Wanzer

One of the letters mailed to the *Washington Evening Star* as part of their attempt to generate tips for the case came from a Charlie Haigh, a quasi-psychic. He claimed that his psychic profile of the killer was a male, light-skinned black, around 22-year-old. The killer would look younger than he was and would have an easy-going nature until something "set him off." His first name was going to be Don or Tom and his last name was something like Werpor or Werner. He lived on a house on South Capitol Street with a street number or license plate having the number 414. The letter was signed "Charlie and Harold."

The FBI field offices in Rhode Island, where the letter originated, determined that the senders were Charlie Haigh and Harold Trudell. Desperate for any leads, the investigators did find a Roger Allen Wanzer who came close enough to the last name the psychics suggested to pique their interest.

As it turned out, in July of 1971, Wanzer had kidnapped a stewardess at knife point and had raped her at his residence, strangling her before she managed to escape. During the assault he had expressed a deep hatred for all women, something that set off further alarm bells with the investigators.

Little is known about Wanzer other than a few almost random notes in his files. He played pool and had been employed as a karate instructor at the Police Boys Club. He had an alibi for the time of the murder of Brenda Woodard, claiming to be in West Virginia. His employment records showed, however, that he had been discharged from the job two months before the Woodard murder – more than enough time to return to Washington. Furthermore, he had no alibis for the other Freeway Phantom murders up to that point.

The West Virginia authorities considered Wanzer as a suspect in two rapes in their state and may still to this day. There is no indication that he had been cleared of suspicion in the Freeway Phantom crimes.

Kenneth Viars

In April of 1976, Kenneth Viars was picked up by Gulfport, Mississippi, police and while in custody, told them he wanted to talk to them about a murder along the Suitland Parkway in Washington DC. The FBI and MPD detectives interviewed Viars, and what they got was a bizarrely convoluted story.

According to Viars, he and a friend traveled from Mississippi to Kannaopolis, North Carolina, burglarizing homes along the way. They split up in Kannapolis, with Viars hitchhiking to Washington DC. Viars contacted his friend's girlfriend who told him that his robbery-buddy was dead.

Viars returned to North Carolina and was picked up by the FBI regarding his friend's death. His accomplice had been shot in the head two times, and the vehicle had been set on fire. Viars underwent five polygraph tests and passed four of them, the last one, however, indicated some hesitation when he was asked if he had killed his friend.

Viars had been diagnosed as a paranoid schizophrenic and admitted that he had no control over his violent personality. He would black out and not be able to remember what he did during those times.

In his interview with the authorities, Viars claimed he had been living in a shack made of branches in the brush off the Suitland Parkway. While there he had seen the Freeway Phantom kill and leave the bodies in the woods. While he never saw the Phantom's face, he described him as Caucasian, between six foot and six foot, two inches tall, wearing coveralls, walking with a limp. His description sounded more like a killer from a 1970s horror movie than a true serial killer.

According to Viars, the Phantom's first victim was a young man, killed on a motorcycle. The victim wore a leather jacket, jeans, and a helmet. The second victim was a white male, in his forties. The third was a blonde-haired, white female, in her early twenties. The fourth victim he saw the Freeway Phantom with was a 13-to-14-year-old black male wearing Converse sneakers. The final victim he witnessed was a 50-to-60-year old white male with a gray mustache. Each time the Freeway Phantom covered the victim's body with leaves or tried to bury them after he killed them.

Initially police were ready to toss his entire confession as the ramblings of a mentally unstable man, but the first victim he talked about matched the description of an unidentified body recovered in 1974 in Prince George's County.

Further digging into Viars life showed that he was a self-described "sex maniac" who had been in and out of mental hospitals since the age of 9. During a short stint in the Marine Corps, he admitted to rigging an explosive device to kill a fellow Marine, which was chalked up as an accident at the time. The child of a prostitute, he witnessed his mother often plying her trade in his youth. In talking with the investigators, he said things such as, "I don't think I'm the Phantom, but maybe I am."

The FBI took his records to psychiatrists for evaluation. They labeled him as a likely sociopath who was incapable of telling the truth even if it would benefit him.

For a string of reasons, sad and otherwise, Viars remained on the list of suspects for the Freeway Phantom cases, though it is unlikely he was involved at all.

The Others…

As of 2001 there were ninety-five names still on the suspect list beyond those listed in this chapter. Many of these, easily more than 25 percent are dead. Another 45 percent are unaccounted for – their current locations are unknown. Many of those who are on the list appear because they committed rapes in the metropolitan Washington DC area during the period of the murders, automatically making them worth investigating.

CHAPTER 21: HUNTING A PHANTOM IN THE NIGHT

> "It's funny. A lot of people think it is an urban myth. They equate it with another urban myth, the Bunny Man. I have talked to people down in South East, who have told me that the Freeway Phantom and the Bunny Man are one-in-the-same."
> —*Former Detective James Trainum to the authors.*

Cold cases leave an investigator, authors, and you as a reader, with more questions than answers. Such is the situation with the Freeway Phantom. Each time the killer struck, he left more questions than clues.

Some of the questions are easy to tackle; others are mind-numbingly difficult. We will try sort through them as much as possible and talk about the solvability of these cases. While some of this ground has been covered in other chapters in greater detail, this is designed to be a summation for you, the reader.

Was it one killer or two?

Some serial killers operate in pairs. It offers a higher degree of control of the victim and a greater sense of security for the killers. When you look at the two primary suspect groups – in this case the Green Vega Gang and Robert Askins, you must wonder what the evidence points to. Was it one murderer, or two (or more)?

There is no physical evidence to support gang rape with the victims. One would expect more bruising, more trauma to sexual organs, etc. In the case of Carol Spinks, she showed signs of repeated rectal sodomy, but not vaginal. Further, there were no signs of semen.

When you look at the victims and their ages/sizes, they were likely chosen because they would be easy to control. Two killers would not have to target young girls; they could select more mature victims because of the control they could exert. The Freeway Phantom targeted young girls because he could intimidate and control them, alone. That, and young girls had some sort of deep meaning to him, something only he could understand.

This points to a single killer, not two or more men.

Why did he bathe and redress his victims?

It is disturbing that the killer had his victims stripped, bathed them, killed them, finally redressing them himself. Was it some sort of ritual with him, somehow tied to his psyche? Is it possible that for the killer, the bathing somehow was a cleansing of his own guilt?

The bathtub itself may be critical in this analysis. It is feasible the bathing was simply a means to get them into the tub, so he could kill them without making any messes or reducing the chance of them getting up and running away.

The Freeway Phantom redressed the victims. That means they were either dead when he put them in the bathtub, or he killed them there.

More realistically, it pointed to someone attempting to wash away any evidence. This means a killer familiar with police techniques at the time. Little did he realize that in the process of trying to wash away any evidence, he left telltale bits of green synthetic fibers that linked five of his victims indelibly.

How did he get away with dropping off the bodies on a heavily traveled set of roads?

Today I-295 is a congested thoroughfare, and in 1971-72 it was also a highly traveled road. The killer pulled over, pulled the bodies of his victims from the car, then sped off. How could he have done this without being seen?

Chances are he *was* seen, but people didn't see him pulling out a body. In their mind it was just another broken down car along the highway. They paid it no mind at all. Key to this was that the bodies were not dragged far from where he would have opened the door to remove them. In fact, they could have been pushed out of the vehicle – though most seemed to show signs of being pulled – their arms out over their heads where he had held onto them.

The sections of roadway where the victims were dumped were well lit. Most were straightaways, except in the case of Brenda Woodard, which was on a sharply curved exit ramp. The killer would have a good field of vision to see approaching headlights, giving him windows of opportunity to perform his grisly task without being seen.

The key was speed. He spent a lot of time with his victims except when depositing their bodies. In that task, he moved quickly.

Why did he stop?

As stated before, the old school thinking of serial killers says that they do not stop unless they are killed or incarcerated. We now know that some do stop, usually as the result of a significant lifestyle change.

The Freeway Phantom was a killer who most likely followed the case, as evident by the note he left, signing it with the name the press had given him. He liked the publicity. If he had moved on to another geographic location to continue his murderous spree, he would have communicated to the authorities there. That did not happen.

Did the Phantom have a close encounter with law enforcement...something that scared him to the point where he knew he had to stop? Were increased police patrols of his hunting grounds making it too risky for him to continue? Both are certainly possible.

Interestingly, with the jailing of the two key suspects – the Green Vega Gang and Robert Askins, the killings stopped.

Were the Suitland Slayings the Work of the Freeway Phantom?

It is impossible to say if the same serial killer was responsible for the Freeway Phantom and Suitland Slayings. This is a considerable cooling off period if it was the same person. There is nothing to physically connect the two serial murder sprees. The time gap tends to point to the crimes not being connected.

While the Prince George's County Police believe they have a suspect in the Suitland Slayings, and they may be correct, but there is a good chance they are wrong. The Suitland Slayer may have stopped simply because he could not use his preferred dumping grounds. So, are the Suitland Slayings the work of another serial killer or the Freeway Phantom after a long cooling off period? Some may argue that such a gap in the killings points to different subjects, and it is a valid argument.

The most compelling link that you can draw between the two sets of murders is that they operated in the same neighborhoods, close to St. Elizabeth's. It is hard to believe that this is pure coincidence...but it could be. Only time, and a conviction, will tell.

Was the Phantom the Green Vega Gang?

At the risk of going over material twice, it is important to summarize the case for and against the Green Vega Gang. Considering the Green Vega Gang forces you to cope with all the anomalies that point away from them.

The gang used a gun, not a knife to get control of their victims. Because of that, the death of Brenda Woodard comes into question since she was stabbed.

None of the green fibers recovered from the victims were linked to any of the gang members. Also where the fibers were found on victims, such as under brassieres or in panties, suggests that they were picked up when the victims were disrobed. The Green Vega Gang were a roving rape gang, they performed their sick acts in different locations, so picking up the fibers on so many victims would have meant that all of them were in the same location.

The Green Vega Gang never mentioned bathing their victims either, which was held back from the public, so only the killer would have known that this occurred with the Freeway Phantom fatalities. If they had mentioned it in their discussions/confessions, it would be have been substantial.

Hair samples were taken from all the Green Vega Gang, and none of them matched the hair samples recovered off the bodies of the victims.

The modus operandi of the gang was to target young women, not children. There are stories of John Davis and Morris Warren attacking teenage girls, but none as young as the youngest victims of the Freeway Phantom.

Carol Spinks had no indication of vaginal intercourse but did show indications of rectal sodomy. The Green Vega Gang only threatened sodomy when their victims refused to engage in vaginal sex. Again, another inconsistency that cannot be overlooked.

The confession of Melvin Gray is completely fictional, and Morris Warren admitted that he had misled investigators. The lies and truths of admitted liars are difficult to unravel and beg questioning their validity.

There is no known evidence that Brenda Woodard was assaulted behind the Pepsi Plant in Prince George's County, where Warren alleged the crime took place. Its only relationship to the murder is that it had access to the exit ramp easily where her body was found.

The geographic profile has an epicenter at St. Elizabeth's Hospital. There was no tangible evidence to support the Green Vega Gang having close ties to that location.

It has been suggested that Morris Warren and Melvin Gray could have gotten much of their information about the cases from newspaper accounts that were relatively easy to access. Ray Banoun discounts that. "I've heard people say that they got the information from the papers…and I can't see that happening. None of these guys were the kind of guys to read *The Washington Post*. Reading wasn't a big thing with any of them."

It all comes down to one figure with the Green Vega Gang, and that is Morris Warren. If you believe his most current story, that he misled authorities, then the gang didn't kill the Freeway Phantom victims. While it could have been the Green Vega Gang, but it also could have been thousands of other people in the District of Columbia.

Was Robert Askins the Freeway Phantom?

Much like the Green Vega Gang, it is necessary to summarize the case of Robert Askins and the Freeway Phantom murders. Askins stands out as the most likely suspect in these cases for a number of reasons. When you look at his previous crimes, especially the last two that he was convicted of committing, Askins kidnapped his victims. In the case of Martinia Stewart, he bathed her in a bathtub. He had Ms. Stewart write a note that he dictated, eerily along the lines of what Brenda Woodard was forced to do with the Freeway Phantom. The note is highly significant. No other rapes or murders before or after the Phantom killings involved someone making someone write a note for the authorities.

Askins was mentally unstable. He spent decades living at St. Elizabeth's Hospital, giving him an anchor point that matches the geographic profile perfectly. He was a violent man who had been killing women for years starting in college. When you look at the note the Freeway Phantom left on the body of Brenda Woodard, "this is tantamount to my insensititivity (sp) to people especially women." Was this Robert Askins renewing his one-man-war on women in DC that he had started back in 1938?

Askins had posed as a police officer before, and he owned both a pistol and a fake police badge. In his youth, he was familiar with police techniques. This would have allowed him to gain control of his victims easily.

Where the Green Vega Gang used multiple locations to commit their crimes, Askins had a house all to himself. In fact, he had lost his roommate just weeks before the first murder. Coincidence?

Robert Askins expressed a hatred of women during his first arrests. The same sentiment is shown in the note left on Brenda Woodard's body.

What works against him is that he is older than what the profiles indicated the killer would have been at the time – with Askins being in his fifties during the time of the Freeway Phantom killings. Profiles are not etched in stone but are meant as a guide to help investigators narrow their focus, so this can be somewhat looked over. Per the FBI profile, "It is not a substitute for a thorough, well-planned investigation and should not be considered all-inclusive. This analysis is based upon probabilities, noting, however, that no two criminal acts or criminal personalities are exactly alike, and therefore, the offender at times may not fit the analysis in every category."

Of all the Freeway Phantom suspects, Robert Askins best fits every possible box on a checklist except there has not, to date, been any physical evidence to connect him to the crimes.

Was the Freeway Phantom a police officer?

Almost from the very beginning there was a thought that the killer could be someone impersonating a police officer or an actual officer. No doubt this was fueled by the murder of Angela Barnes at the hands of police officers. The Metropolitan Police Chief Boyd told *The Washington Post*, "We have investigated some policemen because we thought there might be a tie-in."

Mrs. Spinks, mother of the first Freeway Phantom victim, was not so quick to ignore the thought that a police officer might be involved. "You bring up your children to stop if a policeman calls because this is right. Now today…yes, I'm more suspicious of the police."

The standards for hiring police officers and the checks and balances that keep them from corrupting their positions was very different in the 1970s. Is it possible the killer was a wolf in sheep's clothing, an officer with inside information on the investigation? Yes. Bathing the victims to remove trace evidence shows some knowledge of investigative techniques. Who better to know that than a police officer?

At the same time, there are things that point away from it. An officer would have known to not provide any evidence that was not necessary. The leaving of a note on Brenda Woodard would not have been considered a prudent move – it was literally giving the authorities their best piece of evidence. An officer would not have likely done that.

It is entirely possible that the Freeway Phantom *impersonated* an officer or authority figure. It would explain how he was able to get shy young girls into his vehicle and maintain control over them.

What other murders might be connected to the Freeway Phantom?

In the note left with Brenda Woodard, the killer said he would admit the others. What others? The Washington MPD and FBI had developed a possible list of connected crimes, though many of these are, at best, wild guesses. Some, like the Suitland Slayings, do not appear on the list.

The following are possibly related incidents/killings:

12-23-71   Mary Whitfield   Attempted pickup by a white driver.

1-14-72   Elaine B. Solomon   Kidnapped

1-18-72   Janice Lockhart   Attempted pickup by a white male.

1-27-72   Aelise N. Loftin   Sexual assault by a black male in a green Mustang.

2-7-72   Bertha G. Singleton   Raped.

2-9-72   Edith B. Liggin   Raped and strangled.

2-14-72   Gwendolyn Wilkerson   Assaulted by black male.

4-10-72   Ophelia Gaitwood   Attempted assault by black male.

12-2-74   Manie Woltz   Raped.

12-3-74   Diane Blackshear   Raped.

12-3-74   Edith McConnell   Raped.

12-9-74   Deborah Bailey   Abducted by a black male but managed to escape.

12-18-74   Joyce Ann Petty   Abduction. MPD believes Melvin Gray was responsible

8-22-75   Karen E. Thomas   Missing person

Were one or more of these the women who had been attacked by the Freeway Phantom and had gotten away? That question remains unanswered.

Where are some of the key suspects now?

John Nathanial Davis, the unofficial leader of the Green Vega Gang, was released from prison due to an illness before the end of his sentence in 2002. Oddly, at last check, he isn't even a registered sex offender in the state of Maryland.

Given that his release was for medical reasons, he may very well be dead. We could not locate him or a grave.

Warren Morris remains in prison. He has found God and bemoans that he has remained in jail while others (presumably Davis) have gone free. In a letter to a judge asking for leniency, he wrote: "...petitioner's co-defendant was paroled in 1989, who was the principle crime figure of the offense, who kidnaped, raped, sodomized with arm[ed] 7 victims, which resulted in a 43 count indictment. Petitioner was tried on a [an] 18 count indictment and acquitted of 11 counts, and the DC Court of Appeals ruled in its memorandum and opinion that petitioner had guilty knowledge, rather than mere presence at three offenses. The principal is paroled while the petitioner who had guilty knowledge is denied a parole eligibility..."

Conveniently, in his bemusing of his incarceration, he overlooked the fact that he had been convicted of murder in the 7-Eleven robbery – something not shared with John Davis.

Morris has written a manuscript for a book, but no publisher has touched it. When pressed for details about exactly how he misled investigators, Morris stopped responding to letters from the authors of this book. He has never issued a public apology for what he put the families of the victims through. In 2007 Warren attempted to get his sentence reduced one last time, but the sentence was held in place. Morris Warren, prisoner 05203-016, remains in a federal prison in Petersburg, Virginia, where it is unlikely he will harm anyone in the outside world ever again.

Paul Fletcher and Paul Brooks were both released from prison in July of 2001.

The whereabouts of Melvin Gray are not known at this time. There is no record of him having any other run-ins with the authorities in Washington DC after the convictions of his fellow Green Vega Gang members.

In 1989, Robert Askins argued against a transfer to Lorton's Central Prison Facility because two inmates incarcerated there had threatened to kill him. Prison officials doubted the veracity of these charges. On July 7, 1987, he refused to submit to diagnostic examination. The one inmate, William Terry, allegedly showed Askins a hollowed-out book with a knife hidden in it. Askins turned him over to the guards, and Terry was transferred to the Central Facility where he would have tagged Askins as an informant.

The second incident involved James Fisher in 1983. Askins was a leader of the Catholic-Protestant community in the Maximum Security, and Fisher was the leader of the Seventh Day Adventist community. It was common practice to invite others to "family day" worship services where friends from the outside could visit relatively unsupervised. Both professed religious leaders got into a verbal argument where Fisher, who was transferred to Central, told Askins that he was "living on borrowed time," hardly the words of religious man.

Askins switched religions from Catholicism to Christian Science late in life. In April 2000 he had his last psychiatric examination. The gray-haired, bearded prisoner came in with rumpled clothing, needing eyeglasses to read. His memory was fading at the age of 81, and he worried about being seen going into the evaluation. Askins suffered from stomach problems and mostly subsisted on a diet of rice and beans. He came clutching a letter from the FBI that stated their refusal to provide him with a polygraph. He told his examiner that he harbored the belief that a polygraph would somehow clear him of the crimes of which he was accused. He asked for her help in securing such a test.

"I would never knowingly harm anyone. The reason I got this sentence is based on false accusation. Fabricated accusation...the trial was based on an utterly false – I would *never* kidnap anyone." His anger towards the female sex leaked out during his talks. "Women will do – some people will make any accusation against anybody." He went on to say that he had been "offended" that the jury had found him guilty. Askins refused to express any remorse for the crimes of which he had been convicted.

The final prognosis: "He does not appear to be suffering from a psychotic or mood disorder that would require mental health treatment."

On April 30, 2010 Robert Elwood Askins died of a "lung mass," apparently having refused medical treatment.

Where did the name "Freeway Phantom" come from?

The words, "Freeway Phantom" first appear in print media after the murder of Nenomoshia Yates on October 1, 1971. All the papers carried it, but our own digging pointed to television media as the source. Former detective Jim Trainum filled in that bit of history from his own digging. "I believe that Pat Collins, he's with channel four now, he's the one I believe that started the phrase, "Freeway Phantom." I don't know if it was TV or radio at the time."

Given the lack of a specific source stepping up, Jim Trainum's answer is as good as any.

Could the cases be solved?

In 2018, the FBI and California authorities used genealogical DNA to track down and apprehend the Golden State Killer, Joseph Deangelo. Since then a number of ice-cold cases have used DNA to map out potential relatives and track down killers in more than a dozen high profile cases. It is possible that such a technique could be used to find the Freeway Phantom.

There are hurdles, however. As former-detective Romaine Jenkins relayed to us: "DC destroyed all of its evidence ages ago. They should not have if it is an open case. I had to go to PG County and everybody else because DC had destroyed their stuff. Everything is gone. I did look at the fiber evidence…and we looked at all the evidence and the FBI fiber man, and he said it hadn't been maintained well enough for them to get DNA.

"We don't have the DNA now, you know, because all the evidence has been destroyed. I know because I was wondering, and I went to PG and saw the evidence. I saw the note, I saw everything."

Former-detective Jim Trainum had a similar perspective when asked if the case could be solved. "It may very well not be. Not all cases are. The other rule of thumb is that the suspect's name is somewhere in the case files. Somebody has been interviewed by the cops and was set aside or something like that. A lot of times, the name is already in there."

The Washington Metropolitan Police Department's internal report in 2009 on the Freeway Phantom tackled this issue head-on: "It is to be expected that when reopening a cold case, detectives must face the same problems in their investigation that complicated the case to begin with. However, detectives are also burdened with the issues inherent to the passage of time: the fading of memories, relocation and death of witnesses and subjects, and destruction of evidence.

"There is no doubt that there are a multitude of obstacles facing the reopening of the Freeway Phantom case. It has been over 30 years since a valid lead was pursued, and a number of individuals believed to be central to the case have passed away. The most likely suspects range in age from their mid-70s to late-80s, putting an increased emphasis on the need for rapid investigation. Perhaps most damaging to the case is the fact that the physical evidence gathered from the victims and crime scenes- invaluable forensic trace, perpetrator DNA, and those all-important synthetic green fibers – has since been destroyed. Even the paper materials- the MPD case jackets- are gone, leaving only the limited materials from the FBI field office with which to recreate the investigation.

"As such, without solid physical evidence investigators must turn to alternate methods if they intend to solve the Phantom case. Utilizing the media to saturate the community is a critical step in obtaining any information from individuals still in the area. The success of the Cold Case Unit's partnership with *Fox 5 News* may foreshadow success in this case. As it stands, there is nothing to lose by going public to try and find the Phantom.

"Given the lack of conclusive evidence, any sort of resolution to this case is going to have to come with a confession by the perpetrator. Therefore, it is critical that the suspects from the case are re-interviewed and investigated thoroughly; they are old men now, perhaps wishing for a clear conscience before dying (but not likely). It was noted earlier that none of the Green Vega rapists are currently registered sex offenders; this provides a convenient avenue through which to approach the suspects. Askins is in prison [at the time], and he's not going anywhere. These suspects need to be made a focal point of the reopened investigation and the pressure needs to be heavy-handed.

"Studies have shown that in most cold cases, the name of the offender is somewhere in the case file - it's just a matter of finding it. Dispensing with the proverbial needle-in-a-haystack metaphor, it's time to begin wading through the abundance of names in these case materials and identifying persons of interest. In the absence of DNA testing and hair/fiber comparison, solving this case is going to come down to good old-fashioned detective work."

If that is true, does the Washington MPD have the fortitude and drive to do that old-fashioned detective work?

The lack of cooperation from the Washington DC Metropolitan Police Department and the Prince George's County Police Department

The authors filed numerous Freedom of Information Act (FOIA) requests for material to perform our research and ensure accuracy. Of the more than a dozen filed with the Washington DC MPD, only two were fulfilled, and they were only partially provided. None of our FOIA requests with Prince George's County Police or the Maryland State Police were filled. In fact, we contacted the public relations person from Prince George's County on the phone and three times via email just to interview someone regarding the case. Rather than respond, they ignored our requests entirely.

The authors pointed out to both agencies, in writing, that our books generate new tips and leads for authorities to pursue. Rather than embrace an opportunity to secure new leads, they pursued a strategy of stonewalling.

We even asked the Washington MPD for the search warrant returns from the search of Robert Askins' home or photographs of what was recovered. These are public records but unfortunately have been misfiled at the DC Superior Court, where we might normally have gotten them. We pointed out that this material was over forty-years old and that Askins was dead. If the evidence they had incriminated him, his prosecution would be impossible. They denied our request. On appeal, we received four pages from the mayor's office outlining why they had the right to not respond to our request. It was far more effort than showing us photographs of holes in Robert Askins' yard or of the button that was recovered. It is clear that the mayor's office is complacent in covering up the mishandling of the cases by the MPD.

The FBI surprised us by responding with some material, some of which we had requested from other sources. Our FOIA with the US Park Police is still outstanding after more than a year from submittal. "It is complicated and will take time." We have had FOIAs open with the US Attorney's Office for nine months.

Prince George's County verbally relayed to us via an ombudsman that they were prepared to open their files for us, but that Washington MPD had asked them specifically *not* to cooperate. They deliberately blocked us looking at another jurisdiction's files. The line used was one with which we were familiar, "This is a cold case and we are actively pursuing all leads and tips at this time."

At the time of this writing, these cases were forty-eight years old. It is past time to make them public. The FBI released thousands of pages on Jimmy Hoffa years ago in hopes that it would generate tips. Yet the Washington DC MPD doesn't want anyone to see what they have.

Which begs to question – what are they hiding?

The answer to that is a mismanagement of the cases and physical evidence from the start. What they hope to bury is that they have lost and destroyed the evidence in the cases. It is telling that reporter Del Wilbur found boxes of the material that Jim Trainum used to reconstruct much of the files. Romanie Jenkins has boxes of her notes, photographs, even negatives from the case files in her personal possession.

Rather than own up to their mistakes, the Washington DC MPD seeks to bury them. Rather than embrace a book that might help generate new leads, they have sought to withhold the material. It is a big blue wall of silence from the Washington DC MPD when it comes to the Freeway Phantom cases, a wall that is spray-painted with the word, "Shame!" on it.

So where does that leave us? At the opening of this book, we talked about the note that the killer left on the body of Brenda Woodard. It was his voice, it was him communicating directly to the investigators, the families, and the community as a whole. He taunted the police openly, bragging there were others they had not yet bothered to connect to his bloody murder spree. It is the only time the killer took the time to attempt to engage the authorities, and that makes it significant.

In 2018 the authors attended CrimeCon in Nashville, Tennessee, a relatively new convention of true crime professionals and fans of the genre. There, we met with former

FBI Supervisory Special Agent Jim Fitzgerald. Fitzgerald was the man who created the field of forensic linguistics, which directly led to the capture of the Unabomber. Fitzgerald was the lead character in the Discovery Channel series, *Manhunt: Unabomber.* We approached him about looking at the note left by the Freeway Phantom and corresponded with him over the course of a year on the note itself.

He felt that the word "tantamount" was important, but so was the use of the word, "Free-way" in the message. The hyphenation was significant. According to Fitzgerald, "Not that it matters too much here, but I would surmise that the first DC-area journalist to use the word "freeway" (with or without hyphen) in print, was originally from California. That's because, of course, that word is not used in the DC area to describe a multi-lane limited access highway. Then others followed suit.

"Interesting that a few suspects in the case back in the day were found to have used the word "tantamount" in one writing exemplar or another. I would keep each of those individuals on the short list of suspects, unless they have somehow been conclusively ruled out by other means."

At the suggestion of Fitzgerald, we unleashed not only the power of the internet, but of the Library of Congress's vast newspaper and periodical holdings. Interestingly enough, in two instances, the newspapers did hyphenate "free-way" for page justification purposes. Both were written after the note was found on Brenda Woodard's body – for the most part eliminating the newspapers as the source for the strange spelling of the word.

One source did come up, however, in print form. *Studies in the Psychology of Sex – Sexual Inversion,* By Havelock Ellis. Published in 1906. The book was one of the few books from that era that clinically discussed homosexuality. It would have been found in college libraries or with doctors who worked in the mental health field.

We inquired with St. Elizabeth's Hospital to see if it was one of the books they had in their library available to patients. We never heard back from them, leaving the matter still open.

Jim Fitzgerald offers his perspective into the note that the killer left on Brenda Woodard's body:

"On the very first page of the lengthy Comparative Analysis Report I authored for the FBI regarding the comparison of the Unabom documents to the personal writings of Ted Kaczynski, I quoted a literary theorist by the name of Paul de Man. It read: 'The writer's language is to some degree the product of his own action; he is both the historian and the agent of his own language.' This certainly bore true in 1996 in finally identifying the aforementioned serial killer and it remains true today in identifying other serial offenders when language evidence is involved. The Freeway Phantom left such language evidence behind at the scene of one of his rapes/killings. The note without a doubt reflects the killer's own language, his own history, and his own actions. As with the Unabomber, the language expressed by this man may prove to be tantamount in eventually identifying him."

James R. Fitzgerald, M.S.
Supervisory Special Agent, FBI (Ret.)

Gone now are the dull orange sodium streetlights of the early 1970s in Washington DC. Now white florescent lights turn back the night. Neighborhoods that had suffered after the 1968 riots for decades are bouncing back with new vitality. Many of the landmarks associated with the crimes; the Safeway, some roadways, or homes of the victims, are gone now – replaced with new buildings, homes, exit ramps, and businesses. Many of the neighborhoods have changed, grown, and evolved. The city has a different vibe to it, a different beat. Watergate has been surpassed by a dozen or more scandals/"gates." The Vietnam War protests that dominated the city are history, replaced by protests nearly every weekend over some issue or person. The things that defined DC in the 1970s are fading memories.

Washington DC moved on even if the families of the victims didn't.

There are still murders in DC, far too many. There are still serial killers who have dodged justice up to this point. There is nothing to commemorate the victims of the Freeway Phantom. Gone are the tasks forces and, in some cases, the vital evidence. Many of the officers who worked the cases have passed away, taking with them any legacy information they might have had.

The families of the victims, weary of the media attention, say little any more about the case. It is an old wound for them and picking at that scab yields little. Gone are the days of hoping that a break will come. Our efforts to reach out to them came back with, in one case, "We are tired of dredging this back up…"

What is not gone are the names of those who were taken from us. No one knows what they might have become, what lives they might have touched, what influence on our world they may have had. They are gone, but not forgotten.

Carol Denise Spinks
Darlenia Denise Johnson
Brenda Faye Crockett
Nenomoshia Yates
Brenda Denise Woodard
Diane Dinnis Williams
Teara Ann Bryant

This case remains open to tips and information. Should you have any new information on the Freeway Phantom, please contact: The Synchronized Operations Command Center at 202-727-9099 or at unsolved.murder@dc.gov The reward is open to up to $150,000 depending on the information provided.

ACKNOWLEDGEMENTS

This book could not have been done without the assistance of many people who donated their time, effort and memories, in bringing this book to life.

Romaine Jenkins
Jim Trainum
Ray Banoun
Hilary Szukalowski
David Norman
Jim Fitzgerald
Jean Armstrong – our ever-vigilant genealogical researcher
Adolfo Loeri of the DC Superior Court, Criminal Clerk's Office
Kristina Kelley, US Department of Justice, Federal Bureau of Prisons
C. Darnell Stroble, US Department of Justice, Federal Bureau of Prisons
Chris Anglim, University of the District of Columbia
Del Wilbur
Lisa Warwick, Library Program Coordinator, Washington DC Public Library
Juile Burns, Washington DC Public Library
Michele Casto, Washington DC Public Library
Lisa Archie-Mills, Supervisory FOIA Specialist, Washington DC Metropolitan Police Department

Lisa Kerschner, Office of the Public Access Ombudsman, State of Maryland

Nancy Delaney, Technical Services & Collection Development Coordinator / ILL Services, Culpeper County Library

Inspector Vendette T. Parker, Freedom of Information Act (FOIA) Officer & Interim Director of the Office of Risk Management, Washington DC Metropolitan Police Department

The wonderful folks at CrimeCon who allowed us to connect with some great sources.

Susan Scott, the *Washington Afro-American* Archivist

Crystal L. Hurd, Programs Coordinator, Charles Sumner School Museum and Archives

Cameron Barr, Managing Editor, *The Washington Post*, who offered to share with us the Post's files on the cases.

Timothy Rivenburg – longtime friend who assisted us with some legal research tips.

We also received information from a number of confidential sources, all former police officers, who shared with us material under the promise of keeping their identities secret.

We tried, with numerous letters, to engage with the family members of the victims. Only two ever responded to us and neither wanted to talk. We respected their privacy on these matters.

ABOUT THE AUTHORS:

Blaine Pardoe is a New York Times Bestselling and award-winning author of numerous books in the science fiction, military non-fiction, true crime, paranormal, and business management genres. Born in Newport News, Virginia, he has appeared on a number of national television and radio shows to speak about his books. Mr. Pardoe has been a featured speaker at the US National Archives, the United States Navy Museum, and the New York Military Affairs Symposium. He was awarded the State History Award in 2011 by the Historical Society of Michigan and is a two-time silver medal and one-time gold winner from the Military Writers Society of America. In 2013 Mr. Pardoe won the Harriet Quimby Award from the Michigan Aviation Hall of Fame for his contributions to aviation history.

His books have even been mentioned on the floor of the US Congress. His works have been printed in six languages, and he is recognized worldwide for his historical and true crime works. Mr. Pardoe lives in Culpeper, Virginia.

Victoria Hester became a New York Times Best Selling Author in 2014 for her first true crime work in *The Murder of Maggie Hume*, the first collaboration with her father, Blaine Pardoe. She is a two-time winner of the Michael Carr Award for her work in nonfiction.

Ms. Hester is the Director of Nursing at a correctional center in Virginia. Wife, mother, nurse, and author—Victoria enjoys researching true crimes as much as writing about them. She specializes in cold cases, "Because that is where I feel I can do the most good—generating tips for the authorities and making sure these victims are not forgotten."

APPENDIX: EVIDENCE AND POSSIBLE TROPHIES MISSING FROM THE VICTIMS

Our review of a summary report on the Freeway Phantom case indicates that much of the evidence gathered has been lost and/or destroyed by the Metropolitan Police Department over the decades. Further, forensic techniques in handling evidence have changed significantly over the years, especially with the advent of DNA profiling. In the 1970s however, there were no protocols for handling of physical evidence to prevent cross-contamination.

Carol Spinks
- Negroid hairs found on her shorts, sweater, panties and barrettes.
- Synthetic green fibers in her shorts and panties.
- Human blood recovered from under her fingernails and on her hair barrettes (too small amount for testing/grouping however).

Darlenia Johnson
None due to the decomposition of her remains.

Brenda Crockett
- Negroid hairs in her palm (fragments).

- Black synthetic fibers recovered from the scarf on her neck.
- Synthetic green fibers recovered from insider her blouse, shorts, and panties.
- Semen mixed with blood in her panties.

Nenomoisha Yates

- Negroid hairs in panties, sanitary napkin, sweatshirt, and jeans.
- Synthetic green fibers found on her body.
- Semen found in vaginal smears by the Baltimore medical examiner, but this is contradictory to the FBI analysis on December 15, 1971, which indicated no spermatozoa.
- Tire track found near victim (photograph only).
- One brown lady's loafer, which may be Darlenia Johnson's.

Brenda Woodard

- Note written by Woodard at the direction of her killer.
- Semen recovered from vaginal swabbing.
- Negroid head hairs found on her coat, boots, shirt, and brassiere.
- Synthetic green fibers recovered from inside her socks and panties.
- Caucasian hairs found on her coat and shirt, but these are believed to be contamination from the blanket used.

Diane Williams

- Synthetic green fibers found on brassiere.

- Brown Caucasian hair found on body but believed to have originated from investigators.

- Negroid hairs found on her body. FBI analysis points to these belonging to her – unconfirmed.

- Semen recovered from vaginal swabbing – DNA matched to her boyfriend as the result of consensual sex.

Teara Ann Bryant

Unknown. Prince George's County police refused to release any information regarding this case and do not consider it part of the Freeway Phantom murders.

Possible Trophies

Some serial killers maintain trophies of their victims, often for years after the crimes. These are a way for them to remember their heinous conquests and relive the experiences. If that is the case with the Freeway Phantom, the following items are known to be missing from the victims and may yet be in his possession.

- Carole Spinks blue size 8 ½ tennis shoes

- One or more brown loafer from Darlenia Johnson

- Pink plastic foam hair curlers and white tennis shoes from Brenda Crockett

- Brenda Woodard's schoolbooks and buttons missing from her coat and skirt. *(Modern Algebra, 20th Century Typewriting, and Gregg Shorthand)*

- Shoelaces missing from Diane Williams.

PHOTOS

The photos and maps in this book can also be
viewed at: *wbp.bz/tantamountgallery*

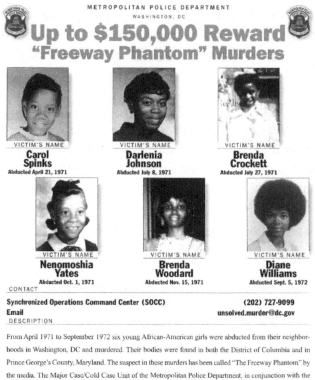

The Freeway Phantom case is still open with
a sizable reward. Police photograph

Washington DC was still reeling from the 1969 riots in 1971. The violence changed the impacted neighborhoods and further strained the relationship between citizens and law enforcement. Photograph From Library of Congress

Protesters in front of the White House speaking out against the Vietnam War the day Carole Spinks' body had been found. Photograph From Library of Congress

Carol Spinks, the first of the Freeway Phantom victims. No one realized this was the start of a string of serial killings.

Denise Johnson was the second victim kidnapped and strangled by the Freeway Phantom. Her body was found fifteen feet from where Carol Spinks's remains had been left along I-295. Police photograph

This is the location where Carol Spinks and Darlenia Johnson were found as it appeared in 2006. Police photograph

Brenda Faye Crockett was kidnapped by the Freeway Phantom and called home twice, attempting to mislead her family and investigators.

Photo of Brenda Crockett where she on Route 50
in Prince George's County, Maryland. Her body is
covered by police. Reprinted with permission of the DC
Public Library, Star Collection © Washington Post

Nenomoshia Yates was found two hours after she
disappeared. It was after her discovery that the media
began to call the serial killer, "The Freeway Phantom."

Brenda Denise Woodard was found near the Prince George's County Hospital exit ramp in Maryland. On her body was a note that she had been forced to write from the Freeway Phantom, taunting police.

This is an aerial photograph of where Brenda Woodward was found with the arrow pointing to the exact location. Police photograph.

These images show the Afro wig worn by Brenda Woodard that had been tossed out by her killer after he had removed her body from his vehicle. Police photographs

This pinpoints where Brenda Woodard was
found alongside the road. Police photograph

Police dressed a life-like mannequin in the same
clothing worn by Brenda Woodard in hopes of
generating leads. Reprinted with permission of the DC
Public Library, Star Collection © Washington Post

Police released a photograph of the books that Brenda Woodard had been carrying in hopes someone had seen them. Reprinted with permission of the DC Public Library, Star Collection © Washington Post

Diane Dinnis Williams. Some authorities consider her the last of the Freeway Phantom victims, but evidence points strongly to Teara Ann Bryant as being the last one. After leaving a bus, she disappeared into the night.

Diane Williams was found face down along the southbound lanes of I-295 as shown in this 2006 police photograph of the location. Very little has changed since 1972.

Morris "Fatsy" Warren. A member of the Green Vega Gang, his confessions related to the Freeway Phantom case has muddied the waters of the investigation for years.

Melvin Gray, a member of the Green Vega Gang, he falsely
confessed to two of the Freeway Phantom murders.

Paul Brooks, member of the Green Vega Gang.
Released from prison in 2001. He was implicated
by his fellow gang members confessions as to being
involved with the Freeway Phantom cases.

Robert Elwood Askins. A murderer with a deep seated hatred of women. He spent years in St. Elizabeth's Hospital before his last kidnappings and rapes which landed him in prison until he died. He remains one of the prime suspects in the Freeway Phantom case. Photo from DC Superior Court File.

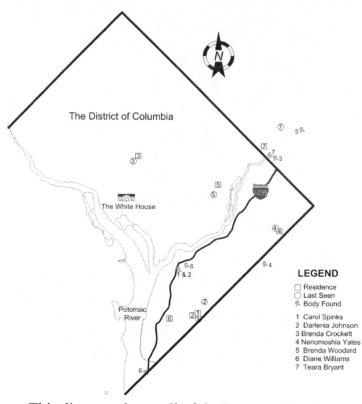

The District of Columbia

The White House

Potomac River

LEGEND

☐ Residence
○ Last Seen
⚚ Body Found

1 Carol Spinks
2 Darlenia Johnson
3 Brenda Crockett
4 Nenomoshia Yates
5 Brenda Woodard
6 Diane Williams
7 Teara Bryant

This diagram shows all of the Freeway Phantom victims in terms of where they lived, where they were last seen, and where they were found.

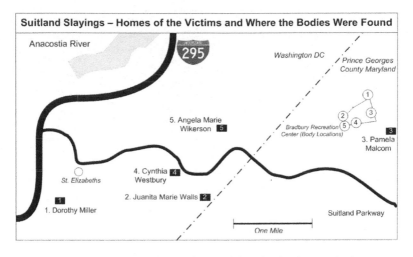

Suitland Slayings – Homes of the Victims and Where the Bodies Were Found

This map shows where the Suitland Slayings victims lived and where they were found. Was this the Freeway Phantom striking again years later?

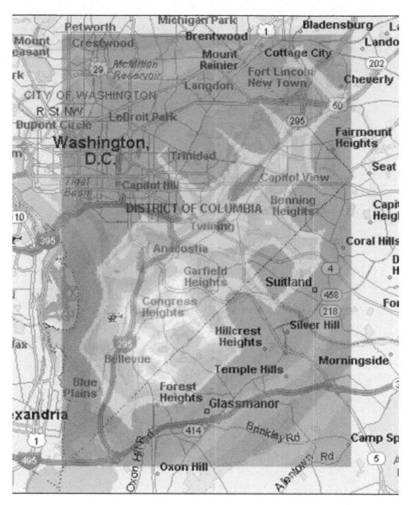

This diagram taken from the Geographic Profile done for Washington MPD in 2006 shows that epicenter of where the Phantom may have operated from – St. Elizabeth's Hospital.

GeoProfile (Victim Encounter Sites)

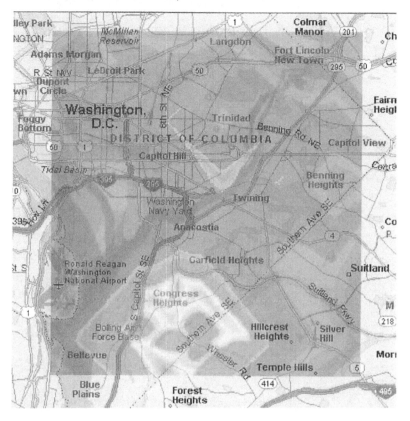

This diagram shows the hot spot of the geographic profile based on where the victims were last seen/encountered the Freeway Phantom – again almost centering on the neighborhoods surrounding St. Elizabeth's Hospital.

*For More News About Blaine Pardoe and
Victoria Hester, Signup For Our Newsletter:*

http://wbp.bz/newsletter

*Word-of-mouth is critical to an author's long-
term success. If you appreciated this book please
leave a review on the Amazon sales page:*

http://wbp.bz/tantamounta

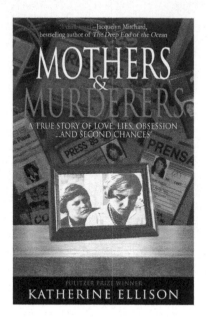

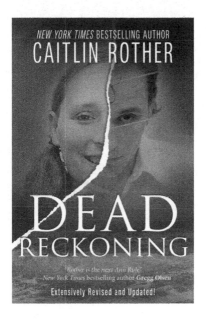

Made in the USA
Las Vegas, NV
17 December 2021

38461973R00184